Imaginación y fantasía

Catorce relatos hispanoamericanos

SIXTH EDITION

DONALD A. YATES

Emeritus, Michigan State University

JOHN B. DALBOR

Emeritus, Pennsylvania State University

Holt, Rinehart and Winston
Harcourt Brace College Publishers

Fort Worth   Philadelphia   San Diego   New York   Orlando   Austin   San Antonio
Toronto   Montreal   London   Syd

D1122606

Publisher	CHRISTOPHER CARSON
Acquisitions Editor	JEFF GILBREATH
Market Strategist	KENNETH S. KASEE
Developmental Editor	MARY K. MAYO
Project Editor	G. PARRISH GLOVER
Art Director	BURL SLOAN
Production Manager	JAMES McDONALD

ISBN: 0-03-023797-1
Library of Congress Catalog Card Number: 98-85706

Address for Orders
Holt, Rinehart and Winston, 6277 Sea Harbor Drive, Orlando, FL 32887-6777
1-800-782-4479

Address for Editorial Correspondence
Holt, Rinehart and Winston, 301 Commerce Street, Suite 3700, Fort Worth, TX 76102

Web Site Address
http://www.hbcollege.com

Holt, Rinehart and Winston will provide complimentary supplements or supplement packages to those adopters qualified under our adoption policy. Please contact your sales representative to learn how you qualify. If as an adopter or potential user you receive supplements you do not need, please return them to your sales representative or send them to: Attn: Returns Department, Troy Warehouse, 465 South Lincoln Drive, Troy, MO 63379.

Printed in the United States of America

8 9 0 1 2 3 4 5 6 7   0 6 6   9 8 7 6 5 4 3 2 1

Holt, Rinehart and Winston
Harcourt Brace College Publishers

To the Memory of
Jorge Luis Borges
(1899–1986)

Contents

Preface to the Sixth Edition

When we were preparing the first edition of *Imaginación y fantasía* some forty years ago, it was our intention to make available to intermediate students of Spanish stories of a type that had not often been represented in other reading texts of that day—tales of imagination and fantasy. It was our belief that narratives of this sort would provide absorbing reading experiences for students who were taking their first step toward dealing with unsimplified literary texts. We thought that stories that were interesting as stories would be appealing.

The growing audience that the book soon found confirmed our idea. In a second edition (1968), we eliminated three stories and added five new ones, raising the total to fourteen. In subsequent editions in 1975 and 1983, we eliminated five stories and, on each occasion, included five new ones. During this time, we were searching for new prose selections that would increasingly challenge students' abilities and stimulate their thinking.

In 1989, numerous helpful suggestions from users of this text led us to the conclusion that the book had become too difficult for its intended audience. Consequently, in that year we submitted the book to its most extensive revision, dropping eight of the fourteen selections and replacing them with eight others. Now, ten years later, once more guided by recommendations offered by frequent users of this reader, we have come up with another minor revision. Five of the tales in the fifth edition have now been replaced, leaving our anthology in what we now consider to be its definitive form.

Collected here are fables, parables, mystery and detective stories, science fiction, and suspense narratives. Also included are stories with elements of fantasy and the macabre. There is a psychological tale and a story by the Uruguayan writer, Horacio Quiroga—which replaces his "Juan Darién" in the previous edition—that almost defies description. In short: a mixed and varied collection of stories grouped around the themes of this text.

We have kept the idea of designating a series of Key Expressions for each story, which are listed beforehand and should be studied in preparation for the reading of each selection. Moreover, most of the other language exercises that follow will draw on these highlighted expressions. These exercises have been prepared with definite purposes in mind. Exercise A, Questions and Opinions, is not only a series of questions, but also a review designed to lead to a full comprehension of the most significant features of the tales. At the end of each of these sections, a few additional questions have been provided that inquire more directly into the student's reaction to the story. These questions, coming at the end, are preceded by a bullet (•). They may be handled in several different ways: as simple queries to be answered concisely, as more probing questions that explore the student's interpretation and evaluation of the story, or as topics that may be assigned for a brief essay or theme.

Exercise B, Verb Practice, deals with verbs that have been defined and explained in the Key Expressions listing. Students are free to compose original sentences using these verbs. The sentences either can parallel those found in the story itself or they can be spontaneous and creative.

Exercise C, Vocabulary Practice, involves the verbs and expressions from the Key Expressions not included in Exercise B. Again, students are encouraged to use these items in sentences of their own design.

Exercise D, Communication Practice, is offered as a means of encouraging one's individual expression in Spanish. There is no single "correct" response here; students are urged to "think themselves into" the contexts described and to find on their own an appropriate way of expressing the given idea without the inhibiting limitation of a specific translation being called for.

Finally, presented under the heading of Exercise E, are various additional and self-explanatory Review Exercises, generally stressing techniques for increasing the student's ability to build a growing "recognition vocabulary." These appear at the end of the first and second stories and occasionally thereafter.

It is our hope that these exercises will increase the value of this text as a language-learning tool and that they will successfully complement its main purpose of serving as an entertaining introduction to the reading of Spanish American imaginative fiction.

D. A. Y.
J. B. D.

A Prefatory Note to the Reader

There are a number of factors that will be of significant value to you in developing, early in your acquaintanceship with the Spanish language, a considerable ability in reading Spanish prose. The stories that follow are presented with the purpose in mind of demonstrating this point. The first selection, "Los dos reyes y los dos laberintos" by the Argentine writer Jorge Luis Borges, provides an excellent illustration of certain immediate advantages that the English-speaking student enjoys.

The author, Borges, who received his education in Europe, was one of his country's most cultured literary figures. His prose is by nature quite formal, and his vocabulary is notable for the use of many "learned" words. You will find that words of this type are among the easiest to comprehend on sight, for a large number of them are English cognates—they resemble their corresponding terms in English.

Thus it is that we start off with a story written in Spanish by a cultured Argentine that has the promise of being quite easy to understand. The story has approximately 300 words. Of these, roughly one-fifth are nouns. Of the 56 individual nouns, 23 are recognizable cognates. In addition, you probably already know many of the remaining nouns. The balance will be new nouns to be learned and retained for future readings.

More than a tenth of the words are verb forms. Of the roughly 30 individual verbs, a third are cognates; it is likely that you will already know another third.

The majority of the remaining words will be familiar to you. Therefore, we feel that you may turn to the Borges story with some feeling of confidence.

As you will see, there are numerous other ways besides spotting cognates of rapidly building up a reading vocabulary in Spanish. In the exercises following several of the stories, these techniques will be discussed and utilized.

We are confident that you will find ahead of you much pleasurable and rewarding reading in this sixth edition of *Imaginación y fantasía*.

Los dos reyes y los dos laberintos

Jorge Luis Borges

JORGE LUIS BORGES (1899–1986) was born in Argentina and educated in Europe. He returned to Buenos Aires in 1921 to begin forging one of the most respected literary reputations ever attained by a Spanish American writer. A leading poet in his early years, in the 1930s and 1940s he turned to prose expression with essays and stories that firmly established him as one of the finest literary stylists ever to write in the Spanish language. He was appointed Director of the National Library in Buenos Aires in 1955, the same year in which he lost his sight. But he continued to compose prose and poetry up until the time of his death, more than three decades later.

Of the numerous themes that run through the writings of Borges, one of the most striking is that of the maze, or labyrinth. A maze is, of course, a system of winding paths designed to confuse all who set foot in it. In Borges, however, the labyrinth becomes a symbol of the universe, an image of what the design of human existence might be. In "Los dos reyes y los dos laberintos" the author has conjured up one more labyrinth, proposing for it a new form—perhaps the most unusual form it could ever acquire.

A PRELIMINARY LOOK AT KEY EXPRESSIONS

The expressions listed below are found in the story and are used in the exercises and activities that follow. By studying these expressions before you read the story, you will facilitate your comprehension of the story and thus increase your enjoyment in reading it. This preliminary study will also help you do the assignments that follow more quickly and accurately, since all constructions and terms used in the activities and exercises appear here first with definitions and, in some cases, with further explanation and examples. The expressions are listed in the same order in which they occur in the story and with page and line numbers.

1. (4:3) **mandar** + *infinitive* When there is no indirect object, the expression means *to have* + *past participle*. For example, **El rey mandó construir un laberinto.** *The king had a labyrinth built.* But if there is an indirect object, the English wording changes: **El rey les mandó construir un laberinto.** *The king ordered them to build (had them build) a labyrinth.*

2. (4:8) **hacer burla de** *to make fun of, make a fool of*

3. (4:9) **hacer** + *infinitive* This expression is similar to Number 1: **El rey hizo construir un laberinto.** *The king had a labyrinth built.* But **El rey les hizo construir un laberinto** is *The king had (made) them build a labyrinth.*

4. (4:11) **dar con** *to find, come across, hit upon, run into* (usually by accident)

5. (4:14) **dar a conocer** *to make known* For example, **Te lo daré a conocer.** *I'll make it known to you.*

6. (4:14) **algún día** *someday* *Any day* (at all) is **cualquier día**

7. (4:14) **luego** *then, next* **Luego** refers to a point in time; **entonces** means *then* in the sense of *at that time, in those days,* etc. Compare **Luego le desaté las ligaduras.** *Then (next) I untied his bonds* with **Entonces yo no era más que un niño.** *Then (at that time) I was just a child.*

8. (4:18) **llevar** *to take, carry* This verb is used when something or someone is taken or transported from one place to another. **Tomar,** on the other hand, means *to take into one's possession:* **Tome Ud. este libro y devuélvalo a la biblioteca.** *Take this book and return it to the library.*

9. (4:20) **querer** (*in preterit*) + *infinitive* *to try* + *infinitive* **Querer** in the preterit indicates that an effort was made to carry out some action: **Me quisiste perder en tu laberinto.** *You tried to get me lost in your labyrinth.* However, in the imperfect **querer** expresses only the desire, whether an attempt was ever made or not: **Yo quería protestar, pero no dije palabra.** *I wanted to protest, but I didn't say a word.*

10. (4:21) **tener a bien** *to see fit*   This phrase is followed by an infinitive with no change of subject: **Dios ha tenido a bien terminarlo.** *God has seen fit to end it.* But it is followed by the subjunctive when there is a change of subject: **Dios ha tenido a bien que yo lo termine.** *God has seen fit that I end it.*

Los dos reyes y los dos laberintos

Cuentan los hombres dignos de fe (pero Alá[1] sabe más) que en los primeros días hubo un rey de las islas de Babilonia que congregó a sus arquitectos y magos y les mandó construir un laberinto tan perplejo y sutil que los varones más prudentes no se aventuraban
5 a entrar, y los que entraban se perdían. Esa obra era un escándalo, porque la confusión y la maravilla son operaciones propias de Dios y no de los hombres. Con el andar del tiempo vino a su corte un rey de los árabes, y el rey de Babilonia (para hacer burla de la simplicidad de su huésped) lo hizo penetrar en el laberinto,
10 donde vagó afrentado y confundido hasta la declinación de la tarde. Entonces imploró socorro divino y dio con la puerta. Sus labios no profirieron queja ninguna, pero le dijo al rey de Babilonia que él en Arabia tenía un laberinto mejor y que, si Dios era servido, se lo daría a conocer algún día. Luego regresó a Arabia,
15 juntó sus capitanes y sus alcaides y estragó los reinos de Babilonia con tan venturosa fortuna que derribó sus castillos, rompió sus gentes e hizo cautivo al mismo rey. Lo amarró encima de un camello veloz y lo llevó al desierto. Cabalgaron tres días, y le dijo: «¡Oh, rey del tiempo y substancia y cifra del siglo!, en Babilonia
20 me quisiste perder en un laberinto de bronce con muchas escaleras, puertas y muros; ahora el Poderoso ha tenido a bien que te muestre el mío, donde no hay escaleras que subir, ni puertas que forzar, ni fatigosas galerías que recorrer, ni muros que te veden el paso.»[2]
25   Luego le desató las ligaduras y lo abandonó en mitad del desierto, donde murió de hambre y de sed. La gloria sea con[3] Aquél que no muere.

[1] *Alá:* Allah (the Moslem name for God)
[2] *que te... paso:* that block your way
[3] *La gloria sea con:* Glory be to

Exercises

A. Questions and Opinions*

1. ¿Qué mandó construir un rey de las islas de Babilonia?

2. ¿Por qué era un escándalo esa obra?

3. ¿Quién vino a la corte del rey?

4. ¿Con qué propósito hizo penetrar en el laberinto a su huésped?

5. ¿Qué hizo el rey árabe antes de pedir socorro?

6. ¿Qué dijo el rey árabe que tenía en Arabia y que le daría a conocer algún día al otro rey?

7. ¿Quién hizo cautivo al rey de las islas de Babilonia?

8. ¿Hasta dónde llevó al rey después de amarrarlo encima de un camello?

9. ¿Es el desierto un laberinto de veras?

10. ¿Quién es «Aquél que no muere»?

•11. ¿Cree Ud. que Dios era servido en este cuento?

•12. ¿Conoce Ud. algún laberinto—existente o legendario?

B. Verb Practice

Here are some of the story's most important and most common Spanish verbal phrases—already presented in the preceding *Key Expressions* section with a brief explanation where necessary. Use each one in an original Spanish sentence—either similar to the one found in the story or, preferably, something completely different and personal. For example, **hacer burla de: El rey de Babilonia hizo burla de la simplicidad de su huésped** (based on the story) or **Nunca hago burla de nadie** (your own). Be prepared to explain the meaning of your sentences.

1. **mandar** + *infinitive*

2. **hacer** + *infinitive*

3. **dar con**

4. **llevar**

5. **querer** (*in preterit*) + *infinitive*

C. Vocabulary Practice Listed in the right-hand column are lexical (vocabulary) items that figure among the *Key Expressions* for this story. Complete the sentences below, matching the expressions on the right with the italicized English words on the left. Be sure to use the correct form of each verb. Then use each expression in an original Spanish sentence and indicate in English what your sentence means.

1. *Next,* llamé a mi compañero.

2. ¿Piensas ir a Arabia *someday*?

3. El jefe *did not see fit* darme un aumento de sueldo.

4. En ese caso, ¿por qué *don't you make known* tus quejas en la oficina del presidente?

5. Creo que los otros *would make fun of me.*

hacer burla de

tener a bien

algún día

luego

dar a conocer

D. Communication Practice The following sentences also involve the *Key Expressions* in the story. Express in Spanish the ideas suggested here, avoiding wherever possible a word-for-word rendering. The purpose here is to encourage you to think in Spanish and arrive at your own way of communicating the idea. For example, say that God saw fit that the King of Arabia show his own labyrinth to the King of Babylonia. (Remember to use the subjunctive.) **Dios tuvo a bien que el rey de los árabes (Arabia) le mostrara su laberinto al rey de Babilonia.**

1. Say that you, too, are going to have a labyrinth built someday.

2. Explain where the King of Arabia took the King of Babylonia.

3. Suggest that maybe tomorrow someone will hit on the solution.

4. Indicate that they have already made known the names.

5. Express the idea that no one saw fit to show you the island.

E. Review Exercise The following words from the story are cognates that you may have been able to recognize because of their resemblance to familiar English words. Review them now and see if you can give their meanings on sight. Check the end vocabulary if necessary.

Nouns: **islas, arquitectos, laberinto, escándalo, confusión, maravilla, operaciones, corte, árabes, simplicidad, capitanes, fortuna, castillos, camello, desierto, substancia, cifra, bronce, galerías, gloria, Babilonia, Alá**

Verbs:　**congregar, construir, aventurarse, entrar, penetrar, implorar, forzar, abandonar**

Adjectives:　**perplejo, sutil, prudente, confundido, divino**

Can you now make any generalizations on how certain groups of English words appear in Spanish? What form, for example, do many English words with the following endings take in Spanish: *-tion, -ty, -nce, -ent?*

Can a Spanish word begin with *sc-, sl-, sm-, sp-,* or *st-?* What is characteristic of the form of the Spanish equivalents of many English words of this type?

El leve Pedro

Enrique Anderson Imbert

ENRIQUE ANDERSON IMBERT (1910–   ) is a native Argentine who came to the United States more than four decades ago to continue a successful and fruitful career as teacher, author, literary critic and historian. His novels *Vigilia* (1934) and *Fuga* (1953) and his collection of short stories *Las pruebas del caos* (1946) established him as one of his country's most gifted writers. In 1954 he published his *Historia de la literatura hispanoamericana,* a valuable work that has since been revised and translated. Professor Anderson has been one of the most frequent and respected contributors to the pages of the principal Argentine literary newspapers and magazines, and is now a distinguished member of the Argentine Academy of Letters.

"El leve Pedro," taken from *Las pruebas del caos,* is that book's opening story. It is the first suggestion the author gives of the form that chaos might take in our comfortable, everyday world—if some imperceptible malfunction of one of the numerous simple "laws of nature" were to occur. If just one infinitesimal impossibility did happen, then, as he proposes elsewhere in his book, a cigarette could smoke a man. Or, in a like manner, we might have the case of—"El leve Pedro."

A PRELIMINARY LOOK AT KEY EXPRESSIONS

Be sure to study these expressions before you read the story.

1. (11:1) **asomarse a** *to peek at, to get a glimpse of; to lean out of* This verb is used to express the position one takes when looking around a corner, leaning out of a window, peeking from a doorway, etc.

2. (11:3) **solito** *all alone, all by oneself* The diminutive ending **-ito** emphasizes the meaning of the adjective **solo** *alone* in a variety of ways. Like most adjectives in Spanish, it changes in form to modify a feminine noun: **La chica estaba solita.** *The girl was all by herself.*

3. (11:14) **animarse a** + *infinitive* *to get up the energy, courage, nerve to + verb*

4. (11:19) **costarle poco (mucho) a uno** *to be easy (hard) for someone* The subject is usually an infinitive: **Le cuesta poco subir la escalera de cinco en cinco.** *It's very easy for him to go up the stairs five at a time.*

5. (11:30) **en cuanto** *as soon as* When the action referred to has not yet occurred, the subjunctive is used: **En cuanto llegue, hablaremos con ella.** *As soon as she gets here, we'll speak with her.*

6. (12:39) **casi** + *present tense* *almost + past tense:* **¡Casi me caigo!** *I almost fell!*

7. (12:39) **caerse** *to fall down*

8. (12:52) **dejar(se) de** + *infinitive* *to stop + present participle*

9. (12:53) **dar un paso** *to take a step*

10. (12:60) **quitarse** + *article of clothing* *to take off + article of clothing*

11. (12:61) **alcanzar a** + *infinitive* *to succeed in, get, manage to + verb*

12. (12:71) **mañana (hoy) mismo** *tomorrow (today) for sure, without fail* **Mismo** emphasizes the time word and is rendered in a variety of ways in English: **ahora mismo** *right now,* **mañana mismo** *tomorrow at the latest,* **ayer mismo** *just yesterday.*

13. (12:74) **sentirse** + *adjective* *to feel + adjective*

14. (13:75) **tener ganas de** + *infinitive* *to feel like + present participle*

15. (13:77) **dar las buenas noches (los buenos días,** etc.) *to say goodnight (good morning,* etc.)

16. (13:78) **al otro día** *(on) the next day*

17. (13:82) **al fin** *at last, finally*

18. (13:86) **tener que** + *infinitive* *to have to + verb*

19. (13:89) **ponerse a** + *infinitive*   *to start, begin + infinitive*   This expression usually implies voluntary action or sudden movement: **Se puso a tirar de la cuerda.** *She began to pull on the cord.* **Comenzar a** or **empezar a** is used for a more static or passive situation: **Comenzó a leer el cuento.** *He began to read the story.*

20. (13:97) **hacerse** + *noun*   *to become, turn into + noun*

El leve Pedro

Durante dos meses se asomó a la muerte. El médico murmuraba que la enfermedad de Pedro era nueva, que no había modo de tratarla y que él no sabía qué hacer... Por suerte el enfermo, solito, se fue curando. No había perdido su buen humor, su oronda calma provinciana. Demasiado flaco y eso era todo. Pero al levantarse después de varias semanas de convalecencia se sintió sin peso.[1]

—Oye —dijo a su mujer— me siento bien pero no sé... el cuerpo me parece... ausente. Estoy como si mis envolturas fueran a desprenderse dejándome el alma desnuda.[2]

—Languideces —le respondió su mujer.

—Tal vez.

Siguió recobrándose. Ya paseaba por el caserón, atendía el hambre de las gallinas y de los cerdos, dio una mano de pintura verde[3] a la pajarera y aun se animó a hachar la leña y llevarla en carretilla hasta el galpón. Pero según pasaban los días[4] las carnes de Pedro perdían densidad. Algo muy raro le iba minando, socavando, vaciando el cuerpo. Se sentía con una ingravidez portentosa.[5] Era la ingravidez de la chispa y de la burbuja, del globo y de la pelota. Le costaba muy poco saltar la verja, trepar las escaleras de cinco en cinco,[6] agarrar de un brinco[7] la manzana alta.

—Te has mejorado tanto —observaba su mujer— que pareces un chiquillo acróbata.

Una mañana Pedro se asustó. Hasta entonces su agilidad le había preocupado, pero todo ocurría como Dios manda.[8] Era extraordinario que, sin proponérselo, convirtiera la marcha de los humanos en una triunfal carrera en volandas sobre la quinta.[9] Era extraordinario pero no milagroso. Lo milagroso apareció esa mañana.

Muy temprano fue al potrero. Caminaba con pasos contenidos porque ya sabía que en cuanto taconeara iría dando rebotes por el corral.[10] Arremangó la camisa, acomodó un tronco, cogió el hacha y asestó el primer golpe. Y entonces, rechazado por el impulso de su propio hachazo, Pedro levantó vuelo.[11] Prendido todavía del hacha, quedó un instante en suspensión, levitando

---

[1] *sin peso:* weightless
[2] *Estoy... desnuda:* I feel as if my skin were peeling off, leaving just my naked soul.
[3] *dio... verde:* he applied a coat of green paint
[4] *según pasaban los días:* as the days went by
[5] *Se... portentosa:* He felt himself to be marvellously free of gravity.
[6] *de cinco en cinco:* five at a time
[7] *de un brinco:* with one leap
[8] *todo... manda:* nothing out of the ordinary happened
[9] *convirtiera... quinta:* he turned a normal human's walk into a triumphal series of soaring flights over the small farm
[10] *en... corral:* as soon as he put his heels down, he would start bouncing all over the yard
[11] *levantó vuelo:* took off

35 allá, a la altura de los techos; y luego bajó lentamente, bajó como un tenue vilano de cardo.

Acudió su mujer cuando Pedro ya había descendido y, con una palidez de muerte, temblaba agarrado a un tronco.

—¡Hebe! ¡Casi me caigo al cielo!

40 —Tonterías. No puedes caerte al cielo. Nadie se cae al cielo. ¿Qué te ha pasado?

Pedro explicó la cosa a su mujer y ésta, sin asombro, le reconvino:

—Te sucede por hacerte el acróbata.[12] Ya te lo he prevenido. 45 El día menos pensado[13] te desnucarás en una de tus piruetas.

—¡No, no! —insistió Pedro—. Ahora es diferente. Me resbalé. El cielo es un precipicio, Hebe.

Pedro soltó el tronco que lo anclaba pero se asió fuertemente a su mujer. Así abrazados volvieron a la casa.

50 —¡Hombre! —le dijo Hebe, que sentía el cuerpo de su marido pegado al suyo como el de un animal extrañamente joven y salvaje, con ansias de huir[14] en vertiginoso galope.— ¡Hombre, déjate de hacer fuerza, que me arrastras![15] Das unos pasos como si quisieras echarte a volar.

55 —¿Has visto, has visto? Algo horrible me está amenazando, Hebe. Un esguince, y ya empieza la ascensión.

Esa tarde Pedro, que estaba apoltronado en el patio leyendo las historietas del periódico, se rió convulsivamente. Y con la propulsión de ese motor alegre fue elevándose como un ludión, como 60 un buzo que se había quitado las suelas. La risa se trocó en terror y Hebe acudió otra vez a las voces de su marido. Alcanzó a cogerlo de los pantalones y lo atrajo a la tierra. Ya no había duda. Hebe le llenó los bolsillos con grandes tuercas, caños de plomo y piedras; y estos pesos por el momento le dieron a su cuerpo la solidez ne- 65 cesaria para tranquear por la galería y empinarse por la escalera de su cuarto. Lo difícil fue desvestirlo. Cuando Hebe le quitó los hierros y el plomo, Pedro, fluctuante sobre las sábanas, se entrelazó a los barrotes de la cama y le advirtió:

—¡Cuidado, Hebe! Vamos a hacerlo despacio porque no 70 quiero dormir en el techo.

—Mañana mismo llamaremos al médico.

—Si consigo estarme quieto[16] no me ocurrirá nada. Solamente cuando me agito me hago aeronauta.

Con mil precauciones pudo acostarse y se sintió seguro.

[12] *Te... acróbata:* It's happened because of your playing the acrobat.
[13] *El día menos pensado:* One of these days
[14] *con ansias de huir:* anxious to flee
[15] *déjate... arrastras!* stop pulling, you're dragging me!
[16] *Si consigo estarme quieto:* If I manage to stay still

75 —¿Tienes ganas de subir?

—No. Estoy bien.

Se dieron las buenas noches[17] y Hebe apagó la luz.

Al otro día cuando Hebe despegó los ojos vio a Pedro durmiendo como un bendito,[18] con la cara pegada al techo. Parecía
80 un globo escapado de las manos de un niño.

—¡Pedro, Pedro! —gritó aterrorizada.

Al fin Pedro despertó, dolorido por el estrujón de varias horas contra el cielo raso. ¡Qué espanto! Trató de saltar al revés, de caer para arriba, de subir para abajo. Pero el techo lo succionaba
85 como el suelo succionaba a Hebe.

—Tendrás que atarme de una pierna y amarrarme al ropero hasta que llames al doctor y vea qué es lo que pasa.

Hebe buscó una cuerda y una escalera, ató un pie a su marido[19] y se puso a tirar con todo el ánimo. El cuerpo adosado al
90 techo se removió como un lento dirigible. Aterrizaba.

En eso[20] se coló por la puerta un correntón de aire que ladeó la leve corporeidad de Pedro y, como a una pluma, la sopló por la ventana. Ocurrió en un segundo. Hebe lanzó un grito y la cuerda se le escapó de las manos. Cuando corrió a la ventana ya su ma-
95 rido, desvanecido, subía por el aire inocente de la mañana, subía en suave contoneo como un globo de color fugitivo en un día de fiesta, perdido para siempre, en viaje al infinito. Se hizo un punto y luego nada.

[17] *Se dieron... noches:* They said goodnight to each other
[18] *un bendito:* a baby; literally a "blessed one"
[19] *ató... marido:* tied one of her husband's feet
[20] *En eso:* At that moment

Exercises

A. Questions and Opinions

1. ¿Qué dijo el médico de la enfermedad de Pedro?

2. ¿Cómo se sintió Pedro al levantarse después de varias semanas de convalecencia?

3. ¿Por qué dijo la mujer de Pedro que éste parecía un chiquillo acróbata?

4. ¿Qué ocurrió cuando Pedro dio un golpe con su hacha?

5. ¿Podría ser el cielo un precipicio de veras?

6. ¿Qué le pasó a Pedro una tarde cuando se rio convulsivamente?

7. ¿Con qué le llenó Hebe los bolsillos a su marido?

8. Al despertarse la mañana siguiente, ¿qué vio Hebe?

9. ¿Cómo se le escapó de las manos la cuerda?

10. ¿Hasta dónde subió el leve Pedro?

•11. ¿Qué le parece a Ud. la idea de que el cielo es un precipicio?

•12. ¿Ha tenido Ud. ganas alguna vez de echarse a volar? ¿Sería divertido?

B. Verb Practice   Use each of the following verbal phrases in an original sentence in Spanish, either based on the story or of your own design. Be prepared to explain the meaning of your sentences.

1. **animarse a** + *infinitive*

2. **costarle poco (mucho) a uno**

3. **caerse**

4. **dejar(se) de** + *infinitive*

5. **quitarse** + *article of clothing*

6. **alcanzar a** + *infinitive*

7. **sentirse** + *adjective*

8. **tener que** + *infinitive*

9. **ponerse a** + *infinitive*

10. **hacerse** + *noun*

C. Vocabulary Practice   Complete the sentences below, matching the expressions on the right with the English words on the left. Be sure to use the correct form of each verb. Then use each expression in an original Spanish sentence and indicate in English what your sentence means.

1. *Finally* Pedro empezó a aterrizar.

2. Cada vez que *he took a step* brincaba como un acróbata.

3. Cuando la esposa de Pedro le quería *say good morning,* no lo veía en ninguna parte.

asomarse a

solito

ayer mismo

casi + *present tense*

4. No quiero de ningún modo *get a glimpse of* la muerte.

5. Pedro *felt like* subir al cielo.

6. *Just yesterday* me asusté por mi propia agilidad.

7. Hebe, *as soon as* taconee levantaré vuelo.

8. Hebe prometió llamar al médico *the next day.*

9. Déjame, que puedo aterrizar *all by myself.*

10. ¡*I almost went up* (**subir**) al techo!

dar un paso

en cuanto

**dar los
buenos días**

al otro día

tener ganas de +
infinitive

al fin

D. Communication Practice

1. Ask a close friend how she feels today.

2. Say you don't feel like going to the city with the others.

3. Indicate that Pepe is becoming just a dot in the sky.

4. Say you began to clean your apartment at eight-thirty.

5. Ask your classmates if they managed to finish all the sentences.

E. **Review Exercise** The following words, which appeared in the last two stories, carry the diminutive endings **-ito, -cito, -illo, -cillo,** and **-uelo.** What different translations can these words have? What do these diminutive suffixes suggest (1) with regard to the object itself and (2) about the point of view of the speaker or author?

pueblecito	**bolsillos**	**arroyuelo**
solito	**criadito**	**callejuelas**
casita	**vientecillo**	
carretilla	**chiquillo**	

Being aware of the widespread use of the various diminutive endings in Spanish is a valuable asset in recognizing new (and, at first glance, apparently unknown) words, and in expanding your own active vocabulary as well.

Jaque mate en dos jugadas

Isaac Aisemberg

ISAAC AISEMBERG (1919–1997) was one of the foremost Argentine cultivators of the detective story—a type of fiction that for decades has enjoyed great popularity in the principal cities of Spanish America. Thanks to Aisemberg and others of his Buenos Aires colleagues, the detective story has had a greater and more varied development in Argentina than in any other Spanish-speaking country—including Spain. Aisemberg brought an interesting background to the writing of detective short stories and novels. He studied law (with the intention of entering politics), worked on Buenos Aires newspapers, and did program planning for Radio Nacional in the capital. He also wrote for Argentine movies and television. His *Tres negativos para un retrato* (1949) and *Manchas en el Río Bermejo* (1950) are two of the most imaginative and well-executed detective novels that have been written in Argentina.

"Jaque mate en dos jugadas" is an ironic tale of revenge, set against the backdrop of Buenos Aires by night. One of Aisemberg's most successful stories, it has been published in translation in the United States and has appeared in other short-story anthologies. Beginning with the story's first three words and continuing on to the surprise climax, the reader is absorbed in the thoughts of Claudio Álvarez and experiences with him the elation and subsequent creeping doubt and terror of a man who has committed a crime in the hope of going unpunished for it before the law.

A PRELIMINARY LOOK AT KEY EXPRESSIONS

Be sure to study these expressions before you read the story.

1. (19:1) **quedar** + *past participle   to be, become + adjective*   This expression is similar to **estar** + *past participle* except that **quedar** emphasizes the change or result. **Está liberado** means *He is free,* but **Queda liberado** means *He gets free* or *He is freed.*

2. (19:11) **acostumbrarse a** *to get used to*

3. (19:14) **a pesar de** *in spite of*

4. (19:16) **hacerse** + *adjective   to become, get + adjective*   This expression is used for relatively fundamental or important changes: **Se hizo intolerable.** *He became unbearable,* as opposed to **ponerse,** which is used for more superficial, temporary changes: **Me puse triste.** *I got sad.*

5. (19:21) **dedicarse a** + *infinitive   to devote oneself to + verb,* or *to spend a lot of time +* *present participle:* **Se dedica a jugar al ajedrez.** *He spends a lot of time playing chess.*

6. (20:66) **tener inconveniente en** + *infinitive   to mind + present participle* or *to* *object to + verb:* **El médico no tendría inconveniente en suscribir el certificado de defunción.** *The doctor would not object to signing the death certificate.*

7. (21:74) **estar dispuesto a** *to be ready, disposed to + verb:* **Estamos dispuestos a revelarlo todo.** *We're ready to confess everything.* It also means *to be inclined toward + noun:* **Tú siempre estás dispuesto a la tragedia.** *You're always inclined toward tragedy* or *You always make things seem so tragic.*

8. (21:77) **tomársela con** *to pick on, quarrel with, have a grudge against, have it in for:* **¿Por qué mi tío siempre se la toma conmigo?** *Why is my uncle always picking on me?*

9. (21:84) **resolver** *to solve*

10. (21:94) **resultar** *to turn out (to be):* **El veneno resultaba rápido.** *The poison was turning out to be fast.*

11. (21:96) **en paz** *alone, "in peace":* **¡Déjame en paz!** *Leave me alone!, Stop bothering me!*

12. (22:122) **pensar en** *to think of, about*

13. (22:153) **de un trago** *in one gulp, swallow*

14. (23:159) **cerrar el paso** *to block the way*   The person whose way is blocked is the indirect object: **El inspector le cerraba el paso.** *The inspector was blocking his way.*

15. (23:177) **a cargo de** *in charge of*

16. (24:198) **encontrarse con** *to meet, run into*   This is either a planned or a chance meeting.
17. (24:221) **tener entendido** *to understand* in the sense of *be informed:* **Tengo entendido que ustedes jugaban al ajedrez.** *I understand that you used to play chess together.*
18. (24:227) **como es de imaginar** *as you (one) can imagine*
19. (25:244) **con vida** *alive:* **¿Quién fue el último que lo vio con vida?** *Who was the last one to see him alive?*
20. (25:251) **con toda mi** (**su,** etc.) **alma** *with all my* (*his,* etc.) *heart and soul*

Jaque mate en dos jugadas

Yo lo envenené. En dos horas quedaría liberado. Dejé a mi tío Néstor a las veintidós.[1] Lo hice con alegría. Me ardían las mejillas. Me quemaban los labios. Luego me serené y eché a caminar tranquilamente por la avenida en dirección al puerto.

5   Me sentía contento. Liberado. Hasta Guillermo saldría socio beneficiario[2] en el asunto. ¡Pobre Guillermo! ¡Tan tímido, tan inocente! Era evidente que yo debía pensar y obrar por ambos. Siempre sucedió así. Desde el día en que nuestro tío nos llevó a su casa. Nos encontramos perdidos en el palacio. Era un lugar seco,
10 sin amor. Unicamente el sonido metálico de las monedas.

    —Tenéis[3] que acostumbraros al ahorro, a no malgastar. ¡Al fin y al cabo,[4] algún día será vuestro! —decía. Y nos acostumbramos a esperarlo.

    Pero ese famoso y deseado día no llegaba, a pesar de que tío
15 sufría del corazón. Y si de pequeños[5] nos tiranizó, cuando crecimos se hizo cada vez más[6] intolerable.

    Guillermo se enamoró un buen día. A nuestro tío no le gustó la muchacha. No era lo que ambicionaba para su sobrino.

    —Le falta cuna..., le falta roce...,[7] ¡puaf! Es una ordinaria...
20 —sentenció.

    Inútil fue que Guillermo se dedicara a encontrarle méritos.[8] El viejo era testarudo y arbitrario.

    Conmigo tenía otra clase de problemas. Era un carácter contra otro. Se empeñó en doctorarme[9] en bioquímica. ¿Resultado?
25 Un perito en póquer y en carreras de caballos. Mi tío para esos vicios no me daba ni un centavo. Tenía que emplear todo mi ingenio para quitarle un peso.

    Uno de los recursos era aguantarle sus interminables partidas de ajedrez; entonces yo cedía con aire de hombre magná-
30 nimo, pero él, en cambio, cuando estaba en posición favorable alargaba el final, anotando las jugadas con displicencia, sabiendo de mi prisa por salir para el club. Gozaba con mi infortunio saboreando su coñac.

[1] *a las veintidós:* In many parts of the world, the 24-hour system of telling time is often used. "Twenty-two," therefore, is 10 P.M.
[2] *socio beneficiario:* partner in the profits
[3] *Tenéis:* the second-person plural form of the verb used with the subject pronoun *vosotros* (The uncle, who is a Spaniard, uses these forms since they are normal in Spain for the familiar form of address. The nephews, however, like all Spanish-Americans, use *ustedes* with its corresponding third-person plural forms to express the familiar plural.)
[4] *Al fin y al cabo:* After all
[5] *de pequeños:* when we were children
[6] *cada vez más:* more and more
[7] *Le falta cuna... roce:* She has no breeding, no class.
[8] *encontrarle méritos:* point out her good qualities
[9] *Se... doctorame:* He insisted that I get a doctor's degree

Un día me dijo con tono condescendiente:

35 —Observo que te aplicas en el ajedrez. Eso me demuestra dos cosas: que eres inteligente y un perfecto holgazán. Sin embargo, tu dedicación tendrá su premio. Soy justo. Pero eso sí,[10] a falta de diplomas,[11] de hoy en adelante tendré de ti bonitas anotaciones de las partidas. Sí, muchacho, vamos a guardar cada uno los
40 apuntes de los juegos en libretas para compararlas. ¿Qué te parece?

Aquello podría resultar un par de cientos de pesos, y acepté. Desde entonces, todas las noches, la estadística. Estaba tan arraigada la manía en él, que en mi ausencia comentaba las partidas con Julio, el mayordomo.

45 Ahora todo había concluido. Cuando uno se encuentra en un callejón sin salida, el cerebro trabaja, busca, rebusca. Y encuentra. Siempre hay salida para todo. No siempre es buena. Pero es salida.

Llegaba a la Costanera.[12] Era una noche húmeda. En el cielo nublado, alguna chispa eléctrica. El calorcillo mojaba las manos,
50 resecaba la boca.

En la esquina, un policía me hizo saltar el corazón.

El veneno, ¿cómo se llamaba? Aconitina. Varias gotitas en el coñac mientras conversábamos. Mi tío esa noche estaba encantador. Me perdonó la partida.[13]

55 —Haré un solitario[14] —dijo—. Despaché a los sirvientes... ¡Hum! Quiero estar tranquilo. Después leeré un buen libro. Algo que los jóvenes no entienden... Puedes irte.

—Gracias, tío. Hoy realmente es... sábado.

—Comprendo.

60 ¡Demonios! El hombre comprendía. La clarividencia del condenado.

El veneno producía un efecto lento, a la hora,[15] o más, según el sujeto. Hasta seis u ocho horas. Justamente durante el sueño. El resultado: la apariencia de un pacífico ataque cardíaco, sin hue-
65 llas comprometedoras. Lo que yo necesitaba. ¿Y quién sospecharía? El doctor Vega no tendría inconveniente en suscribir el certificado de defunción. ¿Y si me descubrían? ¡Imposible!

Pero, ¿y Guillermo? Sí. Guillermo era un problema. Lo hallé en el *hall* después de preparar la «encomienda» para el infierno.
70 Descendía la escalera, preocupado.

—¿Qué te pasa? —le pregunté jovial, y le hubiera agregado de buena gana: «¡Si supieras, hombre!»

—¡Estoy harto! —me replicó.

[10] *eso sí:* keep in mind
[11] *a falta de diplomas:* since there'll be no diploma
[12] *la Costanera:* a riverside thoroughfare in Buenos Aires, officially named Avenida Costanera Rafael Obligado
[13] *Me perdonó la partida:* He excused me from the game.
[14] *Haré un solitario:* I'll play a game by myself
[15] *a la hora:* after an hour

—¡Vamos! —Le palmoteé la espalda—. Siempre estás dis-
75 puesto a la tragedia...

—Es que el viejo me enloquece. Últimamente, desde que
volviste a la Facultad[16] y le llevas la corriente[17] en el ajedrez, se la
toma conmigo. Y Matilde...

—¿Qué sucede con Matilde?

80 —Matilde me lanzó un ultimátum: o ella, o tío.

—Opta por ella. Es fácil elegir. Es lo que yo haría...

—¿Y lo otro?

Me miró desesperado. Con brillo demoníaco en las pupi-
las; pero el pobre tonto jamás buscaría el medio de resolver su
85 problema.

—Yo lo haría —siguió entre dientes—; pero, ¿con qué vivi-
ríamos? Ya sabes cómo es el viejo... Duro, implacable. ¡Me cortaría
los víveres!

—*Tal vez las cosas se arreglen de otra manera...* —insinué
90 bromeando—. ¡Quién te dice...!

—¡Bah!... —sus labios se curvaron con una mueca amarga—.
No hay escapatoria. Pero yo hablaré con el viejo tirano. ¿Dónde
está ahora?

Me asusté. Si el veneno resultaba rápido... Al notar los
95 primeros síntomas podría ser auxiliado y...

—Está en la biblioteca —exclamé—, pero déjalo en paz.
Acaba de jugar la partida de ajedrez, y despachó a la servidumbre.
¡El lobo quiere estar solo en la madriguera! Consuélate en un cine
o en un bar.

100 Se encogió de hombros.

—El lobo en la madriguera... —repitió. Pensó unos segundos
y agregó, aliviado—: Lo veré en otro momento. Después de todo...

—Después de todo, no te animarías,[18] ¿verdad? —gruñí sal-
vajemente.

105 Me clavó la mirada.[19] Sus ojos brillaron con una chispa
siniestra, pero fue un relámpago.

Miré el reloj: las once y diez de la noche.

Ya comenzaría a producir efecto. Primero un leve malestar,
nada más. Después un dolorcillo agudo, pero nunca demasiado
110 alarmante. Mi tío refunfuñaba una maldición para la cocinera.
El pescado indigesto. ¡Qué poca cosa es todo![20] Debía de estar
leyendo los diarios de la noche, los últimos. Y después, el libro,
como gran epílogo. Sentía frío.

[16] *la Facultad:* the University (really just a school, college, or division of a university)
[17] *le llevas la corriente:* you let him have his way
[18] *no te animarías:* you wouldn't have the nerve
[19] *Me clavó la mirada:* He fixed his gaze on me.
[20] *¡Qué... todo!* How easy it all is!

Las baldosas se estiraban en rombos.[21] El río era una mancha
115 sucia cerca del paredón. A lo lejos luces verdes, rojas, blancas. Los
automóviles se deslizaban chapoteando en el asfalto.

Decidí regresar, por temor a llamar la atención. Nuevamente
por la avenida hacia Leandro N. Alem.[22] Por allí a Plaza de Mayo.[23]
El reloj me volvió a la realidad. Las once y treinta y seis. Si el ve-
120 neno era eficaz, ya estaría todo listo. Ya sería dueño de millones.
Ya sería libre... Ya sería..., *ya sería asesino.*

Por primera vez pensé en la palabra misma. Yo ¡asesino! Las
rodillas me flaquearon. Un rubor me azotó el cuello, me subió a
las mejillas, me quemó las orejas, martilló mis sienes. Las manos
125 traspiraban. El frasquito de aconitina en el bolsillo llegó a pe-
sarme una tonelada. Busqué en los bolsillos rabiosamente hasta
dar con él.[24] Era un insignificante cuentagotas y contenía la
muerte; lo arrojé lejos.

Avenida de Mayo. Choqué con varios transeúntes. Pensarían
130 en un borracho.[25] Pero en lugar de alcohol, sangre.

Yo, asesino. Esto sería un secreto entre mi tío Néstor y mi
conciencia.

Recordé la descripción del efecto del veneno: «en la lengua,
sensación de hormigueo y embotamiento, que se inicia en el
135 punto de contacto para extenderse a toda la lengua, a la cara y a
todo el cuerpo.»

Entré en un bar. Un tocadiscos atronaba con un viejo *rag-
time.*[26] «En el esófago y en el estómago, sensación de ardor intenso.» Millones. Billetes de mil, de quinientos, de cien. Póquer.
140 Carreras. Viajes... «sensación de angustia, de muerte próxima, enfriamiento profundo generalizado, trastornos sensoriales, debilidad muscular, contracciones, impotencia de los músculos.»

Habría[27] quedado solo. En el palacio. Con sus escaleras de
mármol. Frente al tablero de ajedrez. Allí el rey, y la dama, y la
145 torre negra. Jaque mate.

El mozo se aproximó. Debió sorprender mi mueca de ex-
travío, mis músculos en tensión, listos para saltar.

—¿Señor?

—Un coñac...

150 —Un coñac... —repitió el mozo—. Bien, señor —y se alejó.

Por la vidriera la caravana que pasa,[28] la misma de siempre.
El tictac del reloj cubría todos los rumores. Hasta los de mi
corazón. La una. Bebí el coñac de un trago.

[21] *Las... rombos:* The paving stones stretched out in the shape of diamonds. (Frequently the side-walks of Buenos Aires consist of diamond-shaped stones or sections of cement.)
[22] *Leandro N. Alem:* a main street in down-town Buenos Aires, near the waterfront
[23] *Plaza de Mayo:* main square of Buenos Aires
[24] *hasta dar con él:* until I found it
[25] *Pensarían en un borracho:* They must have thought I was drunk.
[26] *rag-time:* synco-pated American mu-sic, mainly composed by African-Americans and popular in the early years of the 20th century
[27] *Habría:* He must have
[28] *la caravana que pasa:* the "passing parade"

«Como fenómeno circulatorio, hay alteración del pulso e
155 hipotensión que se derivan de la acción sobre el órgano central,
llegando, en su estado más avanzado, al síncope cardíaco...» Eso
es. El síncope cardíaco. La válvula de escape.

A las dos y treinta de la mañana regresé a casa. Al principio
no lo advertí. Hasta que me cerró el paso. Era un agente de poli-
160 cía. Me asusté.

—¿El señor Claudio Álvarez?

—Sí, señor... —respondí humildemente.

—Pase usted... —indicó, franqueándome la entrada.

—¿Qué hace usted aquí? —me animé a murmurar.

165 —Dentro tendrá la explicación —fue la respuesta.

En el *hall,* cerca de la escalera, varios individuos de uniforme
se habían adueñado del palacio. ¿Guillermo? Guillermo no estaba
presente.

Julio, el mayordomo, amarillo, espectral trató de hablarme.
170 Uno de los uniformados, canoso, adusto, el jefe del grupo por lo
visto, le selló los labios con un gesto. Avanzó hacia mí, y me ins-
peccionó como a un cobayo.

—Usted es el mayor de los sobrinos, ¿verdad?

—Sí, señor... —murmuré.

175 —Lamento decírselo, señor. Su tío ha muerto... asesinado
—anunció mi interlocutor. La voz era calma, grave—. Yo soy el
inspector Villegas, y estoy a cargo de la investigación. ¿Quiere
acompañarme a la otra sala?

—Dios mío —articulé anonadado—. ¡Es inaudito!

180 Las palabras sonaron a huecas, a hipócritas. (*¡Ese dichoso*[29]
veneno dejaba huellas! ¿Pero cómo... cómo?)

—¿Puedo... puedo verlo? —pregunté.

—Por el momento, no. Además, quiero que me conteste algunas preguntas.

185 —Como usted disponga...[30] —accedí azorado.

Lo seguí a la biblioteca vecina. Tras él se deslizaron suavemente dos acólitos. El inspector Villegas me indicó un sillón y se
sentó en otro. Encendió frugalmente un cigarrillo y con evidente
grosería no me ofreció ninguno.

190 —Usted es el sobrino... Claudio. —Pareció que repetía una
lección aprendida de memoria.

—Sí, señor.

—Pues bien: explíquenos qué hizo esta noche.

[29] *dichoso:* damned (literally, "happy")
[30] *Como usted disponga:* Just as you say

Yo también repetí una letanía.

195 —Cenamos los tres, juntos como siempre. Guillermo se retiró a su habitación. Quedamos mi tío y yo charlando un rato; pasamos a la biblioteca. Después jugamos nuestra habitual partida de ajedrez; me despedí de mi tío y salí. En el vestíbulo me encontré con Guillermo que descendía por las escaleras rumbo a la
200 calle. Cambiamos unas palabras y me fui.

—Y ahora regresa...

—Sí...

—¿Y los criados?

—Mi tío deseaba quedarse solo. Los despachó después de ce-
205 nar. A veces le acometían estas y otras manías.

—Lo que usted dice concuerda en gran parte con la declaración del mayordomo. Cuando éste regresó, hizo un recorrido por el edificio. Notó la puerta de la biblioteca entornada y luz adentro. Entró. Allí halló a su tío frente a un tablero de ajedrez,
210 muerto. La partida interrumpida... De manera que jugaron la partidita, ¿eh?

Algo dentro de mí comenzó a saltar violentamente. Una sensación de zozobra, de angustia, me recorría con la velocidad de un pebete. En cualquier momento estallaría la pólvora. *¡Los*
215 *consabidos solitarios de mi tío!*[31]

—Sí, señor... —admití.

No podía desdecirme. Eso también se lo había dicho a Guillermo. Y probablemente Guillermo al inspector Villegas. Porque mi hermano debía de estar en alguna parte. El sistema de la po-
220 licía: aislarnos, dejarnos solos, inertes, indefensos, para pillarnos.

—Tengo entendido que ustedes llevaban un registro de las jugadas. Para establecer los detalles en su orden, ¿quiere mostrarme su libretita de apuntes, señor Álvarez?

Me hundía en el cieno.

225 —¿Apuntes?

—Sí, hombre —el policía era implacable—, deseo verla, como es de imaginar. Debo verificarlo todo, amigo; lo dicho y lo hecho por usted.[32] *Si jugaron como siempre...*

Comencé a tartamudear.

230 —Es que... —Y después, de un tirón:[33] —¡Claro que jugamos como siempre!

Las lágrimas comenzaron a quemarme los ojos. Miedo. Un miedo espantoso. Como debió sentirlo tío Néstor cuando aquella «sensación de angustia... de muerte próxima..., enfriamiento

[31] *solitarios de mi tío:* games my uncle played alone
[32] *lo... usted:* what you said and what you did
[33] *de un tirón:* all at once

235 profundo, generalizado...» Algo me taladraba el cráneo. Me em-
pujaban. El silencio era absoluto, pétreo. Los otros también estaban callados. Dos ojos, seis ojos, ocho ojos, mil ojos. ¡Oh, qué
angustia!

Me tenían... me tenían... Jugaban con mi desesperación... Se
240 divertían con mi culpa...

De pronto, el inspector gruñó:

—¿Y?

Una sola letra ¡pero tanto!

—¿Y? —repitió—. Usted fue el último que lo vio con vida.
245 Y, además, muerto. El señor Álvarez no hizo anotación alguna
esta vez, señor mío.[34]

No sé por qué me puse de pie. Tenso. Elevé mis brazos, los
estiré. Me estrujé las manos, clavándome las uñas, y al final chillé
con voz que no era la mía:
250 —¡Basta! Si lo saben, ¿para qué lo preguntan? ¡Yo lo maté!
¡Yo lo maté! ¿Y qué hay?[35] ¡Lo odiaba con toda mi alma! ¡Estaba
cansado de su despotismo! ¡Lo maté! ¡Lo maté!

El inspector no lo tomó tan a la tremenda.[36]

—¡Cielos! —dijo—. Se produjo más pronto de lo que yo es-
255 peraba. Ya que se le soltó la lengua,[37] ¿dónde está el revólver?

El inspector Villegas no se inmutó. Insistió imperturbable.

—¡Vamos, no se haga el tonto[38] ahora! ¡El revólver! ¿O ha
olvidado que lo liquidó de un tiro? ¡Un tiro en la mitad de la
frente, compañero! ¡Qué puntería!

[34] *señor mío:* my good man
[35] *¿Y qué hay?* And what of it?
[36] *no... tremenda:* did not seem too surprised
[37] *Ya... lengua:* Since your tongue's loosened up
[38] *no... tonto:* don't play dumb

Exercises

A. Questions and Opinions

1. ¿Qué crimen había cometido el narrador, Claudio Álvarez?

2. ¿Qué guardaban Claudio y su tío en sus libretas?

3. ¿Por qué odiaba a su tío el hermano de Claudio?

4. ¿Qué ultimátum le había lanzado Matilde a Guillermo?

5. ¿Cree Ud. que Claudio insultó a su hermano, diciendo «Después de todo, no te animarías, ¿verdad?»?

6. ¿Qué hizo Claudio con el frasquito de veneno?

7. ¿En dónde entró Claudio para calmar los nervios?

8. ¿Quiénes esperaban a Claudio cuando regresó a casa?

9. ¿Dijo la verdad Claudio en todo lo que declaró al inspector?

10. ¿Cómo murió el tío Néstor?

•11. ¿Por qué confesó Claudio Álvarez?

•12. ¿Cree Ud. que pueda haber «un crimen perfecto»? ¿Por qué?

B. Verb Practice Use each of the following verbal phrases in an original sentence in Spanish, either based on the story or of your own design. Be prepared to explain the meaning of your sentences.

1. **quedar** + *past participle*

2. **acostumbrarse a**

3. **hacerse** + *adjective*

4. **dedicarse a** + *infinitive*

5. **tener inconveniente en** + *infinitive*

6. **tomársela con**

7. **resolver**

8. **resultar**

9. **pensar en**

10. **encontrarse con**

C. Vocabulary Practice Complete the sentences below, matching the expressions on the right with the English words on the left. Be sure to use the correct form of each verb. Then use each expression in an original Spanish sentence and indicate in English what your sentence means.

1. *I understand* que a su tío le gustaba jugar al ajedrez casi todos los días.

2. Ahora odia a su tío *with all his heart and soul.*

3. Creo que mi tío habrá tomado el veneno *in one swallow.*

a pesar de

estar dispuesto a

en paz

cerrar el paso

4. Estaba preocupado *in spite of* que el veneno no dejaba huellas.

5. Siempre *I was inclined toward* el pesimismo.

6. Cuando el sobrino quería entrar en la sala, el policía le *blocked the way.*

7. Quería que su tío no le molestara y que lo dejara *alone.*

8. ¿Quién está *in charge of* la investigación?

9. *As you can imagine,* el sobrino estaba terriblemente asustado.

10. Nunca lo volvieron a ver *alive.*

de un trago

a cargo de

tener entendido

como es de imaginar

con vida

con toda mi (su, etc.) **alma**

D. Communication Practice

1. Say you think a lot about your future.

2. State that yesterday everyone left you alone.

3. Express the idea that Claudio would never become accustomed to being poor.

4. Say that Jorge's brother is always picking on you.

5. Indicate that you wouldn't mind helping with the party.

El señor Alcides

Manuel Peyrou

MANUEL PEYROU (1902–1974) was an Argentine novelist, short story writer, and journalist who for many years worked on the editorial staff of the Buenos Aires newspaper *La Prensa*. He was also a frequent contributor to the prestigious Argentine literary review *Sur*. His first novel, *El estruendo de las rosas* (1948), published in the early years of the dictatorship of Juan Domingo Perón, gave the appearance of being a detective story set in a nightmarish pseudo-Germanic setting. It actually amounted, however, to a brilliant satire on the inevitable absurdities and shortcomings of any totalitarian state. Peyrou also published several collections of detective short stories with turn-of-the-century Buenos Aires settings. Perhaps the most significant part of his work will prove to be the series of novels he wrote between 1959 and 1966, which undertakes to depict the mood of moral deterioration that descended over Argentina during and immediately after the rule of Perón.

"El señor Alcides" is a whimsical tale that draws its effect from the subtle exaggeration of certain aspects of massive bureaucracy, still today one of the most evident features of Buenos Aires life. After a while, one observes, reason is no longer a valid standard for conduct within a bureaucratic system. The employee in this story slowly comes to the conclusion that, in the end, it is the system, not the individual, that is really important.

A PRELIMINARY LOOK AT KEY EXPRESSIONS

Be sure to study these expressions before you read the story.

1. (31:3) **acercarse** *to approach, come up to*   This is an intransitive reflexive verb: **me acerqué** *I approached,* **se acercó** *s/he approached,* etc. The nonreflexive **acercar** is transitive (takes an object) and means *to bring (something) closer:* **Acerqué mi silla a la mesa.** *I pulled my chair up to the table.*

2. (31:12) **retirarse** *to withdraw, go away, leave, "get out of the picture"*   **Jubilarse** is *to retire* in the sense of leaving work and taking one's pension.

3. (31:14) **un mueble** *a piece of furniture*   The plural **muebles** means *furniture.*

4. (31:16) **ignorar** *not to know*   This simply means **no saber.** *To ignore* is **no hacer caso de** or **a.**

5. (31:25) **simpatía** *friendliness* or *"niceness"*   the adjective is **simpático.** *Sympathy* is **compasión, condolencia, lástima.**

6. (31:34) **a tiempo** *in time*

7. (32:54) **por decirlo así** *so to speak, to put it one way*

8. (32:65) **ponerse** + *adjective*   *to become, get* + *adjective*   This expression is used with conditions subject to change such as **engorroso** (*bothersome*), **triste, satisfecho, enfermo, mejor,** etc.

9. (32:68) **como de costumbre** *as usual*

10. (32:73) **verse** + *adjective*   *to be* + *adjective:* **Me veía obligado.** *I was obliged.*

11. (33:82) **volver a** + *infinitive*   *verb* + *again:* **Volvió a comentar el caso.** *He commented on the matter again.*

12. (33:110) **al rato** *in a short while*

13. (34:120) **la razón** *correctness, being right:* **Combaten la razón porque no la tienen.** *They are against what's right because they are wrong themselves.*

14. (34:133) **preocuparse de** + *infinitive*   *to worry, bother about* + *present participle:* **El intruso no se preocupa de complacer al señor Alcides.** *The intruder doesn't worry about pleasing Mr. Alcides.*

15. (34:135) **bastar con** + *infinitive*   *to be enough* + *infinitive:* **Bastaba con haber insinuado la cosa.** *It was enough to have insinuated the matter.*

16. (34:138) **terminar de** + *infinitive*   *to finish* + *past participle*   **Dejar de** + *infinitive* is *to stop* + *present participle.* Compare **Terminó de archivar los papeles** *He finished filing the papers* with **Por fin dejó de fumar** *He finally stopped smoking.*

17. (35:157) **al mismo tiempo** *at the same time*
18. (35:159) **de algún modo** *somehow, in some way*
19. (35:170) **de pie** *standing (up), on foot*   This is opposed to **sentado** *sitting* or **acostado** *lying (down).*
20. (35:179) **dar vueltas** *to walk (go) around:* **Di varias vueltas por la mesa.** *I walked around the table several times.*

El señor Alcides

En la cálida penumbra de la oficina, que agitaba apenas el ventilador silencioso, apareció suavemente, dejó unos papeles en la mesa de mi secretaria y, luego de dos o tres vueltas indecisas, se acercó a mi escritorio. Me deseó los buenos días, hizo una observación ocasional sobre el estado del tiempo, y me pidió permiso para dejar su portafolio en un estante, mientras bajaba a tomar no sé qué bebida o alimento. Regresó una hora después, tomó su portafolio y salió.

Desde mi ascenso a director, producido hacía un mes,[1] después de veinte años de trabajos, lo veía todos los días. Entraba por la puerta del archivo, dejaba unas boletas en la mesa de mi secretaria, y se retiraba silenciosamente. Durante todo el mes había mantenido su cartera bajo el brazo; ésa era la primera vez que me solicitaba permiso para dejarla sobre un mueble. Era representante de una persona, o de un grupo de personas, ante una entidad oficial o particular, cuyas actividades o funciones yo ignoraba.

El día siguiente era domingo. Estuve en el campo y el lunes fui de la estación directamente a la oficina. A las diez de la mañana llegó. Después de un mes de mirarlo casi sin verlo, lo seguí con curiosidad en sus evoluciones por la oficina. Dejó unas boletas sobre un escritorio, hojeó distraídamente un diario, y sin pedirme permiso, dejó el portafolio y salió.

Durante un mes más hizo lo mismo, con regularidad, con una permanente expresión bondadosa y frecuentes manifestaciones de simpatía que, muy contenidas y discretas, traslucían, no obstante, algo como un leve deseo de comunicación amistosa. Llamé entonces a la señorita Bafico y al contador. La señorita Bafico era rubia, bien formada, de cutis mate. Parecía una joven culta, pero yo había observado que sus lecturas eran insuficientes o superficiales. Leía el libro de moda, el que conviene conocer para luego tener algo de qué hablar en las reuniones de burgueses ricos. A veces, yo hubiera querido hablarle de Félix Greitz, o de Marcel Schwob,[2] o de cualquier otro de mis autores preferidos, pero siempre me había contenido a tiempo. ¿Para qué modificar

[1] *producido... mes:* which had occurred the month before
[2] *Félix Greitz... Marcel Schwob:* Félix Greitz is not a writer. He is, playfully enough, the protagonist of Peyrou's first novel, *El estruendo de las rosas* (1948); Marcel Schwob (1867–1905) was a French journalist and author.

35 las costumbres literarias de una mujer de treinta años? Eso se intenta una vez en la vida y generalmente se fracasa. Además, no tenía por qué sorprender o asombrar a nadie. La señorita Bafico creía que yo era un hombre como casi todos los que las mujeres padecen en Buenos Aires. Ignoraba mis gustos: suponía, segura-
40 mente, que una insuficiencia mental, o alguna rareza de mi temperamento, eran la causa de que no me conmovieran las hazañas deportivas del *chauffeur* de turno o la rueda interminable del fútbol.[3]

Expliqué al contador y a la señorita Bafico que no me pare-
45 cía lógico permitir que personas extrañas se familiarizaran con el trabajo de nuestra oficina. Los intereses que se nos confiaban eran valiosos; el conocimiento de nuestras prácticas podía redundar en perjuicio general.[4] Tanto el contador como mi secretaria opinaron que el señor Alcides —así se llamaba— era incapaz de per-
50 judicar a nadie. Contesté que en el mundo hay seguramente numerosas personas incapaces de hacer mal a nadie; que esa cualidad, aunque negativa, debe ser un timbre de honor para ellas y sus parientes, ascendientes, descendientes y colaterales, pero observé que esa virtud es, por decirlo así, de uso interno.[5] No auto-
55 riza a reclamar derechos o a ejercer ninguna actividad. Si todas las personas incapaces de hacer mal a nadie —agregué— tuvieran derecho de utilizar nuestras oficinas, la aglomeración consiguiente haría imposible el trabajo. Me contestaron jovialmente que nadie, salvo el señor Alcides, entraba a ellas,[6] y que no había
60 ningún peligro de que el trabajo se entorpeciera. Repuse que ellos parecían acordar un derecho al señor Alcides por el hecho de ser el único extraño que penetraba en las oficinas, y opiné que la falta de entorpecimiento del trabajo no contribuía indudablemente a afianzar esa prerrogativa. Como tenía mucho que hacer,
65 y la discusión se ponía engorrosa, despaché al contador y encargué a la señorita Bafico unas cartas.

Pasaron diez días más durante los cuales el señor Alcides concurrió como de costumbre a la oficina y dejó su portafolio por una hora sobre el estante. Una tarde, con un tono amable, cor-
70 dial, pero no obsecuente, me pidió permiso para guardar en uno de los cajones de mi escritorio unos papeles que retiraría el día siguiente. Vivamente interesado por el sesgo que tomaba su actitud, accedí al pedido, agregando que me veía obligado a concederlo por unas horas, porque después necesitaría el cajón para

[3] *eran... fútbol:* were the reason for my not being moved by the athletic feats of the on-duty driver or by the endless jabbering about soccer
[4] *podía... general:* could be detrimental to all of us
[5] *por... interno:* to put it one way, of limited application
[6] *a ellas:* them, i.e., the offices (*oficinas*)

75 guardar unos documentos. Al día siguiente llegó y retiró los papeles. Era un jueves. El viernes visitó la oficina, dejó su portafolio, pero no utilizó el cajón. El sábado, sin consultarme, dejó unos papeles en el cajón, mientras hacía su habitual observación sobre el estado del tiempo. Esperé el lunes con gran interés. El señor Al-
80 cides llegó muy temprano y, con un visible apresuramiento, como si se encontrara en falta,[7] retiró los papeles, mientras balbuceaba no sé qué disculpas. El martes volvió a utilizar el cajón para guardar unos papeles y un libro, y el miércoles, al llegar, los retiró, pero antes de salir los guardó nuevamente. Desde ese día utilizó el ca-
85 jón diariamente, sin ocuparse ya de retirar los documentos que depositaba.

Volví, entonces, a comentar el caso con mi secretaria. Le dije que no sabía cómo encarar el asunto. El señor Alcides me producía una mezcla de irritación y de lástima, y estos dos sentimien-
90 tos actuaban en mi ánimo en una forma contradictoria. Muchas veces había tomado la decisión de prohibirle la entrada y otras tantas[8] mi voluntad se había quebrado ante su presencia. Parecía tan endeble y vacío que daba la sensación de existir apenas. Dije a mi secretaria que la solución estaba en expedir una orden ge-
95 neral prohibiendo el acceso a la oficina de toda persona extraña. Ante mi sorpresa, la señorita Bafico se opuso terminantemente. Quise argumentar en favor de mi decisión y noté que las razones exhibidas anteriormente eran descartadas con indudable desprecio, como si el hecho de tener ya unas semanas de existencia anu-
100 lara de pleno derecho su eficacia.

«Eso ya lo dijo usted el otro día», argumentó mi secretaria. Le contesté que muchísimas cosas son dichas y repetidas en el mundo varias veces y a pesar de esa lamentable circunstancia conservan su validez o significan siempre el mismo concepto. Me
105 contestó que no era lo mismo porque el señor Alcides era un hombre muy bueno. A esto repuse rápidamente que eso ya lo había dicho la señorita Bafico la semana pasada, de modo que de acuerdo con su lógica ya no servía.[9] Con sequedad me contestó que no era cuestión de broma y pidió permiso para retirarse.
110 Al rato llamé al contador y le sometí el asunto. Me pareció que estaba de acuerdo con mi secretaria, pero que no quería defenderla frente al jefe. Optó por buscar un argumento conciliatorio. Me dijo que siempre se había permitido el acceso de personas extrañas a las oficinas.

[7] *como... falta:* as if he had done something wrong
[8] *otras tantas:* just as many times
[9] *ya no servía:* it was no longer true

115   —Esperaba que dijera eso[10] —contesté—; es una de las fala-
cias del mundo moderno. Siempre que se quiere justificar lo in-
justificable se dice que siempre ha sucedido. Cuando se habla de
un ladrón y ya se han disparado en su defensa los últimos cartu-
chos lógicos, se dice que siempre ha habido ladrones.[11] Es una ne-
120 cia defensa, útil a todos los que combaten la razón, porque no la
tienen.[12]

El contador apreció con ligero asombro el ímpetu que yo
había puesto en mis palabras y se retiró.

Al rato llegó el señor Alcides y, después de depositar su
125 portafolio en el sitio habitual, abrió el cajón de mi escritorio y sacó
unos papeles. Los revisó con detenimiento y luego, observando el
diario que había quedado sobre mi escritorio, me dijo que le daría
un «vistazo». Yo sabía que iba a pronunciar esa palabra; yo sabía
que no iba a decir: voy a «leer» el diario. El «vistazo» es fugaz, no
130 indica detenimiento ni atención excesiva. Tampoco expresa posesión. El vocablo formaba parte sutil de un juego gradual que el
señor Alcides desarrollaba. Otra cosa que comprendí en seguida
fue que, iniciada la lectura,[13] el señor Alcides no se preocuparía
de cumplir exactamente la implicación de la palabra «vistazo».
135 Bastaba con haber insinuado con ella la levedad de una acción, el
escaso interés en molestar, para luego afirmarse con tranquila
persistencia, como un animal o una planta.

Cuando terminó de leer el diario me pidió permiso para
hablar por teléfono. Le contesté que por el momento era imposi-
140 ble porque esperaba una comunicación importante. Observé que
su reacción era la esperada; su gesto, permanentemente afable, se
transformó: palideció y una fugaz irritación apareció en sus ojos.
Un segundo después su cara era normal, como si la hubieran
lavado. El contraste entre la amabilidad empleada para solicitar
145 algo y la irritación exhibida cuando recibía una negativa fue uno
de los elementos más preciosos que tuve para estudiar su personalidad. Muchas veces, en el curso de los días siguientes, me mostré
reacio a algunas de sus solicitudes con el único objeto de obser-
var el juego variable de su fisonomía.

150   Dos o tres días después noté que el señor Alcides había ocu-
pado con documentos y papeles un segundo cajón de mi escritorio. Advertí, también, algunas otras señales muy leves del juego.
Una de ellas era colaborar, por decirlo así, con la institución, pero
en forma deliberadamente ínfima o casi imperceptible. En reali-
155 dad, la expresión no es exacta; no colaboraba: hacía una observa-

[10] *Esperaba... eso:* I was expecting you to say that (*Esperar*, of course, also means *to hope* and *to wait*.)
[11] *siempre... ladrones:* there have always been thieves
[12] *todos... tienen:* all those who are against what's right because they are wrong themselves
[13] *iniciada la lectura:* once he began to read

ción, o realizaba un acto mínimo, que no podía crear precedentes
o establecer una obligación, pero que, al mismo tiempo, vincu-
laba sutilmente al señor Alcides con la entidad. Era un acto generalmente inútil, pero despojado de egoísmo; de algún modo, la
160 institución quedaba obligada ante el señor Alcides. Unas veces
era apagar una luz excesiva; otras, era una oportuna observación
sobre el peligro de trabajar entre corrientes de aire.

Al llegar el invierno[14] el señor Alcides ocupó un tercer cajón
de mi escritorio y dos o tres personas empezaron a llamarlo por
165 teléfono con regularidad. En julio[15] me tomé diez días de vaca-
ciones, y al volver sin previo aviso a la oficina lo encontré sentado
en mi escritorio. Se levantó rápidamente y explicó que no esperaba mi regreso. Dijo que se retiraría para dejarme trabajar con
tranquilidad y salió. Media hora después volvió silenciosamente,
170 sacó unos papeles del escritorio y, de pie, empezó a revisarlos. Al
día siguiente también estaba sentado frente a mi mesa cuando
llegué. Se levantó en seguida, pero no salió de la pieza. Esta situación se repitió durante un mes. Una mañana, a principios de
setiembre, lo encontré, al llegar, instalado en mi escritorio, aten-
175 diendo a un grupo de hombres. Estaban sentados alrededor de él,
y escuchaban sus consejos sobre no sé qué asunto. Me dijo que en
seguida dejaría libre mi despacho, pero siguió hablando con sus
clientes con naturalidad. El hecho me produjo una impresión
penosa. Salí de la oficina y di varias vueltas por la mesa de en-
180 tradas y la contaduría, para ganar tiempo. Cuando regresé a mi
oficina el señor Alcides y sus clientes habían desaparecido. Estuve
un rato cavilando en diversas cosas; no tenía deseos de trabajar y
me sentía cansado. Habría pasado una media hora cuando llegó
un hombre alto, bien vestido, de aire enérgico. Me preguntó por
185 el señor Alcides. Le repuse que se había retirado y me dejó en
forma imperativa un mensaje para él. Contesté, con voz ligera-
mente quebrada, que el mensaje sería trasmitido.

He llegado al término de mis cavilaciones. Pensaba jubilarme
el año que viene, con la máxima mensualidad, pero he cambiado
190 de opinión. Me amparé en la razón y he sido derrotado por los
hechos. Prefiero perder una suma cualquiera[16] por mes y reti-
rarme en seguida. Pediré hoy una licencia[17] prolongada y, entretanto, tramitaré mi jubilación. Ya no volveré a esta oficina.

Aunque sea difícil explicarlo, aquí no hay ningún misterio.
195 Sé muy bien quién es el señor Alcides y sé que no quiere perjudi-
carme. Lejos de aborrecerlo, debo quedarle agradecido de que en

[14] *invierno:* Keep in mind that in the Southern Hemisphere the seasons are "reversed" from our point of view. July in Buenos Aires falls in the middle of its coolest season.
[15] *julio:* See note 14.
[16] *una suma cualquiera:* whatever amount
[17] *licencia:* leave of absence. *License* is often *permiso* in Spanish.

la consecución de sus propósitos se haya portado tan gentilmente conmigo; ha sido amable, ha ejercido la menor presión posible, ha esperado todo el tiempo necesario. Si esto fuera una ficción,
200 podría imaginarle un final humorístico. Decir, por ejemplo: «Entré al despacho del señor Alcides por la puerta del archivo, dejé unas boletas en la mesa de su secretaria y, después de dar dos o tres vueltas, me acerqué a su escritorio. Le deseé los buenos días, hice una observación sobre el estado del tiempo y le pedí permiso
205 para dejar mi portafolio sobre un estante...»

Exercises

A. *Questions and Opinions*

1. ¿Qué hizo el señor Alcides cuando apareció por primera vez en la oficina del director?

2. ¿Le habló al director en esa ocasión?

3. ¿Cuánto tiempo hacía que el director lo veía todos los días?

4. ¿Sabía el director a quién representaba el señor Alcides?

5. ¿Qué opinión tenían el contador y la señorita Bafico del señor Alcides?

6. ¿Por qué encargó el director unas cartas a la señorita Bafico?

7. ¿Por qué permitió el director que el señor Alcides guardara unos papeles en su escritorio?

8. ¿Se enojó el señor Alcides cuando el director no le dio permiso para hablar por teléfono?

9. Al llegar el invierno, ¿qué nuevo aspecto de las operaciones del señor Alcides se reveló?

10. Cuando el señor Alcides se puso a ocupar el escritorio del director, ¿qué otras personas ahora entraban a su oficina?

•11. ¿Cree Ud. que el director hizo bien en jubilarse? ¿Por qué?

•12. Si el final de este cuento es igual al comienzo, ¿qué nos está diciendo el autor?

B. Verb Practice Use each of the following verbal phrases in an original sentence in Spanish, either based on the story or of your own design. Be prepared to explain the meaning of your sentences. (If necessary, refer to *Key Expressions* to check the meaning of each phrase and the way in which it is used.)

1. **acercarse**
2. **retirarse**
3. **ignorar**
4. **ponerse**
5. **verse**
6. **volver a**
7. **preocuparse de**
8. **bastar con**
9. **terminar de**
10. **dar vueltas**

C. Vocabulary Practice Match the lexical expression on the right with the italicized English words on the left. Where required, put the verb in the correct form. Check *Key Expressions,* if necessary. Then use each expression in an original Spanish sentence and explain what your sentence means.

1. El padre de Sara me esperaba *standing* en la veranda.	**muebles**
2. *Somehow,* no me gustó su actitud.	**simpatía**
3. Sí, Carlos vino, pero tarde, *as usual.*	**a tiempo**
4. Diego me criticó, pero *at the same time* me sonreía.	**por decirlo así**
5. Corriendo, pudimos llegar *on time.*	**como de costumbre**
6. Creo que el salón necesita más *furniture.*	**al rato**
7. Nos encanta Elena por su *friendliness.*	**la razón**
8. *In a short time,* el señor director volvió.	**al mismo tiempo**
9. *Being right* es lo que te importa más.	**de algún modo**
10. Pepe no es un gigante intelectual, *to put it one way.*	**de pie**

D. *Communication Practice*

1. Tell Mariano to come a little closer.

2. Say you hope that Adela finishes writing her exams soon.

3. State that Luisa has no idea (doesn't know) what happened between them.

4. Indicate that what you want is for Mr. Alcides to go away.

5. Say that you always get sad when you read sentimental novels.

E. *Review Exercise* Following is a list of verbs found in this story. You can probably guess their meanings—if they are not immediately clear—since the core of each is a noun or adjective with which you are likely already familiar. See if you can spot the familiar elements in these verbs and give their meanings; then give the meanings of the verbs themselves. This exercise suggests another way of increasing your recognition vocabulary.

hojear	**traslucir**	**opinar**
encarar	**palidecer**	**ejercer**

El hombre muerto

Horacio Quiroga

HORACIO QUIROGA (1878–1937), an Uruguayan by birth, spent much of his life in the Argentine province of Misiones. Throughout his career as a writer, this tropical region along the Paraná River offered him a colorful background for dozens of the memorable tales that justify his reputation as one of Spanish America's finest short-story writers. His life was marked by tragedy and poor health, and this was reflected in a good part of his work. In addition to the influence of Edgar Allan Poe and the French Parnassians, which Quiroga acknowledged in his somber stories, one notes a significant literary debt to Rudyard Kipling. This British author's *The Jungle Books* and *Just So Stories,* written for a young audience, undoubtedly inspired many of Quiroga's brighter tales, such as those included in his widely known *Cuentos de la selva* (1918).

"El hombre muerto" is one of Quiroga's most celebrated darker stories. It recounts how in one unguarded moment a man's life can be irrevocably brought to a tragic end. This stark narrative may well have its source buried deep in Quiroga's imagination, for when the author was only two months old, his father died as the result of a similar pointless, pathetic farm accident.

A PRELIMINARY LOOK AT KEY EXPRESSIONS

Be sure to study these expressions before you read the story.

1. (43:1) **acabar de** + *infinitive* *to have just* + *past participle:* **El hombre acaba de caerse.** *The man has just fallen down.* The expression in the imperfect has the same meaning, only in the past: **El hombre y su machete acababan de limpiar la quinta calle del bananal.** *The man and his machete had just cleared the fifth pathway in the stand of banana trees.* However, when this expression is used in the preterit, the best English rendition is *to finish* + *present participle:* **Por fin acabaron de comer.** *They finally finished eating.* **Acabar de** occurs frequently in this story; watch for it.

2. (43:2) **faltarle a uno** *to be missing* or *lacking* Just as with **gustar** and **bastar,** the thing missing or lacking or yet to come is the subject in Spanish, and the person missing it or waiting for it is the indirect object. Often, however, other English phrasing is used to express this concept: **Les faltaban dos calles más.** *They had two pathways still to go.* In the story, **faltábanles** is literary style for the more common **les faltaban.**

3. (43:4) **echar una mirada** *to take a look*

4. (43:10) **tener la impresión** *to have the impression, feeling* The preposition **de** is always used to connect this expression with following elements: **Tuvo la impresión de no ver el machete de plano en el suelo.** *He had the impression that he didn't see the machete lying flat on the ground.* **De** is used even when the following element is a clause: **El hombre tenía la impresión de que se acercaba alguien.** *The man had the feeling that someone was approaching.*

5. (43:12) **acostado** *lying (down)* In Spanish, expressions of physical position are usually past participles unlike in English, where they are present participles: **sentado** *sitting (down),* **colgado** *hanging,* **arrimado** *leaning,* etc. This expression of physical position must be distinguished from the action itself. Compare **Están sentándose** *They are (in the act of) sitting down* vs. **Están sentados en el fondo** *They are sitting (seated) in the back.*

6. (43:19) **intentar** + *infinitive* *to try* + *infinitive* **Intentar** is synonymous with **tratar de** before infinitives, but is much more common before nouns and pronouns. Compare **Intentó mover la cabeza** or **Trató de mover la cabeza,** both *He tried to move his head,* with **Al menos intenté la cosa** *At least I tried the thing,* where **tratar** would not be used.

7. (44:36) **deber** + *infinitive* *must (have to)* + *verb* In the present tense, **deber** is used to express strong obligation: **Debes terminar el trabajo para mañana.**

You must finish the assignment by tomorrow. In the conditional or past subjunctive, however, **deber** expresses milder obligation, i.e., a recommendation: **Deberías (debieras) adelgazar un poco.** *You should (really) lose a little weight.*

8. (44:41) **considerar** + *direct object* + *adjective   to consider* + *direct object* + *adjective:* **La considero sumamente inteligente.** *I consider her extremely intelligent.* This construction is also frequently used reflexively, as in the story: **Puede considerarse muerto.** *He can consider himself dead.*

9. (44:52) **deber** + *infinitive   must (should)* + *verb*   **Deber** can also be used before an infinitive to express probability: **Deben ser las doce.** *It must be (is probably) noon.* Only context can distinguish between this usage and an expression of strong obligation, as in no. 7 above: **Deben vivir en otro apartamento.** *They must (have to) live in another apartment* or *They must (probably) live in another apartment.* In the example cited here in the story, **Pronto deben ser las doce,** only the probability interpretation makes any sense: *It must be going on 12 o'clock.* Often **de** is used between **deber** and the infinitive in this sense: **Deben de haber pasado ya varios minutos.** *Several minutes must have gone by already.*

10. (44:53) **allá arriba** *up there*   In Spanish expressions of location such as this one, the two elements are in reverse order from their occurrence in English: **allá abajo** *down there* (44:57), **mar adentro** *out ("inward") to sea,* **allí afuera** *out there,* **aquí mismo** *right here,* etc.

11. (44:54) **monte** *woods, uncultivated fields, wilderness, countryside*   **Monte** is a very broad concept, occasionally meaning *hill* or *mountain,* but more often meaning the wild, uncultivated area of the countryside containing grassy areas and bushes and even a tree here and there. If the area is mostly wooded, then it is a **bosque** *forest.*

12. (44:57) **en el fondo** *in the bottom*   **Fondo** is also the back of a room, for example: **en el fondo del bar** *in the back of the bar,* or even the background of a picture: **En el fondo se ven unas casitas.** *In the background you can see some small houses.*

13. (45:86) **resistirse a** + *infinitive   to resist* + *present participle* or *to refuse* + *infinitive:* **Siempre se resiste a acompañar a mis tíos.** *She always resists going (refuses to go) with my aunt and uncle.*

14. (45:100) **doblar** *to fold; to double; to dub* (a film); *to turn*   The most common use of this verb is the last one: **Aquí tienes que doblar a la izquierda.** *Here you have to make a left turn.*

15. (45:110) **soltarse (de)** *to let go (of), break away (from), get free (of), escape:* **No quería soltarse de la mano de su madre.** *He didn't want to let go of his mother's hand.* Just **soltar** is *to release, drop,* or *let go of:* **Soltó el machete.** *He let go of (dropped) the machete.*

16. (45:112) **efectivamente** *really, in fact, in effect*   This is what is known as a false cognate, like **actual** *present-day* or **casualmente** *just by chance. Effectively* is **eficazmente.**

17. (46:123) **alejarse (de)** *to leave, to go, walk away (from), get farther away (from)*
    This is the exact opposite of **acercarse (a)** *to approach, get nearer (to).*

18. (46:125) **de siempre** *usual, customary*   This expression can be used as an adjectival clause to modify a noun: **el paisaje de siempre** *the same old landscape, the landscape we always see.*

19. (46:133) **ante** *before, in the presence of:* **Tuvo que comparecer ante el juez.** *He had to appear before the judge;* **¡No digas esas cosas ante tu mamá!** *Don't say those things in front of your mother! Before,* in the sense of preceding in time, is **antes de.**

20. (46:137) **decidirse a** + *infinitive*   *to decide, make up one's mind* + *infinitive*

El hombre muerto

El hombre y su machete acababan de limpiar la quinta calle del bananal. Faltábanles aún dos calles; pero como en éstas abundaban las chircas y malvas silvestres, la tarea que tenían por delante era muy poca cosa.[1] El hombre echó en consecuencia[2] una mi-
5 rada satisfecha a los arbustos rozados, y cruzó el alambrado para tenderse un rato en la gramilla.

Mas al bajar el alambre de púa y pasar el cuerpo, su pie izquierdo resbaló sobre un trozo de corteza desprendida del poste, a tiempo que el machete se le escapaba de la mano. Mientras caía,
10 el hombre tuvo la impresión sumamente lejana de no ver el machete de plano en el suelo.

Ya estaba tendido en la gramilla, acostado sobre el lado derecho, tal como él quería. La boca, que acababa de abrírsele en toda su extensión, acababa también de cerrarse. Estaba como hubiera
15 deseado estar, las rodillas dobladas y la mano izquierda sobre el pecho. Sólo que tras el antebrazo, e inmediatamente por debajo del cinto, surgían de su camisa el puño y la mitad de la hoja del machete; pero el resto no se veía.

El hombre intentó mover la cabeza, en vano. Echó una mi-
20 rada de reojo a la empuñadura del machete, húmeda aún del sudor de su mano. Apreció mentalmente la extensión y la trayectoria del machete dentro de su vientre, y adquirió, fría, matemática e inexorable, la seguridad de que acababa de llegar al término de su existencia.

25 La muerte. En el transcurso de la vida se piensa muchas veces en que un día, tras años, meses, semanas y días preparatorios, llegaremos a nuestro turno al umbral de la muerte. Es la ley fatal, aceptada y prevista; tanto, que solemos dejarnos llevar placenteramente por la imaginación a ese momento, supremo entre to-
30 dos, en que lanzamos el último suspiro.

Pero entre el instante actual y esa postrera espiración, ¡qué de[3] sueños, trastornos, esperanzas y dramas presumimos en nuestra vida! ¡Qué nos reserva aún esta existencia llena de vigor, antes

[1] *muy poca cosa:* really not much
[2] *en consecuencia:* as a result
[3] *de:* Does not translate.

de su eliminación del escenario humano! Es éste el consuelo, el
35 placer y la razón de nuestras divagaciones mortuorias: ¡Tan lejos
está la muerte, y tan imprevisto lo que debemos vivir aún!

¿Aún?... No han pasado dos segundos: el sol está exactamente a la misma altura; las sombras no han avanzado un milí-
metro. Bruscamente, acaban de resolverse para el hombre tendido
40 las divagaciones a largo plazo:[4] Se está muriendo.

Muerto. Puede considerarse muerto en su cómoda postura.

Pero el hombre abre los ojos y mira. ¿Qué tiempo ha pasado?
¿Qué cataclismo ha sobrevenido en el mundo? ¿Qué trastorno de
la naturaleza trasuda el horrible acontecimiento?[5]
45 Va a morir. Fría, fatal e ineludiblemente, va a morir.

El hombre resiste —¡es tan imprevisto ese horror! Y piensa:
Es una pesadilla; ¡esto es! ¿Qué ha cambiado? Nada. Y mira: ¿No
es acaso ese bananal su bananal? ¿No viene todas las mañanas a
limpiarlo? ¿Quién lo conoce como él? Ve perfectamente el ba-
50 nanal, muy raleado, y las anchas hojas desnudas al sol. Allí están,
muy cerca, deshilachadas por el viento. Pero ahora no se mue-
ven... Es la calma de mediodía; pronto deben ser las doce.

Por entre los bananos, allá arriba, el hombre ve desde el duro
suelo el techo rojo de su casa. A la izquierda, entrevé el monte y
55 la capuera de canelas. No alcanza a ver más, pero sabe muy bien
que a sus espaldas está el camino al puerto nuevo; y que en la dirección de su cabeza, allá abajo, yace en el fondo del valle el Paraná[6] dormido como un lago. Todo, todo exactamente como
siempre; el sol de fuego, el aire vibrante y solitario, los bananos
60 inmóviles, el alambrado de postes muy gruesos y altos que pronto
tendrá que cambiar.

¡Muerto! ¿Pero es posible? ¿No es éste uno de los tantos días
en que ha salido al amanecer de su casa con el machete en la
mano? ¿No está allí mismo, a cuatro metros de él, su caballo, su
65 malacara,[7] oliendo parsimoniosamente el alambre de púa?

¡Pero sí! Alguien silba... No puede ver, porque está de espaldas al camino; mas siente resonar en el puentecito los pasos del caballo... Es el muchacho que pasa todas las mañanas hacia el puerto
nuevo, a las once y media. Y siempre silbando... Desde el poste
70 descascarado que toca casi con las botas, hasta el cerco vivo de
monte que separa el bananal del camino, hay quince metros lar-
gos. Lo sabe perfectamente bien, porque él mismo, al levantar el
alambrado, midió la distancia.

[4] *acaban... plazo:* the long-range speculations have just been resolved for the man lying on the ground
[5] *¿Qué... aconteci-miento?* What upheaval in nature is causing the horrible event?
[6] *Paraná:* The Paraná River divides Paraguay and Argentina along the western border of the Argentine province of Misiones.
[7] *malacara:* Since horses are such an important element in the culture of rural Argentina, there is an abundance of very specialized terms for horses, their breeds, their use and care, the areas where they are kept, etc. A horse owner often finds the term *caballo* too general, even meaningless, and prefers to use a more descriptive term when referring to his animal. Thus the author uses *caballo,* quickly followed by the more specific *malacara,* i.e., a reddish-brown horse with a white forehead.

75 ¿Qué pasa, entonces? ¿Es ése o no un natural mediodía de los tantos en Misiones,[8] en su monte, en su potrero, en su bananal ralo? ¡Sin duda! Gramilla corta, conos de hormigas, silencio, sol a plomo[9]...

Nada, nada ha cambiado. Sólo él es distinto. Desde hace dos minutos su persona, su personalidad viviente, nada tiene ya que

80 ver ni con el potrero, que formó él mismo a azada, durante cinco meses consecutivos; ni con el bananal, obra de sus solas manos. Ni con su familia. Ha sido arrancado bruscamente, naturalmente, por obra de una cáscara lustrosa y un machete en el vientre. Hace dos minutos: Se muere.

85 El hombre, muy fatigado y tendido en la gramilla sobre el costado derecho, se resiste siempre a admitir un fenómeno de esa trascendencia, ante el aspecto normal y monótono de cuanto mira.[10] Sabe bien la hora: las once y media... El muchacho de todos los días acaba de pasar sobre el puente.

90 ¡Pero no es posible que haya resbalado...! El mango de su machete (pronto deberá cambiarlo por otro; tiene ya poco vuelo[11]) estaba perfectamente oprimido entre su mano izquierda y el alambre de púa. Tras diez años de bosque, él sabe muy bien cómo se maneja un machete de monte. Está solamente muy fatigado del

95 trabajo de esa mañana, y descansa un rato como de costumbre.

¿La prueba?... ¡Pero esa gramilla que entra ahora por la comisura de su boca la plantó él mismo, en panes de tierra distantes un metro uno de otro! ¡Y ése es su bananal; y ése es su malacara, resoplando cauteloso ante las púas del alambre! Lo ve perfecta-

100 mente; sabe que no se atreve a doblar la esquina del alambrado, porque él está echado casi al pie del poste. Lo distingue muy bien; y ve los hilos oscuros de sudor que arrancan de la cruz y del anca.[12] El sol cae a plomo, y la calma es muy grande, pues ni un fleco de los bananos se mueve. Todos los días, como ése, ha visto las mis-

105 mas cosas.

...Muy fatigado, pero descansa sólo. Deben de haber pasado ya varios minutos... y a las doce menos cuarto, desde allá arriba, desde el chalet de techo rojo, se desprenderán hacia el bananal su mujer y sus dos hijos, a buscarlo para almorzar. Oye siempre,

110 antes que las demás, la voz de su chico menor que quiere soltarse de la mano de su madre: ¡Piapiá![13] ¡Piapiá!

—¿No es eso?... ¡Claro, oye! Ya es la hora. Oye efectivamente la voz de su hijo...

[8] *Misiones:* a small northeastern province of Argentina that juts up between Paraguay and Brazil between the Paraná and the Uruguay Rivers.
[9] *sol a plomo:* sun beating down (literally, "falling like lead")
[10] *cuanto mira:* everything that he is looking at
[11] *tiene... vuelo:* it doesn't have a good grip anymore
[12] *cruz... anca: La cruz* is the withers of the horse, i.e., the highest part of its back at the base of the neck; *el anca* is the rump.
[13] *¡Piapiá!* Daddy! The word is from Guaraní, the language of the Indians, also called Guaraní, who live in this part of Argentina, as well as in Paraguay and southern Brazil.

¡Qué pesadilla!... ¡Pero es uno de los tantos días, trivial como
115 todos, claro está! Luz excesiva, sombras amarillentas, calor silencioso de horno sobre la carne, que hace sudar al malacara [14] inmóvil ante el bananal prohibido.

...Muy cansado, mucho, pero nada más. ¡Cuántas veces, a
mediodía como ahora, ha cruzado volviendo a casa ese potrero,
120 que era capuera cuando él llegó, y que antes había sido monte vir-
gen! Volvía entonces, muy fatigado también, con su machete
pendiente de la mano izquierda, a lentos pasos.

Puede aún alejarse con la mente, si quiere; puede si quiere
abandonar un instante su cuerpo y ver desde el tajamar por él
125 construido, el trivial paisaje de siempre: el pedregullo volcánico
con gramas rígidas; el bananal y su arena roja; el alambrado em-
pequeñecido en la pendiente, que se acoda hacia el camino. [15] Y
más lejos aún ver el potrero, obra sola de sus manos. Y al pie de
un poste descascarado, echado sobre el costado derecho y las pier-
130 nas recogidas, exactamente como todos los días, puede verse a él
mismo, como un pequeño bulto asoleado sobre la gramilla, des-
cansando, porque está muy cansado...

Pero el caballo rayado de sudor, e inmóvil de cautela ante el
esquinado del alambrado, ve también al hombre en el suelo y no
135 se atreve a costear el bananal, como desearía. Ante las voces que
ya están próximas —¡Piapiá!—, vuelve un largo, largo rato las orejas inmóviles al bulto: y tranquilizado al fin, se decide a pasar entre el poste y el hombre tendido —que ya ha descansado.

[14] *al malacara: malacara* is an adjective describing the horse. Thus *al* is used to refer to the omitted masculine noun *caballo.*
[15] *el alambrado... camino:* the wire fence, growing smaller in the distance as it descends the slope, that merges with the road

Exercises

A. *Questions and Opinions*

1. ¿Qué había estado haciendo el hombre?

2. ¿Qué pasó cuando quiso cruzar el alambrado?

3. ¿Por qué no podía ver el machete de plano en el suelo?

4. ¿Se dio cuenta en seguida que iba a morir?

5. ¿A quién oyó silbar?

6. ¿Notó algún cambio a su alrededor?

7. ¿Por qué no se atrevía el caballo a doblar la esquina del alambrado?

8. ¿Quiénes lo iban a buscar a las doce menos cuarto?

9. ¿Quién le gritó «¡Piapiá!»?

10. Al final, ¿qué hizo el caballo? ¿Por qué?

• 11. ¿A Ud. le parece violenta o estoica la reacción del hombre?

• 12. ¿Cree Ud. que el cuento es más o menos eficaz por esta razón?

B. Verb Practice Use each of the following verbal phrases in an original sentence in Spanish, either based on the story or of your own design. Be prepared to explain the meaning of your sentences. (If necessary, refer to *Key Expressions* to check the meaning of each phrase and the way in which it is used.)

1. **acabar de**

2. **faltarle a uno**

3. **echar una mirada**

4. **tener la impresión**

5. **intentar**

6. **deber** (*obligation*)

7. **considerar**

8. **deber** (*probability*)

9. **alejarse de**

10. **decidirse a**

C. Vocabulary Practice Match the lexical expression on the right with the italicized English words on the left. Where required, put the verb in the correct form. Then use each expression in an original Spanish sentence and explain what your sentence means.

1. *Turn* a la derecha en la próxima calle.   **acostado**

2. *In fact,* Ud. sí tiene razón.   **allá arriba**

3. Lola siempre *resists* aceptar mis ideas.   **monte**

4. Con mucho gusto lo repetiré *before* el juez.   **en el fondo**

5. ¿Has visto que es la *same old* comida?   **resistirse a**

6. El libro está *up there* en el estante.   **doblar**

7. Cuando la vi esta tarde, estaba *lying down*.   **soltar**

8. El caballo desapareció en el *wilderness*.   **efectivamente**

9. Había otro baño *in the back* de la casa.   **de siempre**

10. ¡*Drop* ese cuchillo!   **ante**

D. Communication Practice

1. Say that you think that we are short (missing) three dollars.

2. Tell José that we must work tonight.

3. State that you have decided to stay another day.

4. Say that Pedro has just arrived home.

5. Indicate that you'll take a look at the house tomorrow.

Orden jerárquico

Eduardo Goligorsky

EDUARDO GOLIGORSKY (1931–   ) is an Argentine author, editor, journalist, and transla-
tor who began early in his career to cultivate several types of literature of the imagination—
fantasy, science fiction, and crime and mystery fiction. He has won several important
literary prizes in his native Buenos Aires and is remembered particularly as the coauthor,
with Alberto Vanasco, of two collections of futuristic short stories—*Memorias del futuro*
(1966) and *Adiós al mañana* (1967).

Goligorsky's narratives characteristically look ahead to a time when the abuses afflict-
ing modern society and the pervasive amoral treatment of individuals are extended logically to frightening extremes. This view of a future that may well be awaiting us is grim and
sobering. The setting of "Orden jerárquico" is apparently contemporary, but the stress on
the disregard for human life that the author ascribes with unmistakeable irony to certain
powerful international cartels dramatically suggests that even today some basic values
seem already to be slipping out of our control.

A PRELIMINARY LOOK AT KEY EXPRESSIONS

Be sure to study these expressions before you read the story.

1. (52:2) **ser de** + *time of day* to be + *time of day:* **Ya era casi de madrugada.** *It was almost dawn.*

2. (52:3) **sin embargo** *however, nevertheless*

3. (52:3) **inquietarse** *to get nervous, restless, uneasy* **Inquieto** is the opposite of **quieto** *quiet* in the sense of *still* or *motionless.* **Callado** is *quiet* in the sense of *silent* or *not speaking.*

4. (52:11) **empezar a** + *infinitive* to begin + *infinitive*

5. (52:22) **preguntarse** *to wonder* (literally, *to ask oneself*)

6. (52:27) **mejor dicho** *rather, more precisely*

7. (52:35) **confianza** *trust, "closeness"* **Personas de confianza** are people to whom you are close, people whom you can trust and rely on.

8. (53:37) **cada vez más...** *more and more...:* **cada vez más grande** *bigger and bigger*

9. (53:39) **de todos modos** *anyway, at any rate*

10. (53:48) **ahí nomás** *right on the spot, right there* In some Latin American countries, particularly Argentina, the phrase **nomás** (also spelled as two words: **no más**) is used in a variety of ways for emphasis: **ayer no más** *just yesterday,* **Pase no más, señor** *Come right in, sir,* **Sírvase no más** *Please help yourself.*

11. (53:60) **llevar encima** *to carry on one(self):* **No llevaba plata encima.** *I wasn't carrying any money on me.*

12. (54:87) **en cambio** *on the other hand*

13. (54:89) **complacerse en** + *infinitive* to take pleasure in, enjoy, be pleased with + *present participle:* **Se complace en desarmar su pistola.** *He enjoys taking his pistol apart.*

14. (54:106) **tratarse de** *to be a question (matter) of*

15. (54:108) **a la vez** *at the same time* **Al mismo tiempo** is also *at the same time,* but in a broader, more general way; **a la vez** is narrower and often has the meaning of *simultaneously.* Compare **Los dos estaban en Caracas al mismo tiempo** *The two were in Caracas at the same time* with **La Luger servía de arma y símbolo de la jerarquía a la vez** *The Luger served as a weapon and also as a symbol of the chain of command at the same time.*

16. (54:113) **tocarle a uno** *to be one's turn* The person whose turn it is is the indirect object in Spanish: **Ahora le toca a él morir.** *Now it's his turn to die.* In the

story, the phrase **el turno** adds emphasis: **cuando le tocara el turno** *when his time came.*

17. (55:118) **advertir** *to warn, inform; to notice, observe*   The danger that one is being warned of is the direct object in Spanish, and the person being warned is the indirect object: **Su instinto le había advertido algo.** *His instinct had warned him of something.*

18. (55:139) **de antemano** *beforehand, in advance*

19. (55:142) **o sea** *that is to say, I mean, "like"*   **O sea** is a very common filler phrase in Spanish, used either to give the speaker some time to think or explain himself, similar to the conversational "I mean" or "like" in American English.

20. (56:158) **dejar caer** *to drop*   This act of dropping is deliberate, as the verb **dejar** *to let, allow* indicates. **Caérsele a uno** is used for an accidental dropping: **Se le cayó el pasaje.** *He dropped the ticket* (that is, it fell out of his hand).

———————————— ▽ ————————————

Orden jerárquico[1]

Abáscal lo perdió de vista, sorpresivamente, entre las sombras de la
calle solitaria. Ya era casi de madrugada, y unos jirones de niebla
espesa se adherían a los portales oscuros. Sin embargo, no se in-
quietó. A él, a Abáscal, nunca se le había escapado nadie. Ese in-
5   feliz no sería el primero. Correcto. El Cholo[2] reapareció en la
esquina, allí donde las corrientes de aire hacían danzar remolinos
de bruma. Lo alumbraba el cono de luz amarillenta de un farol.

    El Cholo caminaba excesivamente erguido, tieso, con la rigi-
dez artificial de los borrachos que tratan de disimular su condi-
10   ción. Y no hacía ningún esfuerzo por ocultarse. Se sentía seguro.

    Abáscal había empezado a seguirlo a las ocho de la noche.
Lo vio bajar, primero, al sórdido subsuelo de la Galería Güemes,[3]
de cuyas entrañas brotaba una música gangosa. Los carteles multi-
colores prometían un espectáculo estimulante, y desgranaban los
15   apodos exóticos de las coristas. El también debió sumergirse, por
fuerza, en la penumbra cómplice,[4] para asistir a un monótono
desfile de hembras aburridas. Las carnes fláccidas, ajadas, que los
reflectores acribillaban sin piedad, bastaban, a juicio de Abáscal,
para sofocar cualquier atisbo de excitación.[5] Por si eso fuera poco,
20   un tufo en el que se mezclaban el sudor, la mugre y la felpa apoli-
llada, impregnaba el aire rancio, adhiriéndose a la piel y las ropas.

    Se preguntó qué atractivo podía encontrar el Cholo en ese
lugar. Y la respuesta surgió, implacable, en el preciso momento
en que terminaba de formularse el interrogante.[6]

25   El Cholo se encuadraba en otra categoría humana, cuyos gustos y placeres él jamás lograría entender. Vivía en una pensión de
Retiro, un conventillo, mejor dicho, compartiendo una pieza
minúscula con varios comprovincianos recién llegados a la ciudad. Vestía miserablemente, incluso cuando tenía los bolsillos
30   bien forrados:[7] camisa deshilachada, saco y pantalón andrajosos,
mocasines trajinados y cortajeados. Era, apenas, un cuchillero[8]
sin ambiciones, o con una imagen ridícula de la ambición. Útil en
su hora, pero peligroso, por lo que sabía, desde el instante en que
había ejecutado su último trabajo, en una emergencia, cuando
35   todos los expertos de confianza y responsables,[9] como él, como

[1] *«Orden jerárquico»:*
literally, "Hierarchical
Order," but a better
translation might
be "Chain of Com-
mand," referring, as
you will see, not only
to the crime organi-
zation itself but to
the weapons used by
the individuals on the
various levels of the
organization.
[2] *Cholo:* a common
term in Latin America,
here with the mean-
ing of *mestizo,* that is,
a biracial individual
(of Indian and white
parentage)
[3] *la Galería Güemes:*
a commercial arcade
in downtown
Buenos Aires
[4] *la penumbra cóm-
plice:* the protective
semidarkness
[5] *excitación:* excite-
ment, often referring
to sexual arousal.
A more general term
for "excitement" is
emoción.
[6] *terminaba... interrogante:* the question
was formed
[7] *los... forrados:* his
pockets well lined,
i.e., full of money
[8] *cuchillero:* thug
[9] *todos... responsables:*
all the reliable and
trustworthy experts

Abáscal, se hallaban fuera del país. Porque últimamente las operaciones se realizaban, cada vez más, en escala internacional, y los viajes estaban a la orden del día.[10]

40 Recurrir al Cholo había sido, de todos modos, una imprudencia. Con plata en el bolsillo, ese atorrante no sabía ser discreto. Abáscal lo había seguido del teatrito subterráneo a un piringundín de la 25 de Mayo,[11] y después a otro, y a otro, y lo vio tomar todas las porquerías que le sirvieron, y manosear a las coperas, y darse importancia hablando de lo que nadie debía hablar.

45 No mencionó nombres, afortunadamente, ni se refirió a los hechos concretos, identificables, porque si lo hubiera hecho, Abáscal, que lo vigilaba con el oído atento, desde el taburete vecino, habría tenido que rematarlo ahí nomás, a la vista de todos, con la temeridad de un principiante.

50 No era sensato arriesgar así una organización que tanto había costado montar, amenazando, de paso, la doble vida que él, Abáscal, un verdadero técnico, siempre había protegido con tanto celo. Es que él estaba en otra cosa, se movía en otros ambientes. Sus modelos, aquellos cuyos refinamientos procuraba copiar, los

55 había encontrado en las recepciones de las embajadas, en los grandes casinos, en los salones de los ministerios, en las convenciones empresarias. Cuidaba, sobre todo, las apariencias: ropa bien cortada, restaurantes escogidos, *starlets* trepadoras, licores finos, autos deportivos, vuelos en cabinas de primera clase. Por

60 ejemplo, ya llevaba encima, mientras se deslizaba por la calle de Retiro,[12] siguiendo al Cholo, el pasaje que lo transportaría, pocas horas más tarde, a Caracas. Lejos del cadáver del Cholo y de las suspicacias que su eliminación podría generar en algunos círculos.

En eso, el Doctor había sido terminante. Matar y esfumarse.

65 El número del vuelo, estampado en el pasaje, ponía un límite estricto a su margen de maniobra. Lástima que el Doctor, tan exigente con él, hubiera cometido el error garrafal de contratar, en ausencia de los aténticos profesionales, a un rata como el Cholo. Ahora, como de costumbre, él tenía que jugarse el pellejo[13] para

70 sacarles las castañas del fuego a los demás.[14] Aunque eso también iba a cambiar, algún día. Él apuntaba alto, muy alto, en la organización.

Abáscal deslizó la mano por la abertura del saco, en dirección al correaje que le ceñía el hombro y la axila. Al hacerlo rozó,

75 sin querer, el cuadernillo de los pasajes. Sonrió. Luego, sus dedos

[10] *los... día:* trips were the order of the day
[11] *la... Mayo:* The 25th of May Street, a street in one of the seamier sections of the city
[12] *la... Retiro:* the street near Retiro. Retiro is one of the main train stations of the city.
[13] *jugarse el pellejo:* to risk his neck (literally, his skin)
[14] *para... demás:* to pull the others' chestnuts out of the fire (i.e., to get them out of trouble)

encontraron las cachas estriadas de la Luger,[15] las acariciaron, casi sensualmente, y se cerraron con fuerza, apretando la culata.

El orden jerárquico también se manifestaba en las armas. Él había visto, hacía mucho tiempo, la herramienta predilecta del
80 Cholo. Un puñal de fabricación casera, cuya hoja se había encogido tras infinitos contactos con la piedra de afilar. Dos sunchos apretaban el mango de madera, incipientemente resquebrajado y pulido por el manipuleo. Por supuesto, el Cholo había usado ese cuchillo en el último trabajo, dejando un sello peculiar, incon-
85 fundible. Otra razón para romper allí, en el eslabón más débil, la cadena que trepaba hasta cúpulas innombrables.[16]

En cambio, la pistola de Abáscal llevaba impresa, sobre el acero azul, la nobleza de su linaje. Cuando la desarmaba, y cuando la aceitaba, prolijamente, pieza por pieza, se complacía en fanta-
90 sear sobre la personalidad de sus anteriores propietarios. ¿Un gallardo «junker» prusiano,[17] que había preferido dispararse un tiro en la sien antes que admitir la derrota en un suburbio de Leningrado?[18] ¿O un lugarteniente del mariscal Rommel,[19] muerto en las tórridas arenas de El Alamein?[20] Él había comprado la Luger,
95 justamente, en un zoco de Tánger[21] donde los mercachifles remataban su botín de cascos de acero, cruces gamadas y otros trofeos arrebatados a la inmensidad del desierto.

Eso sí, la Luger tampoco colmaba sus ambiciones. Conocía la existencia de una artillería más perfeccionada, más mortífera,
100 cuyo manejo estaba reservado a otras instancias del orden jerárquico, hasta el punto de haberse convertido en una especie de símbolo de status. A medida que él ascendiera, como sin duda iba a ascender, también tendría acceso a ese arsenal legendario, patrimonio exclusivo de los poderosos.
105 Curiosamente, el orden jerárquico tenía, para Abáscal, otra cara. No se trataba solo de la forma de matar, sino, paralelamente, de la forma de morir. Lo espantaba la posibilidad de que un arma improvisada, bastarda, como la del Cholo, le hurgara las tripas. A la vez, el chicotazo de la Luger enaltecería al Cholo, pero tampoco
110 sería suficiente para él, para Abáscal, cuando llegara a su apogeo. La regla del juego estaba cantada y él, fatalista por convicción, la aceptaba: no iba a morir en la cama. Lo único que pedía era que, cuando le tocara el turno, sus verdugos no fueran chapuceros y supiesen elegir instrumentos nobles.

[15] *Luger:* a German automatic 9-millimeter pistol
[16] *la... innombrables:* the chain that reached all the way to higher-ups that could not be named
[17] *"junker" prusiano:* Prussian Junker, that is, a member of the Prussian aristocracy, influential in Germany in the 19th and early 20th centuries. They were highly militaristic and helped the Nazis rise to power in 1933.
[18] *Leningrado:* a city in northwest Russia, also known in the past as St. Petersburg and Petrograd, the scene of many important historical events, including the 1917 Communist Revolution and critical World War II battles
[19] *mariscal Rommel:* Field Marshal Irwin Rommel, the "Desert Fox," commander of German forces in North Africa in World War II
[20] *El Alamein:* town in Egypt, site of a decisive British victory over the Germans in World War II
[21] *Tánger:* Tangiers, a seaport in Morocco

115   La brusca detención de su presa, en la bocacalle siguiente, le cortó el hilo de los pensamientos. Probablemente el instinto del Cholo, afinado en los montes de Orán[22] y en las emboscadas de un Buenos Aires traicionero, le había advertido algo. Unas pisadas demasiado persistentes en la calle despoblada. Una vibración
120 intrusa en la atmósfera. La conciencia del peligro acechante lo había ayudado a despejar la borrachera y giró en redondo, agazapándose. El cuchillo tajeó la bruma, haciendo firuletes, súbitamente convertido en la prolongación natural de la mano que lo empuñaba.
125   Abáscal terminó de desenfundar la Luger. Disparó desde una distancia segura, una sola vez, y la bala perforó un orificio de bordes nítidos en la frente del Cholo.
       Misión cumplida.

* * *

       El tableteo de las máquinas de escribir llegaba vagamente a
130 la oficina, venciendo la barrera de aislación acústica. Por el ventanal panorámico se divisaba un horizonte de hormigón y, más lejos, donde las moles dejaban algunos resquicios, asomaban las parcelas leonadas del Río de la Plata.[23] El smog formaba un colchón sobre la ciudad y las aguas.
135   El Doctor tomó, en primer lugar, el cable fechado en Caracas que su secretaria acababa de depositar sobre el escritorio, junto a la foto de una mujer rubia, de facciones finas, aristocráticas, flanqueada, en un jardín, por dos criaturas igualmente rubias. Conocía, de antemano, el texto del cable: «Firmamos contrato». No
140 podía ser de otra manera. La organización funcionaba como una maquinaria bien sincronizada. En eso residía la clave del éxito.
       «Firmamos contrato», leyó, efectivamente. O sea que alguien —no importaba quién— había cercenado el último cabo suelto, producto de una operación desgraciada.
145   Primero había sido necesario recurrir al Cholo, un malevito marginado, venal, que no ofrecía ninguna garantía para el futuro. Después, lógicamente, había sido indispensable silenciar al Cholo. Y ahora el círculo acababa de cerrarse.[24] «Firmamos contrato» significaba que Abáscal había sido recibido en el aeropuerto de
150 Caracas, en la escalerilla misma del avión, por un proyectil de un rifle Browning calibre 30, equipado con mira telescópica Leupold

[22] *Orán:* a seaport in Algeria
[23] *Río... Plata:* the river that forms the northern boundary of the city of Buenos Aires
[24] *acababa de cerrarse:* had just been completed

M8-100. Un fusil, se dijo el Doctor, que Abáscal habría respetado
y admirado, en razón de [25] su proverbial entusiasmo por el orden
jerárquico de las armas. La liquidación en el aeropuerto, con ese
155 rifle y no otro, era, en verdad, el método favorito de la filial Caracas, tradicionalmente partidaria de ganar tiempo y evitar sobresaltos inútiles.

Una pérdida sensible, reflexionó el Doctor, dejando caer el
cable sobre el escritorio. Abáscal siempre había sido muy eficiente,
160 pero su intervención, obligada, en ese caso, lo había condenado
irremisiblemente. La orden recibida de arriba había sido inapelable: no dejar rastros, ni nexos delatores. Aunque, desde luego, resultaba imposible extirpar todos, absolutamente todos, los nexos.
El, el Doctor, era, en última instancia, otro de ellos.

165 A continuación, el Doctor recogió el voluminoso sobre de
papel manila que su secretaria le había entregado junto con el
cable. El matasellos era de Nueva York. El membrete era el de la
firma que servía de fachada a la organización. Habitualmente, la
llegada de uno de esos sobres marcaba el comienzo de otra ope-
170 ración. El código para descifrar las instrucciones descansaba en el
fondo de su caja fuerte.

El Doctor metió la punta del cortapapeles debajo de la solapa del sobre. La hoja se deslizó hasta tropezar, brevemente, con
un obstáculo. La inercia determinó que siguiera avanzando. El
175 Doctor comprendió que para descifrar el mensaje no necesitaría
ayuda. Y le sorprendió descubrir que en ese trance no pensaba en
su mujer y sus hijos, sino en Abáscal y en su culto por el orden
jerárquico de las armas. Luego, la carga explosiva, activada por el
tirón del cortapapeles sobre el hilo del detonador, transformó todo
180 ese piso del edificio en un campo de escombros.

[25] *en razón de:* considering

Exercises

A. Questions and Opinions

1. ¿A quién seguía Abáscal?

2. ¿Por qué lo estaba siguiendo?

3. ¿Por qué se consideraba Abáscal superior al Cholo?

4. ¿Qué quería «el Doctor» que Abáscal hiciera?

5. ¿Qué arma traía Abáscal?

6. ¿A qué destino viajó después de cumplir con su encargo?

7. ¿Qué le pasó cuando bajaba la escalerilla del avión?

8. ¿Por qué creía el Doctor que en el asesinato de Abáscal había cierta dignidad?

9. ¿Qué otra cosa le llegó al Doctor junto con el cable que indicaba «Firmamos contrato»?

10. ¿Cree Ud. que el Doctor esperaba que le iban a quitar la vida también?

• 11. Explique Ud. la ironía en la reflexión del Doctor de que él mismo era otro de los nexos que había que extirpar.

• 12. ¿Podría Ud. sugerir una manera de continuar este cuento después de la explosión final?

B. Verb Practice Use each of the following verbal phrases in an original sentence in Spanish, either based on the story or of your own design. Be prepared to explain the meaning of your sentences.

1. **ser de**

2. **inquietarse**

3. **empezar a**

4. **preguntarse**

5. **llevar encima**

6. **complacerse en**

7. **tratarse de**

8. **tocarle a uno**

9. **advertir**

10. **dejar caer**

C. Vocabulary Practice Complete the sentences below, matching the expressions on the right with the italicized English words on the left. Then use the expression in an original Spanish sentence and indicate in English what your sentence means.

1. *In any case,* te he dado mi palabra.
2. Rodolfo es absolutamente una persona *trustworthy.*
3. Martín es una gran persona, o *rather* uno de mis mejores amigos.
4. Puede ser que Ud. tenga razón; *on the other hand,* no he hablado con Rosa.
5. Ramón me hablaba y, *at the same time,* aceitaba su pistola.
6. *Nevertheless,* lo que hiciste no está bien.
7. Convendría comprar la pizza *beforehand.*
8. *Right there* Uds. tienen una idea de lo duro que es el jefe.
9. Seguramente ellos no van a venir, *I mean,* así me han dicho.
10. La situación se hizo *more and more* complicada.

sin embargo

mejor dicho

de confianza

cada vez más

de todos modos

ahí nomás

en cambio

a la vez

de antemano

o sea

D. Communication Practice

1. Say that you have already begun to make the necessary calls.
2. Ask whose turn it is now.
3. Indicate that you didn't have your passport on you then.
4. Ask what this is all about (a matter of).
5. Say you wonder if there will be many people at the dance.

E. Review Exercise

The following reflexive verbs that appear in this story also have nonreflexive forms. For example, the reflexive **levantarse** *to get up* has the nonreflexive form **levantar** *to raise.* Give the meaning of each member of the pair and then use them in Spanish sentences.

preguntarse	**tratarse**	**caerse**
sentirse	**jugarse**	**complacerse**

Nosotras

María Elena Llana

MARIA ELENA LLANA (1936–   ) was born in Cuba. While still in her twenties, she published *La reja,* a volume of short stories from which the present narrative is taken. She is one of a large group of authors who, writing either in political exile or from the perspective of present-day Cuban life, have brought Cuban literature into a position of prominence that it has never enjoyed before.

In recent years, Spanish American women have assumed a more important and active role in the area of cultural activities. Increasing attention is being given today to the contributions of women to the literature of the Spanish American nations, and these writers have now begun to fill in—sensitively and eloquently—the previously substantial gaps in the depiction of life and customs in the Western Hemisphere.

"Nosotras" is an unusual story, a lucidly narrated and unsettling adventure that takes place in an impressionable dimension of the mind. It all starts out so innocently, with a wisp of a recollection from a dream. But the narrator has soon passed from the state of sleeping and dreaming into a more troubled waking state, one of growing incredulity and self-doubt. The story's ending—deliberately inconclusive—is but one more disconcerting feature of this narrative.

A PRELIMINARY LOOK AT KEY EXPRESSIONS

Be sure to study these expressions before you read the story.

1. (62:2) **alegrarse** *to be happy, glad*

2. (62:4) **justamente** *just, exactly, right*

3. (62:6) **en vez de** *instead of*

4. (62:10) **lavarse los dientes** *to brush* or *clean one's teeth*   As usual with verbs having to do with personal bodily and grooming habits, the part of the body or article of clothing involved is preceded by the definite article rather than the possessive, and the verb in question is accompanied by a reflexive pronoun: **Ella se lavó los dientes.** *She brushed her (own) teeth.* If someone else performs the action on the first party, the latter is expressed by the indirect object: **El dentista le lavó los dientes.** *The dentist cleaned her teeth.*

5. (62:12) **mediodía** *noon*   The definite article is added when the expression contains *at*: **al mediodía.**

6. (62:18) **descolgar** *to lift, pick up (the phone)*   Literally, **descolgar** is *to unhook, take down*. The opposite is **colgar** (literally, *to hang*) *to hang up (the phone)*.

7. (62:25) **bueno** *well, so*   An introductory phrase to indicate that the speaker wants to change the subject, end the conversation, take some action, etc. To indicate approval, *good* is **bien, está bien, de acuerdo,** and other such phrases.

8. (62:26) **preguntar por** *to ask for; to inquire about*   This expression is used both to request to talk to someone and to inquire about one's health. *To ask for,* in the sense of *request,* is **pedir.**

9. (63:41) **arriesgarse (a)** *to take a chance*   Notice that the verb retains the **ie** in all forms: **Tú te arriesgas, Nosotros nos arriesgamos,** etc.

10. (63:48) **recostarse** *to lie down, lean back, stretch out*   This verb is used for a more temporary casual action; **acostarse** normally means *to lie down (to sleep)* or *to go to bed.*

11. (63:55) **sino** *but* (in the sense of *but rather* or *but also*)   This word is used when what follows contradicts or replaces a previous negative element: **no el comienzo sino el final** *not the beginning but (rather) the end.* **No sólo...** always elicits the use of **sino** or **sino que** if a conjugated verb follows: **No sólo la llamó sino que le habló largo rato.** *She not only called her, but talked to her for a long while.*

12. (63:60) **no poder más** *not to be able to go on, stand it*   The phrase almost always stands alone rather than forming part of a longer sentence: **No puedo más.** *I'm all in; I've had it.*

13. (63:62) **mientras** *while*
14. (64:82) **desde luego** *of course, naturally*
15. (64:88) **molestar** *to bother, annoy*   The person bothered is the indirect object: **Eso no le molestó nada.** *That didn't bother her at all.*
16. (64:91) **acabar por** + *infinitive*   *to end (by)* + *present participle:* **Acabé por llamarla.** *I ended up (by) calling her.*
17. (65:130) **sea como sea** *be that as it may*
18. (65:150) **a riesgo de** *at the risk of*
19. (65:156) **a punto de** *on the point of*
20. (66:186) **tranquilizarse** *to calm down*   Like so many verbs that indicate a change in physical or emotional state, this one is usually reflexive. However, it can be used with a direct object when a second party is involved: **El pensamiento mismo me tranquiliza.** *The very thought makes me feel calm.*

Nosotras

Soñé que venían de la Compañía a cambiar el número del teléfono. «Me alegro mucho —dije—, porque se pasan el día llamando a un número parecido y porque otros, cualquiera sabe quién o quiénes,[1] llaman justamente los sábados a las tres de la
5 madrugada...» Bueno, a ellos no les interesó mucho mi alegría. Lo cambiaron y eso fue todo. Y yo, en vez de mirar al redondelito del centro del aparato, ahí donde se escribe el número, les pregunté: «¿Qué número es?» Y me respondieron: «El 20-58».

Brumas. Algo incoherente. Brumas. Despierto y doy los pa-
10 sos de siempre:[2] desayuno, me lavo los dientes, tiendo la cama... Empieza un día como otro. Sin saber por qué, nunca se sabe exactamente por qué, al mediodía un número surge en mi cerebro, aletargado por la blandura de la hora.[3] «El 20...» Ligero gesto de extrañeza. ¿El 20...? Brumas. Algo incoherente. Brumas. ¡El 20-58!
15 Sonrisa. ¡Es verdad, el 20-58! E inmediatamente, el gesto fatal: coger el teléfono y canalizar[4] una infantil curiosidad... Rac-rac-rac-rac. Y un timbrazo opaco y lejano inicia la conversación. Alguien descuelga y, pese a los vericuetos del hilo[5] la voz llega extrañamente lisa, extrañamente familiar.

20 —Oigo.[6]

—¿Qué casa?

—¿A quién desea?

—¿Es el 20-58?

—Sí.

25 Esa voz, esa voz... Bueno, continuemos la tontería. Si se supone que ése es mi nuevo número, preguntaré por mí misma.

—Con... Fulana.[7]

—Es la que habla.

Claro, algo de estupor. Estas cosas nunca pueden evitarse.
30 Momento de vacilación. Algo incoherente pero ahora sin brumas. Insistencia desde el otro lado.

—Sí, soy yo, ¿quién es?

Total desconcierto. Mi misma imagen devuelta...[8] Bueno, hay que salir de esto. No se me ocurre nada más que la verdad y
35 la digo no sin cierto temor.

[1] *cualquiera... quiénes:* I have no idea who
[2] *doy... siempre:* I follow my regular routine
[3] *aletargado... hora:* groggy from the midday heat
[4] *canalizar:* give in to
[5] *pese... hilo:* despite the long tortuous route of the telephone wire
[6] *Oigo:* Hello (literally, "I hear")
[7] *Fulana:* a fictitious name used in Spanish for any woman in general, like Jane Doe, so-and-so, such-and-such, what's-her-name, etc.
[8] *Mi misma imagen devuelta:* My own voice coming right back at me

—Soy yo, Fulana.

Pudo colgar, pudo decir cualquier cosa, pudo no decir nada, pudo hablar en copto,[9] pero lo que no debió decir nunca fue lo que dijo:

40   —Al fin me llamas.

Me arriesgo:

—Pero oye..., soy Fulana... de Tal.[10]

—Sí, ya lo sé. También yo soy Fulana de Tal.

Es demasiado. Un estremecimiento me recorre el espinazo...
45 Ahora ya no sé qué decir. Esta vez, sin contenerme, en espera a que la otra cuelgue, cuelgo yo y me quedo con la mano sobre el auricular, mirando el aparato como si fuera un animalejo que de un momento a otro pudiera echar a andar. Suspiro. Me recuesto en el sofá. ¿Una broma? ¿Habré hablado en sueños? ¿Se enteraría
50 alguien de...?[11] ¡Pero si[12] es imposible!

Y ya todo gira como el rac-rac-rac-rac del 20-58. Puedo ir y venir por la casa, arreglar este adornito, aderezar aquel marco, calentar el café, pero es como si estuviera vigilada. Como si los ojos que me siguen salieran del teléfono; no que estuvieran agazapa-
55 dos en él, sino que simplemente esperaran su momento. Había dicho «Al fin me llamas», y pudiera creerse que llevaba esperando mil años, por sólo hablar de los últimos tiempos. Voy y vengo; rehúyo cruzar muy cerca del teléfono y después me río de mis aprensiones. «¡Como si tuviera garras que fueran a cogerme por
60 la saya!» Hacia las seis de la tarde ya no puedo más. Descuelgo. Me falta un poco la respiración. Rac-rac-rac-rac. El corazón tamborilea mientras aguardo. Cuando al fin oigo su voz ya no sé qué me pasa.

—Oigo.
65   No puedo evitarlo, tartamudeo:

—¿El... 20... 58...?

—Sí.

—¿Quién habla?

La voz me salió valiente,[13] pero la respuesta tuvo el mismo
70 efecto de un cubito de hielo concienzudamente pasado a lo largo de la columna vertebral.

—Sí, soy yo. Ya sé que eres tú otra vez.

—¿Yo? ¿Quién?

—Yo misma.
75   Esto parece complicarse. Ahora me acometen deseos de discutir. Digo con acento de poner las cosas en su lugar.[14]

[9] *copto:* Coptic, an extinct language of ancient Egypt, still used by Egyptian Christians in their liturgy. We might say "Greek" in such a situation.
[10] *Fulana... de Tal: De Tal* is often added as a family name to such imaginary names (see note 7).
[11] *¿Se enteraría alguien de...?* Could anyone have found out about . . . ? Note the use of the conditional to express conjecture in the past.
[12] *si:* Does not translate.
[13] *La... valiente:* My voice came out sounding brave
[14] *con... lugar:* in a very businesslike tone

—Tú misma, no. Yo misma.

—Es igual.

—Pero aunque todo esto fuera algo juicioso, yo estoy
80 primero.[15]

—¿Por qué? ¿No eres Fulana de Tal?

—Sí, desde luego.

—Pero es que yo soy Fulana de Tal.

—Aunque sea verdad, hay que aclarar que tú eres también
85 Fulana de Tal.

—¿Y por qué? Yo soy Fulana de Tal. Tú eres Fulana de Tal
también.

Ahora ya no me desconcierta, me molesta. Estoy enfurecién-
dome, pero de pronto... Sí, pudiera ser... Hay que investigar un
90 poco más, eso es todo. Han sido coincidencias, pero las coincidencias acaban por fallar cuando se razona.[16] Mi voz suena con-
ciliadora, casi gentil, cuando digo:

—Es mejor ir despacio. Veamos:[17] las dos nos llamamos Fulana de Tal y eso es ya una casualidad.
95   —¿Tú crees?

Su tonito irónico, desafiante, me desarma. Continúo todo lo
gentil que puedo, dadas las circunstancias.

—Yo nací en el pueblo de...

—De X, exactamente. Yo nací allí; hija de Zutana y Espe-
100 rancejo.[18]

Trago en seco,[19] pero no me dejo abatir. Le espeto como un
fiscal:

—¡Segundo apellido!

—Tal, querida. Soy Tal y Tal.
105   Ahora ya empiezo a sentirme decididamente mal. ¿Quién
puede saber todo eso? ¿De quién es la broma? ¿De quién el ardid?
Ella toma la iniciativa:

—¿Qué te pasa? ¿Por qué ponerte así? ¿Ves que no miento?
¿Por qué habría de hacerlo?[20]
110   Quisiera contenerme. Si en definitiva es cierto lo que ocurre,
no hay razón para que ella lo tome así, tranquilamente, y yo lo
tome así, arrebatadamente. Pero me siento engañada. Siento que
alguien se ha confabulado. No puedo evitarlo. Entonces, jugándome el todo por el todo,[21] pregunto:
115   —Si somos la misma, debemos serlo en todo, ¿no? ¿Cómo
estoy vestida?

[15] *primero:* here an adverb, thus showing no agreement with the female subject after the verb *estoy*
[16] *las... razona:* coincidences don't hold up when you submit them to logic
[17] *Veamos:* See here
[18] *Zutana y Esperancejo:* These are both imaginary names like *Fulana.*
[19] *Trago en seco:* I gulp (literally, "I swallow dry")
[20] *¿Por qué... hacerlo?* Why would I want to do that?
[21] *jugándome... todo:* forcing the issue (literally, "Gambling everything for everything")

—Con mi bata..., es decir, voy a evitar el posesivo. Con la bata de casa azul. Por cierto que ya el descosido de la manga molesta.[22]

120 —Sí, molesta, pero...

Me detengo. ¿Por qué camino estoy tomando? ¿Es que voy a transigir? No, no. Ahora ella habla otra vez, es decir, no tengo constancia de que sea «ella». Para ser más exacta, me escucho decir:

—La aguja está en una esquina de la gaveta superior de la
125 mesita de noche. La dejaste allí la última vez que la usaste, y yo, desde luego, la volví a colocar.[23] Cuando creíste que se había perdido, era que yo estaba zurciendo la sayuela rosada.

Ahora empiezo a flaquear. Ayer me sorprendió ver la sayuela cosida y deduje que lo había hecho la lavandera, lo que es muy
130 extraño, pero no le vi otra explicación.[24] Sea como sea, algo se ha ablandado en mí. Casi estoy a punto de suplicar cuando digo:

—¿A qué conduce esto?

—No sé. Fuiste tú quien llamó, ¿recuerdas? ¿Por qué lo hiciste?

135 ¿Qué puedo contestarle? ¿Decirle lo del sueño? De pronto me siento infeliz. Todas las fuerzas ceden ante esta repentina autoconmiseración... Ella me hace dar un salto:

—Por favor, me haces sentir mal. ¿Por qué este estado de ánimo?

140 Ya no puedo menos que[25] indignarme.

—¿Hasta cuándo va a durar esto?

—Hasta que tú quieras. Basta que cuelgues.[26] Nunca te he molestado, ¿no?

¿Por qué balbuceo? No lo sé:

145 —¿Y si... si cuelgo...?

—No volverás a saber de mí, como hasta ahora.[27] Todo esto lo empezaste tú.

Estoy dispuesta a colgar. Hay algo irritante en... en..., ¡bueno, en ella! Pero ha sido tan comprensiva, tan paciente, ¿qué derecho
150 tengo para enojarme? Sin embargo, aun a riesgo de parecer infantil, pregunto:

—¿Puedo saber cuál es tu dirección?

—Está en la Guía.

—¿A nombre de quién?

155 —Mío, desde luego.

Estoy a punto de caer en la trampa, pero reacciono:

[22] *Por... molesta:* Of course, those stitches coming out on the sleeve are annoying.
[23] *la volví a colocar:* put it back again
[24] *no... explicación:* I saw no other explanation for it
[25] *no puedo menos que:* I can't help but
[26] *Basta que cuelgues:* All you have to do is hang up.
[27] *No... ahora:* You'll never find out any more about me than you know now.

—Si tu nombre es el mío, lo buscaré y encontraré mi propia dirección.

—Es lógico.

160 Ya vuelvo a desesperarme.

—Pero y entonces, ¿cómo puedes tener un teléfono distinto?

—La que lo tiene distinto eres tú.

¿Se estará[28] poniendo agresiva? Su tono ha sido ya algo molesto. Sonrío. Me empiezo a adueñar de la situación. Quizá con un 165 poco de sangre fría[29] llegue a desconcertarla. Quizá me lo diga todo. Quizá..., ¡pero ahora recuerdo que tengo que hacer una salida urgente! Voy a decírselo cuando ella me interrumpe:

—Bueno, creo que por hoy es bastante. Tengo que hacer.[30] Cuando quieras, ya sabes dónde me tienes.[31]

170 —Sí, sí..., yo también tengo que...

¡Qué curioso! Cuando recuerdo que se hace tarde, ella parece recordar lo mismo. Bueno, no sé si despedirme o no. No quisiera ser grosera, pero tampoco tengo por qué ser[32] amable. Ella, sin embargo, apresura las cosas. En el fondo[33] se lo agradezco.

175 —Hasta otra ocasión, ¿eh?

Y cuelga. Me quedo con el auricular en la mano. Lo miro. Me paso la otra mano por la frente. Otra vez lo inexplicable me cerca, como esas pesadillas en las que no podemos despegar los pies del suelo. La urgencia del tiempo me decide. Cuelgo de una vez y voy 180 a mi habitación, a vestirme. No sé exactamente qué traje ponerme, pero voy directamente hacia el claro, de algodón... Es como si alguien ya hubiese decidido por mí. La idea me desconcierta, pero entonces ya tengo presencia de ánimo para desecharla. «No, no —me digo—, mejor es no pensar en eso. Si está, en el caso de 185 que «esté», es allí, en el teléfono, esperando en el 20-58.» El razonamiento es desesperadamente pobre, pero lo hago por tranquilizarme y me tranquiliza, al menos mientras me visto. Sin embargo..., el germencito no ha muerto; la raicilla de la misma idea se agita buscando sol. Hasta que aflora: «¿Y si la llamo, sin 190 teléfono? Bastará[34] decir su nombre, que es el mío, y esperar a... ¿Contestará?» En esto he terminado de vestirme y voy al tocador. Cuando alzo los ojos estoy a punto de retroceder. Esos ojos, esos ojos, los míos, que acaban de reflejarse en el espejo, no parecen haberse alzado en este momento. Es como si ya hubieran estado 195 mirándome. Me apoyo en la mesa del tocador. ¿Esa sensación de vahído? Sé que estoy a punto de gritar y no quiero, sencillamente no quiero. Así que cojo la cartera y echo a correr hacia la puerta.

[28] *estará:* Note the use of the future for probability in the present.
[29] *sangre fría: sangfroid* (Fr.), lit. "cold blood," meaning "calm," "composure," "coolness"
[30] *Tengo que hacer:* I've got things to do.
[31] *dónde me tienes:* where you can reach me
[32] *por qué ser:* any reason to be
[33] *En el fondo:* Secretly
[34] *Bastará:* It will be enough for me

Ya en la escalera estoy casi en disposición de sonreír; como si me hubiera escapado de una trampa. Pienso que el aire de la
200 calle me refrescará, que todo esto ha de pasar, como si la salida[35] de la casa pudiera significar un cambio en las cosas, y al regreso todo esté olvidado.

Empiezo a bajar la escalera. Aún el ¡pram! de la puerta al cerrarse resuena en el fondo de mis tímpanos, cuando me detengo.
205 Sé que he hecho ese gesto de sorpresa, un gesto cortado que nos mantiene con la mirada fija al frente por un instante y que hace que los labios balbuceen algo...

—Las llaves..., no metí las llaves en la cartera.

Suspiro. Estoy casi derrotada. Hago memoria[36] y veo las
210 llaves, claramente, encima del aparador. Allí las dejé anoche, cuando volví del cine. Allí estaban mientras hablé por teléfono..., ¡esa maldita conversación! Desde el sofá las veía cada vez que mis ojos recorrían la pieza, mientras hablaba. Y la salida precipitada, la estúpida huída de mi casa, me hizo olvidarlas... ¿Y ahora? De
215 momento siento la necesidad imperiosa de volver. No puedo irme sabiendo que al regreso no podré entrar. Subo los dos o tres escalones que he bajado. Me paro a mirar tontamente la puerta cerrada. Vacilo. De pronto se me ocurre y no me doy tiempo a rechazar la idea. Toco el timbre y retrocedo expectante... No sé si
220 la sangre ha aumentado su velocidad dentro de cada vena, de cada arteria, de cada humilde vasito capilar. No sé si, por el contrario, se ha detenido. Como tampoco sé si es frío o calor lo que me invade, deseos de reír tranquila o de echar a correr despavorida, cuando la puerta empieza a abrirse, lentamente, frente a mí.

[35] *la salida:* my going out
[36] *Hago memoria:* I try to remember

Exercises

A. Questions and Opinions

1. ¿Qué cosa había soñado la narradora?

2. ¿Qué hizo la mujer para satisfacer su «infantil curiosidad»?

3. ¿Con quién se comunicó la mujer llamando el 20-58?

4. ¿Por quién se sentía vigilada la narradora?

5. ¿Por qué volvió a llamar a las seis de la tarde?

6. ¿Qué datos íntimos sabía la otra mujer acerca de la narradora?

7. ¿Por qué preguntó a la otra mujer cómo estaba vestida?

8. ¿Con qué pretexto finalmente terminó la narradora la conversación?

9. ¿Qué cosa rara notó la mujer en el espejo del tocador?

10. Cuando volvió la narradora a su casa por las llaves, ¿quién le abrió la puerta?

• 11. ¿Cuál puede ser la explicación de lo que ocurre en este cuento?

• 12. ¿A Ud. le ha pasado alguna vez algo parecido?

B. Verb Practice Use each of the following verbal phrases in an original sentence in Spanish, either based on the story or of your own design. Be prepared to explain the meaning of your sentences.

1. **alegrarse**

2. **lavarse los dientes**

3. **descolgar**

4. **preguntar por**

5. **arriesgarse**

6. **recostarse**

7. **no poder más**

8. **molestar**

9. **acabar por** + *infinitive*

10. **tranquilizarse**

C. Vocabulary Practice Complete the sentences below, matching the expressions on the right with the English words on the left. Be sure to use the correct form of each verb. Then use each expression in an original Spanish sentence and indicate in English what your sentence means.

1. *Instead of* llamarme a mí misma, vine a visitarme.   **justamente**

2. *Well,* ¿vas a seguir llamándome?   **en vez de**

3. *¡Of course!*   **mediodía**

4. Estaba *on the point of* caer en la trampa.   **bueno**

5. Pero, ¡llamarme todos los sábados *exactly* a las tres de la madrugada!

6. *At the risk of* mostrar demasiada curiosidad, pregunté: —¿Quién eres?

7. ¡No fue ella *but* yo!

8. ¿Te decidiste a llamar al *noon,* o a la medianoche?

9. *Be that as it may,* creo que es hora de llamar a la policía.

10. Yo me quedo aquí *while* tú llamas.

sino

mientras

desde luego

sea como sea

a riesgo de

a punto de

D. Communication Practice

1. Say you've already brushed your teeth.

2. State that you can't go on any longer.

3. Indicate that someone called and asked for Elsa.

4. Express the idea that you'd like to lie down for a few minutes.

5. Indicate that you're glad that no one calls you at three o'clock in the morning.

El papel de plata

Alfonso Ferrari Amores

ALFONSO FERRARI AMORES (1903–1980) was born in Buenos Aires, and there he pursued his subsequent literary career. He was a journalist by profession and a fiction writer during "outside" hours. His short stories appeared in the leading Argentine newspapers and magazines, and his novel *Gaucho al timón* (1948) received a literary prize. Also honored by a similar award was his radio script "Mástiles quebrados". In addition, he had several stage dramas produced in the Argentine capital. To round out his varied background, we might add that Ferrari wrote a number of tangos that enjoyed great popularity in his country and abroad.

Ferrari was widely known as a mystery-story writer—an author of "whodunits." Under pseudonyms, as well as under his own name, he published over a dozen detective novels with scenes laid outside Argentina. His detective short stories, written under his own name, are clever tales usually set against a typically Argentine backdrop. His best work in the field of crime fiction was done in the shorter form, as you may well judge from this ingenious story—"El papel de plata".

A PRELIMINARY LOOK AT KEY EXPRESSIONS

Be sure to study these expressions before you read the story.

1. (72:4) **saludar** *to greet, say hello to*
2. (72:7) **salir** *to go out*   Although **salir** sometimes means *to leave*, it more often means *to go out* or *come out*, or even *to go out on a date.*
3. (72:7) **a pesar mío** *in spite of myself, against my better judgment*   This expression can also be **a pesar tuyo, a pesar suyo,** etc.
4. (72:15) **en frente** *in front of, before one*
5. (72:23) **sacar en limpio** *to gather, conclude:* **Espero que saques algo en limpio.** *I hope you gather something out of it.*
6. (72:24) **acomodarse** *to settle oneself, settle down:* **Me acomodé lo mejor posible en mi silla.** *I settled down as best I could in my chair.* This verb also means *to get a "soft" job* or *to marry into money* (73:41).
7. (73:40) **de repente** *suddenly*
8. (73:41) **dar que hablar** *to give occasion for talk, comment:* **Eso dio que hablar.** *That caused a lot of talk (gossip).*
9. (73:49) **ganarse el pan** *to earn a living* (literally, *to earn bread for oneself*)
10. (73:63) **por separado** *separately:* **Hay que servir los dos tipos de hongos por separado.** *You have to serve both types of mushrooms separately.*
11. (73:65) **por si acaso** *just in case*
12. (73:66) **mostrarse** *to appear, look:* **Se mostró muy interesado.** *He looked very interested.*
13. (73:66) **en seguida** *at once, right away*
14. (73:74) **convenir** *to be desirable, suitable, fitting, proper*   This is a deceptive cognate, which only rarely means *to be convenient.* It is often used with an indirect object: **Le conviene hacer eso.** *She really ought to do that.*
15. (74:81) **olvidarse de** *to forget*
16. (74:86) **casarse con** *to marry, get married to*
17. (74:89) **soler** + *infinitive*   *to be in the habit of, be accustomed to*   This verb is used only in the present and imperfect because of the nature of its repetitive meaning.
18. (74:92) **comunicarse con** *to get in touch with*
19. (74:99) **tal como** *just as:* **Hazlo tal como te dije.** *Do it just as I told you to.*
20. (74:107) **de paso** *in passing, while doing so, in the process:* **Se comprobó, de paso, que yo no era el culpable.** *It was proved, in the process, that I was not the guilty one.*

El papel de plata

Joaco Migueles, aquel borracho filósofo que fue uno de mis amigos más divertidos, vino de la calle trayendo en la mano un papel plateado, de los que se usan como envoltura de chocolatines y cigarrillos. Antes de saludarme fue hasta una caja y lo echó en ella. Explicó:

—Calafate para el techo. Mira. —Señaló una línea de hoyuelos en el piso de tierra—. Una gotera. Esta tarde salí a pesar mío —gruñó, rascándose la nuca. —El solazo me mata. Yo no hubiera querido salir, pero necesitaba vino, y no tuve más remedio que salir.[1] Sin embargo, ya ves, encontré el papel plateado, que es lo mejor que hay para tapar las goteras. Ahí tienes una lección optimista que nos da el azar. No hay mal que por bien no venga,[2] como dice el refrán.

En esto se le volvió la sed y llenó de nuevo el vaso que tenía en frente. Los vasos en que echó Joaco el vino eran como floreros; poco faltaba para que alguno contuviese[3] tanto como la propia botella.

—Tú sabes que yo anduve por la Patagonia[4] cuando era mozo. Fue una experiencia brava; y de no haberla sufrido,[5] sin embargo, no hubiera conocido la felicidad.

Me di cuenta en ese momento de que Joaco Migueles iba a contarme otra de sus memorables historias. A él no le gustaba sino charlar filosóficamente sobre lo que había sacado en limpio de sus experiencias en este mundo. Me acomodé lo mejor posible en mi silla y me puse a escuchar el relato que sirvió para distraerme del mucho calor que hacía.

Acariciando su vaso, Joacó fijó vagamente su mirada en el techo, y me narró la historia que sigue y que he llevado al papel sin cambiar una letra.

—En un rincón de mi memoria donde nunca he barrido para no tener que avergonzarme con lo que saldría a... (iba a decir a relucir, pero no es la miseria cosa que reluzca),[6] hay un tanque de cemento. Un depósito de agua que quedó convertido por mí en dormitorio. Fue en Río Negro,[7] justamente, en El Ñireco.[8] Tan despilchado andaba en aquel tiempo, que ni ganas de remendarme

[1] *no... salir:* I had no choice but to go out
[2] *No hay... venga:* "Every cloud has a silver lining." (Literally, "There is no ill that does not come to good.")
[3] *poco... contuviese:* one of them was almost big enough to hold
[4] *Patagonia:* region comprising the southern part of continental Chile and Argentina
[5] *de... sufrido:* if I hadn't gone through it
[6] *no... reluzca:* misery isn't something that glitters
[7] *Río Negro:* a province in southern Argentina, just north of Patagonia
[8] *El Ñireco:* small town in Río Negro province

tenía, porque hubiera sido lo mismo que calafatear un barco hundido. En ese entonces muchos otros muchachos hicieron plata[9] con los caminos, trabajando de sol a sol[10] en las cuadrillas de Vialidad.[11] Yo no tengo pasta para andar entablado,[12] tú sabes, como
40 animal de tropilla. Seguí pobre, pero no por mucho tiempo. De repente, me acomodé. Eso dio que hablar a muchos. Todo el mundo opinó. Que esto, que lo otro, que lo de más allá.[13] Yo voy a referirme al caso, ya que también lo conozco, y después tú sacarás la conclusión que mejor te parezca. Lo que dije del tanque al prin-
45 cipio viene a que por él te explicarás fácilmente[14] que no podía yo negarme a disfrutar, cuando empezaron las nieves en Viedma,[15] de una cama en la trastienda de una herboristería, en la que me ofrecieron empleo como vendedor. Entre seguir en el tanque de cemento en El Ñireco y ganarme el pan en Viedma, ¿quién iba a
50 titubear? Así, quedé como único ocupante del boliche, y una tarde llegó allí a visitarme el viejo gringo[16] avaro, don Hellmuth. Charlamos de mil cosas, y en cierto momento le dije que si era verdad que la diabetes consiste en un exceso de glucosa, a mí me parecía que la ingestión de hongos venenosos, que matan por pri-
55 var a la sangre de aquella substancia, podría ensayarse, en ciertas dosis, para curar a los diabéticos. Era una simple cuestión de lógica. Entonces don Hellmuth me preguntó:

—¿Usted tiene hongos venenosos?

Por toda respuesta saqué[17] dos bolsitas del hueco del mos-
60 trador y se los mostré.

—Éstos son los buenos, y éstos son los malos. ¿No parecen idénticos? Don Hellmuth asintió, maravillado.

—Calcule usted —continué—. Si uno los sirve por separado, en dos platos, nadie podría diferenciar los venenosos de los otros.
65 Claro que sería conveniente disponer de un antídoto, por si acaso.

—¿Cuál? —preguntó don Hellmuth, que se mostró en seguida muy interesado.

—La misma glucosa.[18] Una solución muy concentrada, claro. Puede beberse o inyectarse.
70 —Déme hongos de las dos clases —dijo él—. Y el contraveneno.

Mientras le cobraba los hongos y el frasco, le dije:

—Claro que si ha de estar al alcance de un enemigo que haya comido los hongos venenosos, convendría disfrazar el antídoto,
75 para que no lo tome.

[9] *plata:* money, "dough"
[10] *de sol a sol:* from sunup to sundown
[11] *Vialidad:* highway department
[12] *Yo... entablado:* I'm not cut out for being herded around
[13] *Que esto... allá:* This, that, and the other thing.
[14] *viene... fácilmente:* was said so that you can easily understand
[15] *Viedma:* Coastal city of Río Negro province
[16] *gringo:* In some Latin American countries, *gringo* refers to an American, but in others, like Argentina, it refers to any foreigner.
[17] *Por toda respuesta saqué:* My only reply was to take out
[18] *La misma glucosa:* Glucose, as I said.

—¿Y cómo? —preguntó don Hellmuth.

Yo tomé de un cajón una etiqueta donde se veía una calavera en rojo, y debajo de ella la palabra «Veneno», y la pegué en el frasco.

80 —Ya está —le dije—. Ahora únicamente nosotros dos sabemos que esto no es lo que dice la etiqueta. Trate de no olvidarse de este detalle.

Casualmente[19] aquella misma noche vino a refugiarse en mi botica la mujer de don Hellmuth, una criollita joven y linda a
85 quien el gringo acostumbraba moler a palos,[20] y eso después de haberse casado con ella, o tal vez de rabia por haberlo hecho; y me contó que después de haber comido juntos un guiso con hongos, la había echado de su casa corriéndola con un látigo. Don Hellmuth, que era hombre tan rico como avaro, solía tener arre-
90 batos, pero nunca como esa vez, y la muchacha lloraba como una Magdalena.[21] (¡Y tanto que escaseaban por allá las mujeres![22]) Yo hice girar la manivela del teléfono, me comuniqué con don Hellmuth y le grité, asustado:

—¡Oiga! ¡Equivoqué las etiquetas de los hongos! Los comes-
95 tibles son los venenosos, y los...

Dicen que lo encontraron al otro día envenenado con cianuro de potasio. El forense analizó el contenido del frasco que había vaciado de un trago don Hellmuth, y declaró:

—Veneno, tal como lo indica la etiqueta. Sin duda, don Hell-
100 muth se suicidó.

No faltaron después quienes me miraron de reojo porque me casé con la viuda. Claro que la criollita era un bombón. Fue mi papel de plata, como el que hoy encontré para remediarme. Pero, ¿asunto a qué murmuraban?[23] De envidiosos, no más.[24] En
105 todo ven el dinero. ¿Por qué no se les ocurre pensar que un hombre, por más pobre que sea, puede ser desinteresado? A don Hellmuth le hicieron la autopsia; con ese motivo[25] se comprobó, de paso, que los hongos eran inofensivos. ¡Que iba a vender yo hongos venenosos![26]

[19] *Casualmente:* By chance
[20] *acostumbraba moler a palos:* used to beat regularly
[21] *Magdalena:* Mary Magdalene, the repentant sinner depicted in the Bible
[22] *¡Y... mujeres!* And women were so scarce there, too!
[23] *¿asunto a qué murmuraban?* was that anything for them to gossip about?
[24] *De envidiosos, no más:* They were jealous, that's all.
[25] *con ese motivo:* in this way
[26] *¡Que... venenosos!* What would I be doing selling poisonous mushrooms!

Exercises

A. Questions and Opinions

1. ¿Qué había encontrado Joaco Migueles para impermeabilizar el techo?
2. ¿A qué refrán se refirió Joaco?
3. ¿Sobre qué cosas le gustaba a Joaco charlar?
4. ¿Por qué no trabajaba Joaco en los caminos de Río Negro con los otros muchachos?
5. ¿Qué trabajo le ofrecieron a Joaco en Viedma?
6. ¿Quién llegó un día a la tienda a visitar a Joaco?
7. ¿Qué dijo Joaco acerca de los hongos venenosos?
8. ¿Qué acabó por comprar don Hellmuth?
9. ¿Quién vino a refugiarse en la tienda aquella misma noche?
10. ¿Cómo murió don Hellmuth?
• 11. ¿Considera Ud. que Joaco Migueles es un asesino? ¿Por qué?
• 12. ¿Es justificable lo que hizo Migueles? ¿Por qué?

B. Verb Practice
Use each of the following verbal phrases in an original sentence in Spanish, either based on the story or of your own design. Be prepared to explain the meaning of your sentences.

1. **saludar**
2. **salir**
3. **acomodarse**
4. **ganarse el pan**
5. **mostrarse**
6. **convenir**
7. **olvidarse de**
8. **casarse con**
9. **soler** + *infinitive*
10. **comunicarse con**

C. *Vocabulary Practice* Complete the sentences below, matching the expressions on the right with the English words on the left. Be sure to use the correct form of each verb. Then use each expression in an original Spanish sentence and indicate in English what your sentence means.

1. Joaco *had gotten a lot out of* sus viajes por Patagonia.

2. Si tienes hongos buenos y hongos malos, te conviene servirlos *separately.*

3. Me enamoré de la esposa de don Hellmuth *in spite of myself.*

4. Lo hice *just as* me dijeron.

5. Examinó con cuidado los hongos que tenía *before him.*

6. Y, *in the process,* la policía descubrió que no había hongos venenosos.

7. Y don Hellmuth *suddenly* notó algo raro en el guiso.

8. Mejor que tenga glucosa en la casa, *just in case.*

9. La criollita venía a visitarme con frecuencia y eso *caused a lot of talk.*

10. Yo traté de comunicarme con don Hellmuth *right away.*

a pesar mío

en frente

sacar en limpio

de repente

dar que hablar

por separado

por si acaso

en seguida

tal como

de paso

D. *Communication Practice*

1. Say that you usually get up before 7:30.

2. Ask Carlos who Ana is marrying.

3. Indicate that it would be desirable to eat after the theater.

4. Tell Martin not to forget to call the restaurant.

5. Say you'll get in touch with Alice tomorrow afternoon.

E. Review Exercise The following words from the story are based on shorter words that you might already know. The shorter words are defined in case you are not familiar with them. See if you know the meaning of the longer words. Check the end vocabulary if necessary.

1. **plata** *silver,* **plateado**

2. **gota** *drop,* **gotera**

3. **flor** *flower,* **florero**

4. **cómodo** *comfortable,* **acomodarse**

5. **vergüenza** *shame,* **avergonzarse**

6. **dormir** *to sleep,* **dormitorio**

7. **vender** *to sell,* **vendedor**

8. **veneno** *poison,* **venenoso**

9. **mostrar** *to show,* **mostrador**

10. **comer** *to eat,* **comestible**

Las abejas de bronce

Marco Denevi

MARCO DENEVI (1922–   ) was born in Sáenz Peña, a suburb of Buenos Aires. He achieved literary fame with *Rosaura a las diez,* the first novel he wrote, winning with it the first prize in a contest held by the Editorial Kraft in Buenos Aires in 1955. It has been reprinted many times, has been translated into several languages, and was made into a movie. In 1961, Denevi submitted a long story entitled "Ceremonia secreta" to the first literary competition sponsored by *Life en Español,* the Latin American edition of *Life* magazine. It won the first prize of $5,000. Since then, he has continued writing (and winning prizes) as a novelist, short-story writer, and playwright.

Much of Denevi's work reveals a fondness for whimsy, fantasy, and—always just below the surface—social satire. The latter is reflected in "Las abejas de bronce", a story that criticizes an aspect of modern life against which Denevi has always rebelled. As a resident of the second largest city in the world south of the equator, he feels compelled here to point out certain consequences of the technological progress characteristic of the great metropolises of our age.

A PRELIMINARY LOOK AT KEY EXPRESSIONS

Be sure to study these expressions before you read the story.

1. (80:2) **aparte de** *apart, aside from*

2. (80:3) **tratar a** *to treat, deal with:* **Nadie como él sabía tratar a las Abejas.** *No one knew how to deal with the Bees as he did.*

3. (80:6) **por otro lado** *furthermore, moreover, on the other hand*   This expression usually follows **por un lado** *on the one hand.*

4. (80:6) **entenderse con** *to handle, get along with:* **El Zorro sabía entenderse con el Oso.** *The Fox knew how to handle the Bear.*

5. (80:8) **llevarse bien** *to get along (well)*   This is another reflexive verb that can be used with one subject or two subjects reciprocally: **El Zorro se lleva bien con el Oso.** *The Fox gets along with the Bear.* And **El Zorro y el Oso se llevan bien.** *The Fox and the Bear get along (well).*

6. (80:9) **al aire libre** *outside*

7. (80:25) **darse prisa** *to hurry*

8. (80:27) **(no) dejar de** + *infinitive*   In the affirmative, this expression means *to stop* + *present participle:* **Dejó de reír.** *He stopped laughing.* But in the negative it means *not to fail* + *infinitive* or *to be sure* + *infinitive:* **No dejes de llamar(me) si me necesitas.** *Be sure to call (me) if you need me.*

9. (81:41) **a coro** *in chorus, all together*

10. (81:53) **de acuerdo** *agreed, OK*

11. (81:60) **de una buena vez** *once and for all*

12. (82:86) **aprender a** + *infinitive*   *to learn* + *infinitive*

13. (82:107) **atreverse a** + *infinitive*   *to dare* + *infinitive*

14. (83:141) **sobre todo** *above all, especially*

15. (85:205) **tener éxito** *to be successful*

16. (85:207) **quejarse** *to complain*

17. (85:213) **tardar** + *time* + **en** + *infinitive*   *to take* + *time* + *infinitive:* **Tardaron diez días en volver.** *It took them ten days to get back.*   Notice that this expression really has nothing to do with the idea of *lateness,* as the adverb **tarde** does.

18. (86:240) **optar por** *to pick, choose*

19. (86:268) **más tarde** *later*

20. (87:278) **ninguna parte** *nowhere*   This expression is usually preceded by a preposition: **No va a ninguna parte.** *He's not going anywhere.* Or **No lo pude encontrar en ninguna parte.** *I couldn't find it anywhere.*

Las abejas de bronce

Desde el principio del tiempo el Zorro vivió de la venta de la miel.
Era, aparte de una tradición de familia, una especie de vocación
hereditaria. Nadie tenía la maña del Zorro para tratar a las Abejas
(cuando las Abejas eran unos animalitos vivos y muy irritables) y
5   hacerles rendir al máximo. Esto por un lado.[1]

Por otro lado el Zorro sabía entenderse con el Oso, gran con-
sumidor de miel y, por lo mismo,[2] su mejor cliente. No resultaba
fácil llevarse bien con el Oso. El Oso era un sujeto un poco bru-
tal, un poco salvaje, al que la vida al aire libre, si le proporcionaba
10   una excelente salud, lo volvía de una rudeza de manera[3] que no
todo el mundo estaba dispuesto a tolerarle.

(Incluso el Zorro, a pesar de su larga práctica, tuvo que sufrir
algunas experiencias desagradables en ese sentido.) Una vez, por
ejemplo, a causa de no sé qué cuestión baladí, el Oso destruyó de
15   un zarpazo la balanza para pesar la miel. El Zorro no se inmutó ni
perdió su sonrisa. (*Lo enterrarán con la sonrisa puesta,*[4] decía de él,
desdeñosamente, su tío el Tigre.) Pero le hizo notar al Oso que,
conforme a la ley, estaba obligado a indemnizar aquel perjuicio.

—Naturalmente —se rió el Oso— te indemnizaré. Espera
20   que corro a indemnizarte.[5] No me alcanzan las piernas para correr
a indemnizarte.[6]

Y lanzaba grandes carcajadas y se golpeaba un muslo con
la mano.

—Sí —dijo el Zorro con su voz tranquila—, sí, le aconsejo
25   que se dé prisa, porque las Abejas se impacientan. Fíjese, señor.

Y haciendo un ademán teatral, un ademán estudiado, señaló las colmenas. El Oso se fijó e instantáneamente dejó de reír.
Porque vio que millares de Abejas habían abandonado los panales
y con el rostro rojo de cólera, el ceño fruncido y la boca crispada,
30   lo miraban de hito en hito,[7] y parecían dispuestas a atacarlo.

—No aguardan sino mi señal[8] —agregó el Zorro, dulce-
mente—. Usted sabe, detestan las groserías.

El Oso, que a pesar de su fuerza era un fanfarrón, palideció
de miedo.

[1] *Esto por un lado:* This on the one hand
[2] *por lo mismo:* by the same token
[3] *lo... manera:* gave him such a crude manner
[4] *con la sonrisa puesta:* with that smile on his face
[5] *Espera... indemnizarte:* You just wait. I'll break my neck running to pay you back for the damage (*sarcastically, of course*).
[6] *No... indemnizarte:* I can't hurry fast enough to pay you back for the damage.
[7] *de hito en hito:* from head to foot
[8] *No... señal:* They're just waiting for my signal

35   —Está bien, Zorro —balbuceaba—, repondré la balanza.
Pero por favor, dígales[9] que no me miren así, ordéneles que vuel-
van a sus colmenas.

          —¿Oyen, queriditas? —dijo el Zorro melífluamente, diri-
giéndose a las Abejas—. El señor Oso nos promete traernos otra
40 balanza.

          Las Abejas zumbaron a coro. El Zorro las escuchó con ex-
presión respetuosa. De tanto en tanto[10] asentía con la cabeza y
murmuraba:

          —Sí, sí, conforme. Ah, se comprende. ¿Quién lo duda? Se lo
45 transmitiré.

          El Oso no cabía en su vasto pellejo.[11]

          —¿Qué es lo que están hablando, Zorro? Me tienes[12] sobre
ascuas.

          El Zorro lo miró fijo.

50   —Dicen que la balanza deberá ser flamante.

          —Claro está, flamante. Y ahora, que se vuelvan.

          —Niquelada.

          —De acuerdo, niquelada.

          —Fabricación extranjera.

55   —¿También eso?

          —Preferentemente suiza.

          —Ah, no, es demasiado. Me extorsionan.

          —Repítalo, señor Oso. Más alto. No lo han oído.

          —Digo y sostengo que... Está bien, está bien. Trataré de com-
60 placerlas. Pero ordénales de una buena vez que regresen a sus panales. Me ponen nervioso tantas caras de Abeja juntas, mirándome.

          El Zorro hizo un ademán raro, como un ilusionista, y las
Abejas, después de lanzar al Oso una última mirada amonesta-
dora, desaparecieron dentro de las colmenas. El Oso se alejó, un
65 tanto mohino y con la vaga sensación de que lo habían enga-
ñado. Pero al día siguiente reapareció trayendo entre sus brazos
una balanza flamante, niquelada, con una chapita de bronce
donde se leía: *Made in Switzerland.*

          Lo dicho:[13] el Zorro sabía manejar a las Abejas y sabía mane-
70 jar al Oso. Pero ¿a quién no sabía manejar ese zorro del Zorro?[14]

          Hasta que un día se inventaron las Abejas artificiales.

          Sí. Insectos de bronce, dirigidos electrónicamente, a control
remoto (como decían los prospectos ilustrativos), podían hacer el

[9] *dígales:* Note how the Bear, now nervous and fearful, switches to the polite form of address, using *diga* instead of *di.*
[10] *De tanto en tanto:* Every so often
[11] *El Oso... pellejo:* The Bear was beside himself (literally, "He didn't fit in his enormous hide.")
[12] *tienes:* Now the Bear switches back to the familiar form of address.
[13] *Lo dicho:* As I have said
[14] *¿a... Zorro?* who didn't that foxiest of all foxes know how to deal with?

mismo trabajo que las Abejas vivas. Pero con enormes ventajas.
75 No se fatigaban, no se extraviaban, no quedaban atrapadas en las
redes de las Arañas, no eran devoradas por los Pájaros; no se ali-
mentaban, a su vez, de miel, como las Abejas naturales (miel que
en la contabilidad y en el alma del Zorro figuraba con grandes
cifras rojas); no había, entre ellas, ni reinas, ni zánganos; todas
80 iguales, todas obreras, todas dóciles, obedientes, fuertes, activas,
de vida ilimitada, resultaban, en cualquier sentido que se consi-
derase la cuestión, infinitamente superiores a las Abejas vivas.

El Zorro en seguida vio el negocio, y no dudó. Mató todos
sus enjambres, demolió las colmenas de cera, con sus ahorros
85 compró mil Abejas de bronce y su correspondiente colmenar
también de bronce, mandó instalar el tablero de control, apren-
dió a manejarlo, y una mañana los animales presenciaron, atóni-
tos, cómo las Abejas de bronce atravesaban por primera vez el
espacio.

90 El Zorro no se había equivocado. Sin levantarse siquiera de
su asiento, movía una palanquita, y una nube de Abejas salía ru-
giendo hacia el norte, movía otra palanquita, y otro grupo de
Abejas disparaba hacia el sur, un nuevo movimiento de palanca,
y un tercer enjambre se lanzaba en dirección al este, *et sic de ce-*
95 *teris.*[15] Los insectos de bronce volaban raudamente, a velocidades
nunca vistas, con una especie de zumbido amortiguado que era
como el eco de otro zumbido; se precipitaban como una flecha
sobre los cálices, sorbían rápidamente el néctar, volvían a levantar vuelo, regresaban a la colmena, se incrustaban cada una en su
100 alvéolo, hacían unas rápidas contorsiones, unos ruiditos secos,
tric, trac, cruc, y a los pocos instantes destilaban la miel, una miel
pura, limpia, dorada, incontaminada, aséptica; y ya estaban en
condiciones de recomenzar. Ninguna distracción, ninguna fatiga,
ningún capricho, ninguna cólera. Y así las veinticuatro horas del
105 día. El Zorro no cabía en sí de contento.[16]

La primera vez que el Oso probó la nueva miel puso los ojos
en blanco,[17] hizo chasquear la lengua y, no atreviéndose a opinar,
le preguntó a su mujer:

—Vaya,[18] ¿qué te parece?
110 —No sé —dijo ella—. Le siento gusto a metal.[19]
—Sí, yo también.

Pero sus hijos protestaron a coro:

[15] *et sic de ceteris:* and the same for all the rest (*Latin*)
[16] *no... contento:* was beside himself with joy
[17] *puso... blanco:* he rolled his eyes
[18] *Vaya:* Well now
[19] *Le... metal:* I get a metallic taste from it.

—Papá, mamá, qué disparate. Si se ve a la legua que esta miel es muy superior. Superior en todo sentido. ¿Cómo pueden
115 preferir aquella otra, elaborada por unos bichos tan sucios? En cambio ésta es más limpia, más higiénica, más moderna y, en una palabra, más miel.

El Oso y la Osa no encontraron razones con que rebatir a sus hijos y permanecieron callados. Pero cuando estuvieron solos
120 insistieron:

—Qué quieres,[20] sigo prefiriendo la de antes. Tenía un sabor...

—Sí, yo también. Hay que convenir, eso sí, en que la de ahora viene pasteurizada. Pero aquel sabor...
125 —Ah, aquel sabor...

Tampoco se atrevieron a decirlo a nadie, porque, en el fondo, se sentían orgullosos de servirse en un establecimiento donde trabajaba esa octava maravilla de las Abejas de bronce.

—Cuando pienso que, bien mirado,[21] las Abejas de bronce
130 fueron inventadas exclusivamente para nosotros... —decía la mujer del Oso.

El Oso no añadía palabra y aparentaba indiferencia, pero por dentro estaba tan ufano como su mujer.

De modo que por nada del mundo hubieran dejado de com-
135 prar y comer la miel destilada por las Abejas artificiales. Y menos todavía cuando notaron que los demás animales también acudían a la tienda del Zorro a adquirir miel, no porque les gustase la miel, sino a causa de las Abejas de bronce y para alardear de modernos.[22]

Y, con todo esto, las ganancias del Zorro crecían como un in-
140 cendio en el bosque. Tuvo que tomar a su servicio un ayudante y eligió, después de meditarlo mucho, al Cuervo, sobre todo porque le aseguró que aborrecía la miel. Las mil Abejas fueron pronto cinco mil; las cinco mil, diez mil. Se comenzó a hablar de las riquezas del Zorro como de una fortuna fabulosa. El Zorro se son-
145 reía y se frotaba las manos.

Y entretanto los enjambres iban, venían, salían, entraban. Los animales apenas podían seguir con la vista aquellas ráfagas de puntos dorados que cruzaban sobre sus cabezas. Las únicas que, en lugar de admirarse, pusieron el grito en el cielo, fueron las
150 Arañas, esas analfabetas. Sucedía que las Abejas de bronce atravesaban las telarañas y las hacían pedazos.

[20] *Qué quieres:* Say what you want
[21] *bien mirado:* if one really thinks about it
[22] *alardear de modernos:* brag about being modern

—¿Qué es esto? ¿El fin del mundo? —chillaron las damnificadas la primera vez que ocurrió la cosa.

Pero como alguien les explicó luego de qué se trataba,[23]
155 amenazaron al Zorro con iniciarle pleito. ¡Qué estupidez! Como decía la mujer del Oso:

—Es la eterna lucha entre la luz y la sombra, entre el bien y el mal, entre la civilización y la barbarie.

También los Pájaros se llevaron una sorpresa.[24] Porque uno
160 de ellos, en la primera oportunidad en que vio una abeja de bronce, abrió el pico y se la tragó. ¡Desdichado! La abeja metálica le desgarró las cuerdas vocales, se le embutió en el buche y allí le formó un tumor, de resultas del cual falleció al poco tiempo, en medio de los más crueles sufrimientos y sin el consuelo del canto,
165 porque había quedado mudo. Los demás Pájaros escarmentaron.

Y cuando ya el Zorro paladeaba su prosperidad, comenzaron a aparecer los inconvenientes. Primero una nubecita, después otra nubecita, hasta que todo el cielo amenazó tormenta.

La serie de desastres quedó inaugurada con el episodio de
170 las rosas artificiales. Una tarde, al vaciar una colmena, el Zorro descubrió entre la miel rubia unos goterones grises, opacos, de un olor nauseabundo y sabor acre. Tuvo que tirar toda la miel restante, que había quedado contaminada. Pronto supo, y por la colérica boca de la víctima, el origen de aquellos goterones re-
175 pugnantes. Había sucedido que las Abejas de bronce, desprovistas de instintos, confundieron un ramo de rosas artificiales de propiedad de la Gansa con rosas naturales, y cayendo sobre ellas les sorbieron la cera pintada de que estaban hechas y las dejaron convertidas en un guiñapo. El Zorro no solamente debió de sufrir
180 la pérdida de la miel, sino indemnizar a la Gansa por daños y perjuicios.

—Malditas Abejas —vociferaba mentalmente—. Las otras jamás habrían caído en semejante error. Tenían un instinto infalible. Pero quién piensa en las otras. En fin, nada es perfecto en
185 este mundo.

Otro día, una Abeja, al introducirse como una centella en la corola de una azucena, degolló a un Picaflor que se encontraba allí alimentándose. La sangre del Pájaro tiñó de rojo la azucena. Pero como la Abeja, insensible a olores y sabores, no atendía sino sus
190 impulsos eléctricos, libó néctar y sangre, todo junto. Y la miel

[23] *de qué se trataba:* what it was all about
[24] *se llevaron una sorpresa:* were surprised

apareció después con un tono rosa que alarmó al Zorro. Felizmente su empleado le quitó la preocupación de encima.[25]

—Si yo fuese usted, Patrón —le dijo con su vocecita ronca y
su aire de solterona—, la vendería como miel especial para niños.

195 —¿Y si resultase venenosa?

—En tan desdichada hipótesis yo estaría muerto, Patrón.

—Ah, de modo que la ha probado. De modo que mis subal-
ternos me roban la miel. ¿Y no me juró que la aborrecía?

—Uno se sacrifica, y vean cómo le pagan —murmuró el
200 Cuervo, poniendo cara[26] de dignidad ultrajada—. La aborrezco,
la aborreceré toda mi vida. Pero quise probarla para ver si era venenosa. Corrí el riesgo por usted. Ahora, si cree que he procedido
mal, despídame, Patrón.

¿Qué querían que hiciese el Zorro, sino seguir el consejo del
205 Cuervo? Tuvo un gran éxito con la miel rosa especial para niños.
La vendió íntegramente. Y nadie se quejó. (El único que pudo
quejarse fue el Cerdo, a causa de ciertas veleidades poéticas que
asaltaron por esos días a sus hijos. Pero ningún Cerdo que esté en
su sano juicio[27] es capaz de relacionar la extraña locura de hacer
210 versos con un frasco de miel tinta en la sangre de un Picaflor.)

El Zorro se sintió a salvo. Pobre Zorro, ignoraba que sus tri-
bulaciones iban a igualar a sus Abejas.

Al cabo de unos días observó que los insectos tardaban cada
vez más tiempo[28] en regresar a las colmenas.

215 Una noche, encerrados en la tienda, él y el Cuervo consi-
deraron aquel nuevo enigma.

—¿Por qué tardan tanto? —decía el Zorro— ¿A dónde diablos van? Ayer un enjambre demoró cinco horas en volver. La
producción diaria, así, disminuye, y los gastos de electricidad au-
220 mentan. Además, esa miel rosa la tengo todavía atravesada[29] en
la garganta. A cada momento me pregunto: ¿Qué aparecerá hoy?
¿Miel verde? ¿Miel negra? ¿Miel azul? ¿Miel salada?

—Accidentes como el de las flores artificiales no se han repe-
tido, Patrón. Y en cuanto a la miel rosa, no creo que tenga de qué
225 quejarse.

—Lo admito. Pero ¿y este misterio de las demoras? ¿Qué explicación le encuentra?

—Ninguna. Salvo...

—¿Salvo qué?

[25] *le... encima:* took the worry off his shoulders
[26] *poniendo cara:* taking on an expression
[27] *sano juicio:* right mind
[28] *cada vez más tiempo:* longer and longer
[29] *atravesada:* stuck

230   El Cuervo cruzó gravemente las piernas, juntó las manos y miró hacia arriba.

—Patrón —dijo, después de reflexionar unos instantes—. Salir y vigilar a las Abejas no es fácil. Vuelan demasiado rápido. Nadie, o casi nadie, puede seguirlas. Pero yo conozco un Pájaro
235 que, si se le unta la mano,[30] se ocuparía del caso. Y le doy mi palabra que no volvería sin haber averiguado la verdad.

— ¿Y quién es ese Pájaro?

—Un servidor.[31]

El Zorro abrió la boca para cubrir de injurias al Cuervo, pero
240 luego lo pensó mejor y optó por aceptar. Pues cualquier recurso era preferible a quedarse con los brazos cruzados, contemplando la progresiva e implacable disminución de las ganancias.

El Cuervo regresó muy tarde, jadeando como si hubiese vuelto volando desde la China. (El Zorro, de pronto, sospechó que
245 todo era una farsa y que quizá su empleado conocía la verdad desde el primer día.) Su cara no hacía presagiar nada bueno.[32]

—Patrón —balbuceó—, no sé cómo decírselo. Pero las Abejas tardan, y tardarán cada vez más, porque no hay flores en la comarca y deben ir a libarlas al extranjero.

250   —¿Cómo que no hay flores[33] en la comarca? ¿Qué tontería es esa?

—Lo que oye, Patrón. Parece ser que las flores, después que las Abejas les han sorbido el néctar, se doblan, se debilitan y se mueren.

255   —¡Se mueren! ¿Y por qué se mueren?

—No resisten la trompa de metal de las Abejas.

—¡Diablos!

—Y no termina ahí la cosa. La planta, después que las Abejas le asesinaron las flores...

260   —¡Asesinaron! Le prohíbo que use esa palabra.

—Digamos mataron. La planta, después que las Abejas le mataron sus flores, se niega a florecer nuevamente. Consecuencia: en toda la comarca no hay más flores. ¿Qué me dice, Patrón?

El Zorro no decía nada. Nada. Estaba alelado.

265   Y lo peor es que el Cuervo no mentía. Las Abejas artificiales habían devastado las flores del país. Entonces pasaron a los países vecinos, después a los más próximos, luego a los menos próximos, más tarde a los remotos y lejanos, y así, de país en país, dieron toda la vuelta al mundo y regresaron al punto de partida.

[30] *si... mano:* if you grease his palm
[31] *Un servidor:* Yours truly.
[32] *Su... bueno:* His face didn't indicate good news.
[33] *¿Cómo... flores:* What do you mean there aren't any flowers

270 Ese día los Pájaros se sintieron invadidos de una extraña congoja, y no supieron por qué. Algunos, inexplicablemente, se suicidaron. El Ruiseñor quedó afónico y los colores del Petirrojo palidecieron. Se dice que ese día ocurrieron extraños aconteci-mientos. Se dice que, por ejemplo, los ríos dejaron de correr y las
275 fuentes, de cantar. No sé. Lo único que sé es que, cuando las Abe-jas de bronce, de país en país, dieron toda la vuelta al mundo, ya no hubo flores en el campo, ni en las ciudades, ni en los bosques, ni en ninguna parte.

Las Abejas volvían de sus viajes, anidaban en sus alvéolos, se
280 contorsionaban, hacían tric, trac, cruc, pero el Zorro no recogía ni una miserable gota de miel. Las Abejas regresaban tan vacías como habían salido.

El Zorro se desesperó. Sus negocios se desmoronaron. Aguantó un tiempo gracias a sus reservas. Pero incluso estas reser-
285 vas se agotaron. Debió despedir al Cuervo, cerrar la tienda, perder la clientela.

El único que no se resignaba era el Oso.

—Zorro —vociferaba—, o me consigues miel o te levanto la tapa de los sesos.[34]

290 —Espere. Pasado mañana recibiré una partida del extran-jero —le prometía el Zorro. Pero la partida del extranjero no lle-gaba nunca.

Hizo unas postreras tentativas. Envió enjambres en distintas direcciones. Todo inútil. El tric, trac, cruc como una burla, pero
295 nada de miel.

Finalmente, una noche el Zorro desconectó los cables, des-truyó el tablero de control, enterró en un pozo las Abejas de bronce, recogió sus dineros y a favor de las sombras[35] huyó con rumbo desconocido.

300 Cuando iba a cruzar la frontera escuchó a sus espaldas unas risitas y unas vocecitas de vieja que lo llamaban.

—¡Zorro! ¡Zorro!

Eran las Arañas, que a la luz de la luna tejían sus telas pre-históricas.

305 El Zorro les hizo una mueca obscena y se alejó a grandes pasos.

Desde entonces nadie volvió a verlo jamás.

[34] *te... sesos:* I'll beat your brains out
[35] *a... sombras:* under cover of darkness

Exercises

A. Questions and Opinions

1. ¿De qué había vivido el Zorro desde el principio del tiempo?
2. ¿Qué maña especial tenía el Zorro?
3. ¿Cómo era el mejor cliente del Zorro?
4. ¿Qué experiencia desagradable sufrió el Zorro a causa del Oso?
5. ¿Qué tuvo que traerles el Oso al Zorro y a las Abejas?
6. ¿Cuáles eran las ventajas de las Abejas de bronce?
7. ¿Qué hizo el Oso al probar por primera vez la nueva miel?
8. ¿Por qué acudían todos los animales a la tienda del Zorro a adquirir miel?
9. ¿Qué perjuicios sufrieron las Arañas?
10. ¿Qué le ocurrió a un Pájaro que se tragó una abeja de bronce?
11. ¿Por qué tuvo que tirar el Zorro toda la miel en una ocasión?
12. ¿Por qué exclamó el Zorro: —Malditas Abejas?
13. ¿Qué tiñó de rosa la miel?
14. ¿Qué nueva miel tuvo un gran éxito?
15. ¿Cuánto tiempo demoró un enjambre en volver a la colmena?
16. ¿Qué sospechó el Zorro cuando el Cuervo regresó?
17. ¿Por qué no había flores en toda la comarca?
18. ¿Cuál fue la amenaza del Oso?
19. ¿Qué les ocurrió a algunos Pájaros? ¿Al Ruiseñor? ¿Al Petirrojo?
20. Al final del cuento, ¿cómo resolvió el Zorro el asunto?
• 21. ¿Le tiene Ud. lástima al Zorro? ¿Por qué?
• 22. ¿A Ud. le gustaría comer miel producida mecánicamente? ¿Por qué?

B. Verb Practice Use each of the following verbal phrases in an original sentence in Spanish, either based on the story or of your own design. Be prepared to explain the meaning of your sentences.

1. **tratar a**
2. **entenderse con**
3. **llevarse bien**
4. **darse prisa**
5. **(no) dejar de** + *infinitive*
6. **aprender a** + *infinitive*
7. **atreverse a** + *infinitive*
8. **tener éxito**
9. **quejarse**
10. **tardar** + *time* + **en** + *infinitive*

C. Vocabulary Practice Complete the sentences below, matching the expressions on the right with the English words on the left. Be sure to use the correct form of each verb. Then use each expression in an original Spanish sentence and indicate in English what your sentence means.

1. Las Abejas no pudieron encontrar néctar en *anywhere*.
2. *Aside from* miel contaminada, el Zorro no tenía problemas al principio.
3. El Zorro y el Oso preferían pasar su tiempo *outdoors*.
4. Creo que el Zorro *will go for* el plan del Cuervo.
5. Las Abejas, *later,* llegaron a tierras más lejanas.
6. El Zorro insistió en una balanza flamante, y el Oso respondió: —*You got it!*
7. Por un lado, el Zorro sabía manejar a las Abejas, y, *furthermore,* sabía entenderse con el Oso.
8. *Especially* cuando el Oso tenía ganas de comer miel.
9. ¡Dime *once and for all* si esta miel está contaminada!
10. El Cuervo y el Oso protestaron *in a single voice.*

aparte de
por otro lado
a coro
de acuerdo
de una buena vez
sobre todo
optar por
más tarde
ninguna parte
al aire libre

D. Communication Practice

1. Say that you hope that Mariana is successful.
2. Indicate that you and Rolando always get along well.
3. Tell your friend to hurry up.
4. Say that it was so hot in Acapulco that everyone was complaining.
5. Indicate that you learned to speak Spanish in Buenos Aires.

Un suicida

Marcos Victoria

MARCOS VICTORIA (1901–1975), Argentine physician, poet, and author, taught in both the School of Medicine and School of Arts and Letters of the National University of La Plata. He retired from teaching in 1960 and in 1965 was named Director of Cultural Affairs of the Argentine Department of State. Contributor to *La Nación* and *La Prensa* and member of the Buenos Aires Academy of Medicine, he wrote more than thirty books on scientific and literary subjects. In this respect he was representative of the traditional part-time Spanish American author for whom literature is a separate career, pursued during the hours left free after one's "professional" day is ended.

Marcos Victoria composed many admirable short stories and novelettes, some of these collected in *Un verde paraíso* (1960), *María Rosa en primavera* (1960), *Novela de la ciudad y del río* (1961), and *Las uvas doradas del más allá* (1962). From the last of these we have selected "Un suicida", which offers a chilling, Orwellian vision of what human existence might be like in Buenos Aires in the distant future, four hundred years after Argentina first moved to seek independence from Spain.

A PRELIMINARY LOOK AT KEY EXPRESSIONS

Be sure to study these expressions before you read the story.

1. (94:2) **por ambos lados** *on both sides*
2. (94:6) **hacía cinco minutos** *five minutes before*   **Hacer** with time units renders English *before* when used in the imperfect and *ago* when used with the preterit: **Hace un mes trató de suicidarse.** *He tried to commit suicide a month ago.*
3. (94:20) **detenerse** *to stop, come to a halt*
4. (94:21) **seguir** + *present participle*   *to keep on, continue* + *present participle*
5. (94:28) **por encima de** *over, above*   The expression **encima de** also occurs in our twelfth story, "Cuento para tahures," but with no movement: there is a lamp over (**encima de**) the billiard table. However, when motion is expressed, **por** precedes **encima de** as in "Un suicida", where a helicopter is passing overhead. Compare **El gato está encima de la silla** with **El gato saltó** (*jumped*) **por encima de la silla.**
6. (94:32) **tratar de** + *infinitive*   *to try* + *infinitive*
7. (95:35) **tener que ver (con)** *to have to do with, be relevant*   Unlike English, in Spanish the element **con** + *noun* can be left out: **¿Yo qué tengo que ver?** *What do I have to do with that (what has just been said)?* Or **Eso no tiene nada que ver.** *That has nothing to do with anything* or *That's not relevant.*
8. (95:47) **tener derecho (a)** *to have a right (to)*   The element following **a** can be a verb: **¿Acaso no tengo derecho a concluir mi vida?** *Isn't it possible that I have a right to end my own life?* Or a noun: **No tienes derecho a ese dinero.** *You have no right to that money.*
9. (95:48) **no servir para nada** *to be useless, good for nothing*
10. (96:96) **realizar** *to carry out, make*   This is another deceptive cognate in Spanish: *to realize* in the sense of *be aware* is **darse cuenta (de).**
11. (96:99) **entrometerse** *to intrude, interfere, butt in*   Thus, someone who does this to excess is an **entrometido.**
12. (96:109) **quedarle a uno** *to have left*   This verb is like **gustar, faltar,** and **bastar** in that the subject in English is the indirect object in Spanish: **Me quedan dos días.** *I have two days left* (literally, "Two days remain to me").
13. (96:112) **depender de** *to depend on*
14. (97:125) **querer decir** *to mean*   This expression means the same as **significar,** but is more common in conversation.

15. (97:128) **cinta** *tape*   This word has a wide variety of meanings: *computer* or *recording tape, adhesive tape, ribbon, headband,* and even *shoelace* in some countries.
16. (97:138) **a su disposición** *at your disposal, available, at hand*
17. (97:142) **disponer de** *to have available, have use of*
18. (98:161) **rechazar** *to turn down, reject, refuse*
19. (98:162) **perder tiempo** *to lose, waste time*
20. (98:166) **de acuerdo con** *in accordance with, according to*   This expression is somewhat more formal and precise than the conversational **según.**

Un suicida

El hombre se internó en la avenida que conducía hasta los malecones. Por ambos lados, la cortina de acero y cemento de los depósitos aduaneros. La luz lechosa de los tubos luminosos se elevaba de los cordones de las aceras y descendía de las altas
5 columnas blancas. Una noche de agosto, neblinosa y extremadamente fría.[1] Temblando, apresuró el ritmo de sus pasos. Hacía cinco minutos, había descendido a la entrada del puerto desde una de las torres del ferrocarril suspendido que circundaba a Buenos Aires con sus cables de acero, a cincuenta metros sobre el
10 suelo. En el vagón de ferrocarril la temperatura era soportable. Lo mismo ocurría en el centro de la ciudad que había inaugurado la calefacción electrónica de sus calles y plazas hacía un año, en 2210, precisamente al celebrar la Argentina el cuarto centenario de su nacimiento a la vida libre.[2] El puerto estaba desierto y el viento
15 húmedo del río le quemaba los ojos. El hombre sentía heladas las orejas y la nariz. Un poco más y todo quedaría terminado. Al frente, vislumbró la lámina metálica del Plata,[3] perfectamente iluminada hasta cincuenta metros del malecón, precisamente a causa de casos como el suyo. Doscientos metros más y estaba a salvo.
20 —Deténgase —oyó que le ordenaba desde arriba una voz dura e impersonal. Siguió caminando, aunque no dudó que la voz desconocida se dirigía a él.

—Si da un paso más, disparo —insistió la voz. Se detuvo en seco.[4]
25 —Alce las manos. Escuche. —No sólo alzó las manos sino los ojos.

Las aletas de un diminuto helicóptero se movían silenciosamente, cinco metros por encima de su cabeza.

—Lo hemos seguido desde que descendió del tren elevado.
30 Vino a suicidarse.

—¿Cómo lo sabe?

—No trate de engañarnos. Usted pertenece al circuito A5[5] de la ciudad, donde se produjo la epidemia de suicidios del año pasado. No queremos que se repita este año.

[1] *Una... fría:* Keep in mind that in the Southern Hemisphere the seasons are "reversed," so to speak, from our point of view.
[2] *precisamente... libre:* Argentina began its war of independence from Spain on May 25, 1810.
[3] *del Plata:* the Plate River (*Río de la Plata*), which forms the northern boundary of the city of Buenos Aires
[4] *Se detuvo en seco:* He stopped short.
[5] *circuito A5:* an imaginary division of the city in the twenty-third century
[6] *matrícula:* number (of his identification card)

35   —¿Y yo qué tengo que ver?

—Su carta al comisario de A5, firmada con su matrícula,[6] fue leída hace diez minutos. Hemos llegado a tiempo.

El hombre se sintió vencido. Imposible luchar contra aquella organización perfecta.

40   —Identifíquese. A5-p3213.

—Tupac Pérez.[7]

—¿Estado civil?[8]

—Viudo.

—¿Profesión?

45   —Escritor.

—No hay más escritores. Profesión desconocida.

—Bueno; pensionista del Estado. ¿Acaso no tengo derecho a concluir mi vida? No sirvo para nada desde que se cerraron las últimas editoriales.

50   —Eso lo dirá en el Depósito Central de calle Esmeralda. ¡Baje los brazos, por favor! Voy a descender. Cuando esté sobre la calle, abra la portezuela y entre. Nada de vivezas,[9] ¿eh?

Cuando el helicóptero se posó en tierra, abrió la portezuela y, como lo sospechaba, encontró vacía la cabina. Luz azulada en
55 su interior. Sobre el tablero reluciente, múltiples cuadrantes y lucecitas rojas y verdes. La voz resonó todavía, más suave:

—Ajústese el cinturón de seguridad. —El helicóptero se elevó rápidamente. Un ruido monótono, como el de un reloj (seguramente el mecanismo de control remoto) se escuchaba a sus es-
60 paldas. Pero él continuaba abstraído en su propio problema. Se decía: «Nada que pueda ocurrirme ahora me interesa. Mañana o pasado,[10] esto tiene que terminar». Tan abstraído, que no observó el espectáculo soberbio de Buenos Aires nocturno, con su tránsito aéreo (centenares de helicópteros individuales, y los destellos
65 luminosos con que advertían su vecindad) y el otro tránsito terrestre de las avenidas y la iluminación de los rascacielos. Tan preocupado estaba que no vio las dos avenidas superpuestas (lo que antes se llamaba Avenida de Mayo[11]) y la hoja de trébol de sus conexiones con los tres pisos de Avenida Nueve de Julio,[12] ruti-
70 lantes de luces. La niebla esfumaba los contornos pero daba telón de fondo[13] a los letreros de propaganda[14] y a las noticias de última hora, que proyectaban sobre el cielo sus letras corredizas: «Compre su lote por mensualidades en la Antártida Argentina,

[7] *Tupac Pérez:* This name is significant in the story. Tupac Amaru was a Peruvian Inca who rebelled against the Spaniards and was executed in 1579. Another Incan descendant of the same name met a similar fate for the same reason in 1780. *Pérez,* on the other hand, is such a common Spanish family name that it is often used to represent a typical ordinary person, something like "Smith" or "Jones" in English.

[8] *Estado civil:* Marital status, a line always found on identification cards, passports, etc.

[9] *Nada de vivezas:* No tricks

[10] *pasado: pasado mañana* day after tomorrow   *Pasado* here is masculine to agree with *el mañana* "tomorrow," as opposed to *la mañana* "the morning."

[11] *Avenida de Mayo:* a principal street of Buenos Aires

[12] *Avenida Nueve de Julio:* another main street of Buenos Aires, reputedly the widest in the world

[13] *daba telón de fondo:* served as a backdrop

[14] *propaganda:* This word usually means "advertising" or "promotion," although in certain contexts it can have the same negative meaning as its English cognate.

junto al Hotel de Turismo de Isla Desolación...[15] Es la inversión
75 perfecta...» «Acaba de ser electo Presidente de la Confederación
de Repúblicas Democráticas del Planeta el General Truman Rocke-
feller»... «Coma patay,[16] y sus hijos nacerán fuertes»... Si hubiera
podido abrir la portezuela herméticamente cerrada y aspirar a
plenos pulmones[17] el aire de la noche, a quinientos metros de al-
80 tura, habría podido saborear el profundo silencio de aquella ciudad zigzagueante de luces, pero absolutamente desprovista de
ruidos. La propulsión atómica había proporcionado aquella ventaja, decisiva para la salud mental: la metrópolis enorme y taci-
turna, silenciosa como una película muda.

85 El helicóptero descendía. Se posó sobre una terraza, iluminada por potentes reflectores. La voz mecánica ordenó:

—Descienda por la escalera que tiene a la vista hasta el primer
ascensor. Apriete el botón del Piso XXII.

Tupac Pérez ejecutó las órdenes puntualmente. Quería termi-
90 nar de una vez. Salió del ascensor y se encontró frente a una puerta
de metal liso. Hacia un costado, la placa: «Tribunal Supremo de
Suicidas». Empujó y entró. Se quitó los guantes. Alisó sus cabellos
blancos. Se retocó la corbata. Una sala de audiencias,[18] vacía, con
asientos tapizados de un material plástico de color gris. Se sentó.
95 Al frente, el estrado vacío. Una voz cansada comenzó a hablar.

—Usted ha realizado dos tentativas anteriores.

—Correcto.

—Iba a realizar hoy la tercera.

—La última, si no se hubieran entrometido...
100 —¿Las anteriores?

—La primera, un balazo en el corazón...

—¿Y? —El despecho empañó la voz de Pérez.

—Desgraciadamente, nadie muere ya de balazos en el corazón... La segunda, me arrojé al Subterráneo...[19]
105 —... y detuvo durante media hora toda la red de ferro-
carriles... Y quemó instalaciones por valor de millones de
sarmientos...[20]

—El sistema de seguridad funcionó a las mil maravillas.[21]
No me quedaba más que el agua del Río de la Plata.
110 —Tiene que comprender que esta situación no debe pro-
longarse indefinidamente.

—De ustedes depende...

—El Estado no puede permitir suicidios caros como el suyo.

[15] *Isla Desolación:* Desolation Island, an imaginary name for a likely tourist stop in Antarctica
[16] *patay (m.):* name of an imaginary food
[17] *a plenos pulmones:* in deep breaths
[18] *sala de audiencias:* conference or meeting room
[19] *Subterráneo:* the subway, now called by everyone in Buenos Aires *el subte.* The most common word for "subway" in other Hispanic countries is *el metro.*
[20] *sarmientos:* The author suggests that by the year 2210 the Argentine monetary unit, now the peso, will be the *sarmiento,* honoring one of the early Argentine patriots, former president Domingo Faustino Sarmiento (1811–1888).
[21] *a las mil maravillas:* wonderfully (literally "like a thousand marvels")

—Ahogarme en el río no perjudicaba a nadie.

115 —Podía envenenar las aguas. Los peces podían transmitir agentes patógenos albergados en sus narices. Su tentativa individual encarece el suicidio. Pone usted frente a frente la libre empresa y la estatización[22] de los servicios públicos. Hace muchos lustros[23] que nos hemos decidido por la segunda. Los suicidios

120 irremediables están reservados al Estado y se efectúan con el menor costo posible. Ventajas de la producción en masa. Usted no puede ignorar que su tentativa está violando principios básicos de economía social.

—Enhorabuena.[24]

125 —¿Quiere decir que está de acuerdo con nosotros?

—Terminemos de una vez.

Tupac Pérez ansiaba que concluyera aquel diálogo singular. Tenía la impresión de estar discutiendo con una cinta magnética.

—¿No tiene nada que agregar?

130 —No.

—Cumplamos entonces las formalidades legales. ¿Las conoce?

—Tengo una vaga idea.

—Se le ofrecerán a título gratuito[25] los placeres que más

135 atraen a los hombres. Es una compensación por las privaciones de su vida. Si los rechaza, procederemos al trámite final.

—Comience cuando quiera.

—Ponemos a su disposición el B 608.

—¿Qué es eso?

140 —Un placer erótico tan intenso, embriagador y peligroso que ha pasado a ser propiedad secreta del Estado. Nuestra sociedad se disolvería si cualquier hombre pudiera disponer libremente de él. Escapó a las enumeraciones del Kamasutra.[26] El Caballero Casanova[27] lo describió en un codicilo único, conservado en la

145 Biblioteca Nacional de París y rescatado de sus ruinas por nuestro Servicio de Informaciones. El conde de Bussy, Brantôme y Stendhal,[28] que lo conocieron, no se atrevieron a hacerlo público. Lo reservamos para casos excepcionales, para premiar a los sabios y a los grandes poetas, aunque, por precaución, sólo arriesgamos

150 el ofrecimiento cuando ellos son suficientemente ancianos... Es una recompensa superior al Premio Nobel. ¿Acepta el B 608, Tupac Pérez?

—No me tienta. ¿Qué más me ofrece?

[22] *estatización:* nationalization
[23] *lustros:* five-year periods
[24] *Enhorabuena:* Well and good, all right then.
[25] *a título gratuito:* free of charge
[26] *el Kamasutra:* a 2000-year-old Sanskrit treatise on the art of love
[27] *Casanova:* Giovanni Giacomo Casanova (1725–1798), celebrated Italian narrator of amorous adventures in his autobiographical *Memoirs* (1826–1838).
[28] *El conde... Stendhal:* The Count de Bussy (Roger Robustin, 1618–1693), Brantôme (Pierre de Bourdeilles, 1540–1614), and Stendhal (Henri Beyle, 1783–1842), were French chroniclers of the sexual mores of their respective periods.
[29] *Dijon:* a city in

La voz sin matices siguió enumerando, en un vano intento
155 de corrupción.

—Tenemos para usted viajes espaciales; recetas de cocina, salvadas de la destrucción de Dijon,[29] en la segunda mitad del siglo XX; la posesión temporal de óleos de Corot[30] y acuarelas de Paul Klee,[31] vinos chilenos de hace cien años...

160   —Prefiero beber el agua turbia de nuestro río...

—¿Rechaza todas nuestras proposiciones?

—Estamos perdiendo un tiempo precioso...

No hubo palabras durante unos minutos. Sólo se escuchó un ronroneo sutil y prolongado, como el de los tubos luminiscentes.
165 Era el computador electrónico que justipreciaba las respuestas de aquel suicida y calculaba sus posibilidades de vida, de acuerdo con las estadísticas de los últimos cien años. Al final, la voz decidió.

—El Estado le concede la solución que desea. Nada podemos hacer para impedirlo. Le quedan cinco segundos.

170   Tupac Pérez se puso de pie y avanzó sin vacilar, el paso firme, hacia las puertas anaranjadas de la «Cámara de Desintegración», que se abrieron para dejarlo pasar y se cerraron rápidamente detrás de él.

Los helicópteros siguieron trayendo hasta el alba nuevos
175 suicidas desde el Círculo A5 hasta el Depósito Central de calle Esmeralda 66.

eastern France, an oblique reference to the reputation of French cuisine
[30] *Corot:* Jean Baptiste Corot (1796–1875) was an influential nineteenth-century French painter.
[31] *Paul Klee:* Klee (1879–1940) was a Swiss painter of the abstract and surrealist schools.

Exercises

A. Questions and Opinions

1. ¿Cómo ha llegado el hombre al puerto de Buenos Aires?

2. ¿Cómo está el área del puerto a esa hora?

3. ¿Hacia dónde se dirige el hombre?

4. ¿Qué lo detiene?

5. ¿Desde dónde le hablan?

6. ¿Por qué ya no sirve la profesión de Tupac Pérez?

7. Cuando baja el helicóptero, ¿a quién encuentra Tupac Pérez en la cabina?

8. ¿Adónde lo llevan?

9. ¿Qué cosas le ofrecen a Tupac Pérez para que no se empeñe en suicidarse?

10. Al final, ¿qué solución le permiten al escritor?

• 11. ¿Reconoce Ud. que el suicidio puede llegar a ser preferible a seguir viviendo?

• 12. ¿Cree Ud. que en el futuro de nuestra civilización ocurrirán cosas parecidas a lo que se narra en este cuento?

B. Verb Practice Use each of the following verbal phrases in an original sentence in Spanish, either based on the story or of your own design. Be prepared to explain the meaning of your sentences.

1. **hacía cinco minutos**
2. **detenerse**
3. **seguir** + *present participle*
4. **tratar de** + *infinitive*
5. **tener que ver (con)**
6. **no servir para nada**
7. **quedarle a uno**
8. **depender de**
9. **querer decir**
10. **perder tiempo**

C. Vocabulary Practice Complete the sentences below, matching the expressions on the right with the English words on the left. Be sure to use the correct form of each verb. Then use each expression in an original Spanish sentence and indicate in English what your sentence means.

1. Esto está *in accordance with* todas las leyes y reglas del Estado.

2. El Estado tiene *available* medidas extraordinarias para saber lo que está pasando.

3. En esta sociedad nadie *has a right to* suicidarse.

4. Me ofrecieron un ascenso a cambio de información, pero *I turned it down.*

por ambos lados

por encima de

entrometerse

realizar

tener derecho (a)

cinta

5. Los oficiales del Estado *stick their noses* en los asuntos de todos los ciudadanos.

6. Había una cortina de acero *on both sides* de la avenida.

7. Señor, estoy *at your service* en cualquier momento.

8. Pasa un helicóptero a 10 metros *above* su cabeza.

9. ¿Puedo usar esta *tape* de mi grabadora para mi computadora también?

10. El Estado *has carried out* medidas extraordinarias para impedir el suicidio.

a su disposición

disponer de

rechazar

de acuerdo con

D. Communication Practice

1. Say that you stopped at the corner a moment to speak to Ernesto.

2. Insist that Francisco's money has nothing to do with your friendship.

3. State that one single kiss doesn't mean that they are in love.

4. Say that life without freedom isn't worth anything.

5. Tell Mario not to waste time watching television.

E. Review Exercise The following words from the story are cognates with English words, but they are "deceptive" in the sense that their meanings will not be the obvious ones. If you don't know them, look them up in the end vocabulary.

suicida	**editoriales**	**ignorar**
vagón	**seguridad**	**recetas**
paso	**propaganda**	
comisario	**tentativas**	

El pajarito de los domingos

María de Montserrat

MARÍA DE MONTSERRAT (1915–1995) was born in Camagüey, Cuba, where business had taken her parents, but she spent her life since the age of two in Montevideo, Uruguay. She attended the Women's University there, then married and raised three children. Her first book, *Tres relatos* (1944), was followed by other volumes of short stories, a medium in which she excelled. Her novels, beginning with *Los habitantes* (1968), deal imaginatively and nostalgically with Uruguay's historical past. In 1978 she became a member of the Uruguayan National Academy of Letters.

"El pajarito de los domingos", taken from her collection *El sonido blanco* (1979), is a brief but uncommonly disturbing short story. The reader easily follows the account of the narrator, an adolescent girl, and effortlessly adopts a point of view from which to judge the events she recounts. For this reason, the story's conclusion will likely provide a sudden shock. Apart from this emotional aspect, this tale also seems to invite a moral judgment of the people depicted.

A Preliminary Look at Key Expressions

Be sure to study these expressions before you read the story.

1. (104:4) **esforzarse por** + *infinitive   to make an effort, try* + *infinitive*
2. (104:11) **rodear (de)** *to surround (with)*
3. (104:15) **quedarse** *to stay, remain*
4. (104:21) **educación** *upbringing, breeding*   This refers mainly to the training given in the home to children by parents. *Education* in the sense of "schooling," "instruction," etc., is more often **instrucción, enseñanza,** etc.
5. (104:26) **elegir** *to choose, pick*   In many South American countries, **coger** and to a lesser extent, its derivatives, **escoger** and **recoger,** are taboo words. Thus other words, such as **elegir** for **escoger,** are used.
6. (104:28) **tener** + *definite article* + *part of the body* + *adjective   possessive adjective* + *part of the body* + *to be* + *adjective*   Spanish uses **tener** to express conditions of parts of the body: **Tengo las manos frías** *My hands are cold.* **Tienen colorados los cachetes** *Their cheeks are pink,* etc.
7. (104:30) **cada uno** *each one, every one*   **Cada** is invariable in form: **cada libro, cada mesa, cada dos días.**
8. (104:31) **cargar con** *to carry* (something heavy)
9. (105:36) **rogar** *to beg, ask* (someone to do something)   This is a stronger version of **pedir.**
10. (105:37) **valer la pena** *to be worthwhile, worth it*
11. (105:38) **recién** + *past participle   new(ly)* + *past participle*   This use of **recién** is particularly common with **nacido** *newborn* and **casado** *newlywed.* Also **recién llegado** is *newcomer.*
12. (105:38) **chocar (contra)** *to bump, crash (into, against)*
13. (105:41) **tal vez** *perhaps, maybe*
14. (105:55) **admitir** *to admit, let in*   **Confesar** is used for *admit* in the sense of *confess* or *own up to.*
15. (105:56) **de vez en cuando** *from time to time, once in a while, now and then*
16. (105:59) **apoyado** *leaning*   Spanish uses a past participle to express physical position, in contrast to the present participle of English: **acostado** *lying,* **sentado** *sitting,* **colgado** *hanging,* **arrimado** *leaning,* etc.
17. (105:69) **¿Qué le pasa?** *What's the matter with you (him, her, it)?*

18. (105:71) **impedir** *to prevent, keep from*   This verb is used with an indirect object and often an infinitive: **Me impiden ir tras ella.** *They keep me from going after her.*

19. (105:75) **suceder** *to happen, occur*   This is a slightly more formal synonym of **pasar** and **ocurrir.**

20. (106:77) **avergonzarse** *to be embarrassed, ashamed*   Spanish does not ordinarily distinguish between these two ideas, as English does. Remember also that **embarazada** is *pregnant,* not *embarrassed,* which is **avergonzado(-a).**

El pajarito de los domingos

Mi mejor amiga es Pepita, la hija de los carboneros.[1] Tuve que dar muchas explicaciones a mi familia por esta preferencia y probar que tal amistad no me convierte en una chica sucia y desprolija, que no pierdo mis buenos modales ni nada de lo superior que se
5   esfuerzan por inculcarme.[2]

El lugar más limpio que conozco, y el más cómodo, es la trastienda donde viven los carboneros. Antes hay que pasar por la negrura y el tizne. Pero creo que no debe ser sólo por el contraste que allá lo blanco es más blanco que en cualquier otro sitio.

10   Y cuando Pepita está enferma, admiro sus sábanas dóciles y crujientes, según como ella se revuelve parecen rodearla de países fragantes y soleados.[3] La cama esmaltada no tiene ninguna saltadura y el mosquitero que se frunce en lo alto, dentro de una corona de bronce, está arreglado como un velo de novia.[4]

15   Yo me quedaría para siempre en esta casa, por los cromos de las paredes, por las ventanas y sus cortinas recogidas con moños de cinta desde donde se ve un patiecito[5] lleno de plantas. Aquí se está bien,[6] por frío que esté afuera y siempre hay agua pronta para el té sobre el calorífico de cisco. Se habla poco,[7] las personas son
20   amables y reposadas, no se les nota que les falte por completo la educación como aseguran en casa.[8]

¡Estamos tan contentas! Hoy es sábado y ya hicimos los deberes del lunes. Pepita me ayudó en una redacción y yo la ayudé en los ejercicios de aritmética. Mañana iremos, como todos los
25   domingos, a la feria grande[9] con mi tía Melita y a más de curiosear, de comer bizcochos y comprar calcomanías, elegiremos un lindo pajarito.

Una mañana fría pero hermosa; tenemos los cachetes colorados, los pies calientes, las manos algo paspadas. Mi tía Melita
30   nos ha comprado bizcochos y un bastón de caramelo a cada una. Nosotras cargamos con la cesta llena de naranjas y ella se oculta de los piropeadores[10] con un gran ramo de dalias matizadas. Ahora vamos al puesto de los pájaros. El hombre nos conoce pero nunca es muy amable. Se pone hosco y pregunta: ¿Van a llevar lo
35   mismo? Yo propongo que esta vez llevemos un cardenal. ¡Son tan

[1] *carboneros:* coal peddlers
[2] *lo superior... inculcarme:* feelings of superiority that they have tried to drum into me
[3] *según... soleados:* which, as she moves around in bed, make her seem to be travelling through fragrant and sunny lands
[4] *un velo de novia:* a bridal veil
[5] *patiecito:* little patio (In Hispanic homes, a *patio* is really a small interior courtyard, usually open to the sky.)
[6] *se está bien:* you're comfortable
[7] *Se habla poco:* There's not too much talking
[8] *no... casa:* it's not at all apparent that they have no class or breeding, as they keep telling me at home
[9] *la feria grande:* the market
[10] *piropeadores:* admirers (In Hispanic countries, it is common for males to admire women in public and make remarks as they pass by.)

vistosos! Sobre todo los de penacho rojo. Se lo ruego. Pero mi tía Melita levanta los hombros como hace cuando no vale la pena contestar. Los mistos parecen recién cazados, chocan continuamente contra los alambres. Hay pájaros menos chúcaros y más
40 bonitos. No digo comprar un canario,[11] sería pedir mucho, pero tal vez un gargantillo. ¿Por qué no un gargantillo? Mi tía levanta los hombros por segunda vez y ya no me atrevo a proponer nada más. «Será como siempre —le susurro a Pepita— no tienen un poco de imaginación».[12] Aquí está. Un misto ruin y descolorido.
45 Lo ponen dentro de una bolsa de papel que tiene un agujerito para la respiración. Se la cedo a Pepita; con su mano libre la lleva con muchísimo cuidado.

En la puerta nos despedimos para vernos más tarde. Pero ahora Pepita pide algo. «¿No me dejaría ver la pajarera de los mis-
50 tos, señora?» Mi tía Melita va a contestar con alguna palabra cortante, lo piensa mejor y dice: «¿Quieres verla? Pasa, pasa».

Pepita camina entre nosotras, admirada. Le gustan los sillones de mimbre, tan blancos y floridos, las palmas en sus soportes de mayólica, y más que nada el vitral del techo por el que bajan
55 todos los colores que existen. Estoy contenta. Creo que ya la admitirán de vez en cuando.[13] Llegamos al segundo patio. Le murmuro a mi amiga: «Ahora vas a conocer a toda la familia». Mi madre sale de la cocina secándose las manos, mi tío se levanta con su libro bajo el brazo, mi abuela sale de su cuarto apoyada en
60 el bastón. Todos nos acercamos a la jaula. Tía Melita arrebata a mi amiga la bolsa de papel. Ella se sobresalta y la mira asombrada, aún sin entender.

—¡Aquí tienes el pajarito de los domingos, mi goloso!

Con su habilidad de siempre, tía Melita abre la puerta de la
65 jaula al mismo tiempo que rasga el papel. El misto entra. ¡Tan feíto él![14] Después de un loco revoloteo le viene el chucho como a los otros.[15] El caburé[16] lo mira. Hincha su pechera blanca, levanta su cola rayada. ¡Es tan gracioso! Giro hacia Pepita y veo a una desconocida.[17] ¿Pero qué le pasa? Retrocede alocada. ¡Casi hace
70 caer a mi abuela! Ahora corre atropelladamente. ¡Pepita! ¡Pepita! Quiero ir tras ella pero me lo impiden.

Se ha ido gritándonos algo horrible. ¡Dios mío! El primer día que entraba en esta casa y que le dejábamos ver todo, hasta el precioso caburé en su momento más interesante. «¿Qué te decíamos,
75 eh? Ya sucedió. La carbonerita ha mostrado su hilacha.»[18]

[11] *No... canario:* I don't suggest that we buy a canary
[12] *no... imaginación:* they haven't the slightest bit of imagination
[13] *ya... cuando:* from now on they'll have her in every once in a while
[14] *¡Tan feíto él!* The diminutive *feíto* (from *feo*) is for emphasis: "He's so ugly!"
[15] *le... otros:* it begins to tremble just like all the others
[16] *caburé:* pygmy owl, a bird native to southern South America. Its feathers are highly prized.
[17] *veo a una desconocida:* I can scarcely recognize her (literally, "I see a stranger")
[18] *La carbonerita... hilacha:* The little coal peddler has shown her true colors.

Ahora cada uno vuelve a lo que estaba haciendo antes. No puedo menos que avergonzarme. A causa de Pepita se han perdido la mayor distracción del domingo. El caburé ya se ha zampado la cabecita del misto. Y lo demás no vale tanto la pena.[19]

[19] *Y... pena:* And the rest isn't really worth the trouble to watch.

Exercises

A. Questions and Opinions

1. ¿Por qué tuvo que dar la narradora explicaciones sobre su amistad con Pepita?

2. ¿Cómo es la casa de Pepita?

3. ¿Adónde suelen ir los domingos las dos chicas?

4. ¿Por qué se dirigen al puesto de los pájaros?

5. ¿Por qué prefiere la narradora comprar un cardenal?

6. Por fin, ¿qué tipo de pajarito compran?

7. ¿Por qué quiere Pepita entrar a la casa de la narradora?

8. ¿Cómo es la casa de la narradora?

9. ¿Qué hay en la jaula?

10. ¿Qué le pasa al último pajarito de los domingos?

• 11. ¿Le sorprendió a Ud. el final de este cuento? ¿Por qué?

• 12. ¿Qué opina Ud. de la narradora y de su familia? ¿Y de Pepita?

B. Verb Practice
Use each of the following verbal phrases in an original sentence in Spanish, either based on the story or of your own design. Be prepared to explain the meaning of your sentence.

1. **esforzarse por**

2. **quedarse**

3. **elegir**

4. **cargar con**

5. **rogar**

6. **chocar (contra)**

7. **admitir**

8. **impedir**

9. **suceder**

10. **avergonzarse**

C. Vocabulary Practice Complete the sentences below, matching the expressions on the right with the English words on the left. Be sure to use the correct form of each verb. Then use each expression in an original Spanish sentence and indicate what your sentence means.

1. *Every now and then* su tía nos llevaba con ella.

2. Allí estaba Pepita, *surrounded with* pájaros.

3. *What's wrong with you?*

4. A la chica le falta *breeding.*

5. Pagamos más de diez dólares *each.*

6. Me dijo que *it wasn't worthwhile* ver la jaula.

7. *Leaning* en la jaula, Pepita contemplaba el pajarito.

8. *Perhaps* nadie lo sabrá jamás.

9. *My hands were very warm.*

10. La sala estaba *newly* pintada.

rodear de

educación

tener + *part of the body* + *adjective*

valer la pena

recién + *past participle*

tal vez

de vez en cuando

apoyado

¿qué le pasa?

cada uno

D. Communication Practice

1. Say that the girl would have chosen a cardinal.

2. Tell Carlos that this time it's not worth it.

3. Indicate that Clara admitted to you that she had done it [do not use **admitir**].

4. Say that Angela's mother kept you from seeing her.

5. State that such things happen all the time.

E. Review Exercise The following verbs, which have appeared in previous stories, also figured in "El pajarito de los domingos". Review your mastery of them by composing questions in Spanish using each of these verbs; then answer the questions.

faltarle a uno	**tener que**	**atreverse a**
acercarse a	**ponerse**	**levantarse**

Cuento para tahures

Rodolfo Jorge Walsh

RODOLFO JORGE WALSH (1927–1977) was born in the southern Argentine province of Río Negro, a descendant of Irish immigrants. He later found in Buenos Aires the stimulation that led him into a career in journalism and political activism. During the years following the overthrow of the Argentine dictator Juan Domingo Perón, he found himself in the forefront of investigative journalism—a new field—and wrote a number of exposés of the abuses of the military junta that had replaced Perón. In 1962 he was in Cuba, experiencing firsthand the early years of the Fidel Castro regime. Eventually, after his return to Argentina, his leftist associations and his determination not to let the military government carry out its war on suspected subversives with impunity cost him his life. In March of 1977, after having made public an "Open Letter" critical of the then-ruling military regime, he was ambushed and killed on a street in downtown Buenos Aires.

In addition to his politically motivated writings, Walsh produced a long series of detective short stories, a type of fiction that he was very fond of and one that he helped to develop in Argentina. In 1953, he published *Diez cuentos policiales argentinos,* the first anthology of Argentine detective tales, which encouraged many other authors to write detective fiction. "Cuento para tahures" is an early Walsh story, displaying his ingenuity in plotting and his interest in native Argentine settings. The dice game he describes and his narrator's shrewd interpretation of it combine to create a perfect gem of a tale.

A PRELIMINARY LOOK AT KEY EXPRESSIONS

Be sure to study these expressions before you read the story.

1. (112:2) **importarle a uno** *to matter to one*

2. (112:13) **por fin** *at last*   A common alternate is **al fin.**

3. (112:17) **un montón** *a pile, a lot*   **Un montón** can literally mean "a pile," as it does here in the story, or simply "a great number," "a lot," "a ton": **¡Por favor, ahora no! ¡Tengo un montón de problemas personales!** *Please, not now! I have a million personal problems!*

4. (112:20) **haber que** + *infinitive*   *to be necessary to, to have to* + *verb:* **Hay que saber perder.** *You need* (or *one needs, has*) *to know how to lose.* This expression is very similar to **necesitar** + *infinitive* or **tener que** + *infinitive* except that these latter expressions are personal and must be conjugated accordingly (**Necesitas trabajar mucho** *You need to work hard* or **Tienen que saber perder** *They have to know how to lose*), whereas **haber que** is impersonal, always in the third-person singular, and refers to anyone and everyone in general.

5. (112:32) **antes (de) que** *before*   This time conjunction, unlike most others in Spanish, is always followed by the subjunctive, either in the past or the present, regardless of the sequence of events: **antes de que empezara el alboroto** *before the hubbub began.* **De** is sometimes omitted: **antes que venga la ronda** *before the patrol gets here.*

6. (113:36) **figurarse** *to imagine*   This verb is virtually synonymous with **imaginarse.**

7. (113:49) **marcharse** *to leave, go away*   This verb is a slightly more formal equivalent of **irse.** Remember that with **marcharse** and **irse,** the emphasis is on departing from a given point in space, whereas with **salir,** the emphasis is on going from within a structure to the outside: **Salió del bar.** *He left (came out of) the bar.* Thus in Spanish you cannot **"salir"** if you are already outside; you must **"marcharse"** or **"irse."**

8. (113:59) **encima (de)** *on top (of)*

9. (113:71) **pegarle** *to hit, beat; to shoot*   The person receiving the violent action is always the indirect object in Spanish: **Le pegó.** *He hit him.* When the verb refers to shooting, and this fact is not already clear from context, the noun for *shot,* **tiro,** is used, too: **Le pegaron un tiro en plena calle.**   *They shot him right out in the street.* However, in the sentence appearing in the story, it is clear that we are talking about a shooting; thus **Y le pegaron al otro.** *And someone shot the other man.*

10. (114:77) **de todas maneras** *anyway*   This expression is a sentence introducer used to end the discussion and make a statement intended to move the conversation along, like the English *So anyway . . .*

11. (114:88) **no se podía** + *infinitive*   *one, "you" could not + verb*   In Spanish, **se** with **poder** followed by an infinitive is used to express what one in general can or cannot do. Sometimes the passive is the best equivalent in English: **No se podía encontrar los dados.** *The dice could not be found (No one could find the dice).* Sometimes the infinitive can be only implied and not even stated, as in the Mexican political slogan **¡Sí, se puede!** *Yes, we (one, you) can!*

12. (114:101) **al día siguiente** *(on) the following day*   In such time expressions with **siguiente, a** and the definite article precede the time noun: **al mes siguiente** *the next month.*

13. (114:103) **enterarse** *to find out*   Sometimes just the past participle of **enterar** is used to indicate one's knowledge or awareness of something: **Todavía no están enterados del asunto.** *They are still unaware of the matter.*

14. (114:112) **a la fuerza** *by force, under pressure, against one's will*

15. (115:124) **llegar a** + *infinitive*   *to get to, manage to + verb*   This expression conveys a successful attempt to do something. It is almost synonymous with **alcanzar a** + *infinitive.*

16. (115:129) **jugar sucio** *to cheat*   The person cheated is the indirect object in Spanish, as in the story: **si yo quisiera jugarle sucio a alguien** *if I wanted to cheat someone.*

17. (115:138) **claro (que)** *of course*   If there is no following element, just **claro** is used: **—¿Quieres ir? —¡Claro!** But **que** connects **claro** to following elements: **¡Claro que sí!, ¡Claro que quiero ir!,** etc.

18. (115:140) **tener suerte** *to be lucky*   There are many Spanish expressions with **tener** + *noun* that are equivalents of English expressions with *to be + adjective:* **tener sueño (miedo, frío, hambre,** etc.) *to be sleepy (afraid, cold, hungry, etc.).*

19. (115:150) **darse cuenta (de)** *to realize*   **De** connects this expression with a following noun or pronoun: **Se dio cuenta de lo que pasaba.** *He realized what was going on;* **de que** with a following clause: **Se dio cuenta de que no era pura suerte.** *He realized that it was not plain and simple luck.*

20. (115:152) **pararse** *to stand up; to stop*   These two concepts are related but slightly different. One meaning of this verb contrasts with movement: **El carro se paró en medio de la bocacalle** *The car stopped in the middle of the intersection,* and the other contrasts with a lying or sitting position: **De repente el dueño se paró.** *Suddenly the owner stood up.*

Cuento para tahures

Salió no más el 10[1] —un 4 y un 6— cuando ya nadie lo creía. A mí qué me importaba, hacía rato que me habían dejado seco.[2] Pero hubo un murmullo feo entre los jugadores acodados a la mesa del billar y los mirones que formaban rueda. Renato Flores
5 palideció y se pasó el pañuelo a cuadros por la frente húmeda. Después juntó con pesado movimiento los billetes de la apuesta, los alisó uno a uno y, doblándolos en cuatro, a lo largo, los fue metiendo entre los dedos de la mano izquierda, donde quedaron como otra mano rugosa y sucia entrelazada perpendicularmente
10 a la suya. Con estudiada lentitud puso los dados en el cubilete y empezó a sacudirlos. Un doble pliegue vertical le partía el entrecejo oscuro. Parecía barajar un problema que se le hacía cada vez más difícil. Por fin se encogió de hombros.

—Lo que quieran... —dijo.

15 Ya nadie se acordaba del tachito de la coima.[3] Jiménez, el del negocio, presenciaba desde lejos sin animarse a recordarlo. Jesús Pereyra se levantó y echó sobre la mesa, sin contarlo, un montón de plata.

—La suerte es la suerte —dijo con una lucecita asesina en la
20 mirada—. Habrá que irse a dormir.[4]

Yo soy hombre tranquilo; en cuanto oí aquello, gané[5] el rincón más cercano a la puerta. Pero Flores bajó la vista y se hizo el desentendido.[6]

—Hay que saber perder —dijo Zúñiga sentenciosamente, po-
25 niendo un billetito de cinco en la mesa. Y añadió con retintín—
: Total,[7] venimos a divertirnos.

—¡Siete pases seguidos! —comentó, admirado, uno de los de afuera.

Flores lo midió de arriba abajo.

30 —¡Vos, siempre rezando![8] —dijo con desprecio.

Después he tratado de recordar el lugar que ocupaba cada uno antes de que empezara el alboroto. Flores estaba lejos de la puerta, contra la pared del fondo. A la izquierda, por donde venía la ronda, tenía a Zúñiga.[9] Al frente, separado de él por el ancho

[1] *Salió... 10:* Ten was the number that came up. The definite article *el* is often used when referring to numbers in contexts like this. (This story is about the dice game craps, played with two dice. A first throw of 7 or 11 wins; a first throw of 2, 3, or 12 loses. A first throw of any other number, which becomes one's "point," must be repeated to win. Other numbers, that neither win nor lose, are "passes." But if a 7 is thrown before the point number comes up again, the player loses.)
[2] *hacía... seco:* they had cleaned me out sometime before
[3] *tachito... coima:* the pot for the separate "kitty" (to pay off the owner of the establishment where the game was being played)
[4] *Habrá... dormir:* But you'd have to be half asleep (literally, "one will have to go away to go to sleep"). The unfinished thought, of course, is "not to see what's going on."
[5] *gané:* I managed to get to
[6] *se... desentendido:* played dumb
[7] *Total:* The word *total* is often used to sum something up or "to make a long story short." Here it might be translated *anyway.*

35 de la mesa del billar, estaba Pereyra. Cuando Pereyra se levantó,
dos o tres más hicieron lo mismo. Yo me figuré que sería por el interés del juego, pero después vi que Pereyra tenía la vista clavada
en las manos de Flores. Los demás miraban el paño verde donde
iban a caer los dados, pero él sólo miraba las manos de Flores.

40   El montoncito de las apuestas fue creciendo: había billetes
de todos tamaños y hasta algunas monedas que puso uno de los
de afuera. Flores parecía vacilar. Por fin largó los dados. Pereyra
no los miraba. Tenía siempre los ojos en las manos de Flores.

    —El cuatro —cantó alguno.

45   En aquel momento, no sé por qué, recordé los pases que
había echado Flores: el 4, el 8, el 10, el 9, el 8, el 6, el 10... Y ahora
buscaba otra vez el 4.

    El sótano estaba lleno del humo de los cigarrillos. Flores le
pidió a Jiménez que le trajera un café, y el otro se marchó rezon-
50 gando. Zúñiga sonreía maliciosamente mirando la cara de rabia
de Pereyra. Pegado a la pared, un borracho despertaba de tanto en
tanto y decía con voz pastosa:

    —¡Voy diez a la contra![10] —Después se volvía a quedar
dormido.

55   Los dados sonaban en el cubilete y rodaban sobre la mesa.
Ocho pares de ojos rodaban tras ellos. Por fin alguien exclamó:

    —¡El cuatro!

    En aquel momento agaché la cabeza para encender un ciga-
rrillo. Encima de la mesa había una lamparita eléctrica, con una
60 pantalla verde. Yo no vi el brazo que la hizo añicos. El sótano
quedó a oscuras. Después se oyó el balazo.

    Yo me hice chiquito[11] en mi rincón y pensé para mis aden-
tros: «Pobre Flores, era demasiada suerte». Sentí que algo venía ro-
dando y me tocaba en la mano. Era un dado. Tanteando en la
65 oscuridad, encontré el compañero.[12]

    En medio del desbande, alguien se acordó de los tubos fluo-
rescentes del techo. Pero cuando los encendieron, no era Flores el
muerto. Renato Flores seguía parado con el cubilete en la mano,
en la misma posición de antes. A su izquierda, doblado en su silla,
70 Ismael Zúñiga tenía un balazo en el pecho.

    «Le erraron a Flores», pensé en el primer momento, «y le
pegaron al otro. No hay nada que hacerle, esta noche está de
suerte».[13]

[8] *¡Vos, siempre re-zando!:* You're always complaining (literally, "praying")! In some parts of Spanish America, including Argentina, *vos,* an-other form for *you,* is used, usually in place of *tú.* It is familiar, second-person singular and has its own verb forms: *sos (eres), tenés (tienes), comés (comes), sentate (sién-tate),* etc.

[9] *tenía a Zúñiga:* was Zúñiga (literally, "he had Zúñiga")

[10] *¡Voy... contra!:* I'll lay ten against you!

[11] *Yo... chiquito:* I crouched down (liter-ally, "I made myself little")

[12] *el compañero:* its mate (i.e., the other die)

[13] *esta... suerte:* this is his lucky night

Entre varios alzaron a Zúñiga y lo tendieron sobre tres sillas
75 puestas en hilera. Jiménez (que había bajado con el café) no quiso
que lo pusieran sobre la mesa de billar para que no le mancharan
el paño. De todas maneras ya no había nada que hacer.

Me acerqué a la mesa y vi que los dados marcaban el 7. Entre ellos había un revólver 48.

80 Como quien no quiere la cosa,[14] agarré para el lado de la
puerta y subí despacio la escalera. Cuando salí a la calle había muchos curiosos y un milico que doblaba corriendo la esquina.

Aquella misma noche me acordé de los dados, que llevaba en el
bolsillo —¡lo que es ser distraído!—, y me puse a jugar solo, por
85 puro gusto. Estuve mucho tiempo sin sacar un 7. Los miré bien y
vi que faltaban unos números y sobraban otros. Uno de los «chivos»[15] tenía el 8, el 4 y el 5 repetidos en caras contrarias. El otro,
el 5, el 6 y el 1. Con aquellos dados no se podía perder. No se
podía perder en el primer tiro, porque no se podía formar el 2, el 3
90 y el 12, que en la primera mano son perdedores. Y no se podía
perder en los demás porque no se podía sacar el 7, que es el
número perdedor después de la primera mano. Recordé que Flores había echado siete pases seguidos, y casi todos con números
difíciles: el 4, el 8, el 10, el 9, el 8, el 6, el 10... Y a lo último había
95 sacado otra vez el 4. Ni una sola clavada.[16] Ni una barraca.[17] En
cuarenta o cincuenta veces que habría tirado los dados no había
sacado un solo 7, que es el número más salidor.[18]

Y, sin embargo, cuando yo me fui, los dados de la mesa formaban el 7, en vez del 4, que era el último número que había
100 sacado. Todavía lo estoy viendo, clarito: un 6 y un 1.

Al día siguiente extravié los dados y me establecí en otro barrio. Si me buscaron, no sé; por un tiempo no supe nada más del
asunto. Una tarde me enteré por los diarios que Pereyra había
confesado. Al parecer, se había dado cuenta de que Flores hacía
105 trampa. Pereyra iba perdiendo mucho, porque acostumbraba jugar fuerte, y todo el mundo sabía que era mal perdedor. En aquella racha de Flores se le habían ido más de tres mil pesos. Apagó
la luz de un manotazo. En la oscuridad erró el tiro, y en vez de
matar a Flores mató a Zúñiga. Eso era lo que yo también había
110 pensado en el primer momento.

Pero después tuvieron que soltarlo. Le dijo al juez que lo
habían hecho confesar a la fuerza. Quedaban muchos puntos

[14] *Como... cosa:* Nonchalantly
[15] *"chivos":* dice
[16] *clavada:* losing roll
[17] *barraca:* "boxcars" (i.e., a 12)
[18] *el número más salidor:* the number that comes up most often

oscuros. Es fácil errar un tiro en la oscuridad, pero Flores estaba frente a él, mientras que Zúñiga estaba a un costado, y la distan-
115 cia no habrá sido mayor de un metro. Un detalle lo favoreció: los vidrios rotos de la lamparita eléctrica del sótano estaban detrás de él. Si hubiera sido él quien dio el manotazo —dijeron— los vidrios habrían caído del otro lado de la mesa de billar, donde estaban Flores y Zúñiga.

120   El asunto quedó sin aclarar.[19] Nadie vio al que pegó el manotazo a la lámpara, porque estaban todos inclinados sobre los dados. Y si alguien lo vio, no dijo nada. Yo, que podía haberlo visto, en aquel momento agaché la cabeza para encender un cigarrillo, que no llegué a encender. No se encontraron huellas en el revólver,
125 ni se pudo averiguar quién era el dueño. Cualquiera de los que estaban alrededor de la mesa —y eran ocho o nueve— pudo pegarle el tiro a Zúñiga.

Yo no sé quién habrá sido el que lo mató.[20] Quien más quien menos[21] tenía alguna cuenta que cobrarle.[22] Pero si yo quisiera ju-
130 garle sucio a alguien en una mesa de pase inglés, me sentaría a su izquierda, y al perder yo, cambiaría los dados legítimos por un par de aquellos que encontré en el suelo, los metería en el cubilete y se los pasaría al candidato. El hombre ganaría una vez y se pondría contento. Ganaría dos veces, tres veces... y seguiría ganando.
135 Por difícil que fuera el número que sacara de entrada, lo repetiría siempre antes de que saliera el 7. *Si lo dejaran,* ganaría toda la noche, *porque con esos dados no se puede perder.*

Claro que yo no esperaría a ver el resultado. Me iría a dormir, y al día siguiente me enteraría por los diarios. ¡Vaya usted a echar
140 diez o quince pases[23] en semejante compañía! Es bueno tener un poco de suerte; tener demasiada no conviene, y ayudar a la suerte es peligroso...

Sí, yo creo que fue Flores no más[24] el que lo mató a Zúñiga. Y en cierto modo lo mató en defensa propia. Lo mató para que
145 Pereyra o cualquiera de los otros no lo mataran a él. Zúñiga —por algún antiguo rencor, tal vez— le había puesto los dados falsos en el cubilete, *lo había condenado a ganar toda la noche,* a hacer trampa sin saberlo, lo había condenado a que lo mataran, o a dar una explicación humillante en la que nadie creería.
150   Flores tardó en darse cuenta; al principio creyó que era pura suerte; después se intranquilizó; y cuando comprendió la treta de Zúñiga, cuando vio que Pereyra se paraba y no le quitaba la vista

[19] *El... aclarar:* The matter remained a mystery.
[20] *quién... mató:* who possibly could have killed him. The future perfect (*habrá sido*) is used here in place of the preterit *fue* to express probability or conjecture in the past.
[21] *Quien más quien menos:* Everybody more or less
[22] *tenía... cobrarle:* had an account to settle with him
[23] *¡Vaya... pases:* Just try to throw 10 or 15 passes
[24] *Flores no más:* Flores himself. *No más* is very commonly used in Argentina for emphasis—often in place of *mismo.*

de las manos, para ver si volvía a cambiar los dados, comprendió que no le quedaba más que un camino. Para sacarse a Jiménez de
155 encima,[25] le pidió que le trajera un café. Esperó el momento. El momento era cuando volviera a salir el 4, como fatalmente tenía que salir, y cuando todos se inclinaran instintivamente sobre los dados.

Entonces rompió la bombita eléctrica con un golpe del cu-
160 bilete, sacó el revólver con aquel pañuelo a cuadros y le pegó el tiro a Zúñiga. Dejó el revólver en la mesa, recobró los «chivos» y los tiró al suelo. No había tiempo para más. No le convenía que se comprobara que había estado haciendo trampa, aunque fuera sin saberlo. Después metió la mano en el bolsillo de Zúñiga, le
165 buscó los dados legítimos, que el otro había sacado del cubilete, y cuando ya empezaban a parpadear los tubos fluorescentes, los tiró sobre la mesa.

Y esta vez sí echó clavada, un 7 grande como una casa, que es el número más salidor...

[25] *Para... encima:* To get Jiménez out from behind him (where he could see what was going on)

Exercises

A. Questions and Opinions

1. ¿Quién está jugando con los dados cuando el cuento comienza?

2. ¿Por qué no pasa los dados a otro jugador?

3. ¿Quién parece sospechar que Flores está jugando sucio?

4. ¿Dónde está el narrador cuando de golpe el sótano queda a oscuras?

5. ¿Qué encuentra el narrador en el suelo antes de que se enciendan los tubos fluorescentes?

6. ¿Quién aparece muerto de un balazo?

7. En un primer momento, ¿qué interpretación le da el narrador al asesinato?

8. ¿Qué descubrió el narrador aquella noche cuando se puso a jugar solo con los dados que había encontrado?

9. ¿Cómo era posible que en la última echada de Flores saliera el 7?

10. ¿Quién, pues, mató a Zúñiga y por qué?

• 11. ¿Por qué cree Ud. que no se explica el motivo que tenía Zúñiga para condenar a Flores a ganar—y morir?

• 12. ¿Le parece a Ud. que Flores podía haber encontrado otra solución a su situación peligrosa?

B. Verb Practice Use each of the following verbal phrases in an original sentence in Spanish, either based on the story or of your own design. Be prepared to explain the meaning of your sentences.

1. **importarle a uno**
2. **haber que**
3. **figurarse**
4. **marcharse**
5. **pegarle**
6. **enterarse**
7. **llegar a**
8. **jugar sucio**
9. **tener suerte**
10. **darse cuenta de**

C. Vocabulary Practice Complete the sentences below, matching the expressions on the right with the italicized English words on the left. Be sure to use the correct form of each verb. Then use each expression in an original sentence in Spanish and indicate in English what your sentence means.

1. Sí, le di el dinero, pero sólo *under pressure.*   **por fin**

2. El jugador *stood up* y echó las cartas sobre la mesa.   **un montón de**

3. *The next day,* David me llamó a mediodía.   **antes (de) que**

4. *No one could* encontrar el revólver.   **encima de**

5. No, gracias. Tengo *a ton of* trabajo que hacer.   **de todas maneras**

6. Vamos ahora, *before* todas las tiendas se cierren.   **no poderse**

7. *Of course,* Flores tenía que hacerlo.   **al día siguiente**

8. *At last* salió el 7.   **a la fuerza**

9. Ella posó su mano *on top of* la mía.   **claro**

10. *Anyway,* no one likes to lose.   **pararse**

D. Communication Practice

1. Say that you'll never manage to understand why Luis did it.

2. Indicate to a friend that you realize that he is right.

3. Say that it is necessary to read a lot for that professor.

4. State that you have always been very lucky.

5. Say that you (one) can't win playing with him.

Fósforos de madera

Conrado Nalé Roxlo

CONRADO NALÉ ROXLO (1898–1971) was recognized as a poet, playwright, prose writer, and (rare among Spanish American writers) a humorist. His exuberant poem "El grillo" (1923) is an established anthology piece, and his comedy *Una viuda difícil* (1944) is widely known in the United States, having been adapted and performed on Broadway. His charming novel *Extraño accidente* (1960) had as a principal character an earthbound angel who was easily incorporated into everyday reality. The fanciful manner in which Nalé viewed life, as we can see, allowed ample room for supernatural or fantastic occurrences to take place.

In "Fósforos de madera"—a tale reminiscent of the haunting "Los ojos verdes" by the nineteenth-century Spanish Romantic poet Gustavo Adolfo Bécquer—we encounter an entrancing, otherworldly feminine presence who lures the impressionable protagonist into a mysterious and fatal pact. As in most good stories of fantasy, there is no explanation offered for the puzzling central events. But, as in all such fantastic tales, we also have a few subtle hints that give us some basis for conjecture.

A Preliminary Look at Key Expressions

Be sure to study these expressions before you read the story.

1. (122:4) **quedarse con** *to keep* in the sense of "You can have it; I don't need it back." **Quedarse** without **con,** of course, usually means *to remain* or *stay.*

2. (122:18) **faltar** + *time period* + **para** + *event* This construction has a variety of renditions in English, depending on the context. In the story, **Faltaban veinte minutos para mi tren** means *I still had twenty minutes before my train arrived* or *My train wouldn't be here for another twenty minutes.* Or **Faltan diez días para el final del semestre.** *There are ten days left in the semester.* Or **Faltan cinco minutos para las dos.** *It's five to two (o'clock).*

3. (123:35) **estar por** + *infinitive* *to be about to* + *verb* or *to be on the point of* + *present participle:* **Mi tren estaba por salir.** *My train was about to leave (on the point of leaving).*

4. (123:46) **por** + *adjective* + **que** + *subjunctive* *no matter how (however)* + *adjective* + *might (may) be* This construction can be used in the present: **por ricos que sean** *no matter how rich they are (may be)* or in the past as in the story: **por lógicas que fueran** *however logical they were (might be).*

5. (123:59) **como si** + *verb in past subjunctive* *as if* + *verb* This construction, unlike no. 4 above, is always in the past subjunctive: **como si entendiera** *as if she understood.*

6. (123:69) **olor a** + *substance* *smells like* + *substance:* **olor a polvo** *dusty smell.* This usage extends to the verb **oler: Huele a chocolate** *It smells like chocolate,* as well as to the concept of taste: **sabor a sal** *a salty taste,* **Sabe a ajo** *It tastes like garlic.*

7. (124:77) **lo** + *past participle* *what* + *verbal constructions with past participle:* **lo ocurrido** *what has (had) happened;* **lo dicho** *what was said;* **lo escrito** *what we (I, they, she, etc.) have written.*

8. (124:80) **el colmo** *the height, extreme, the last word* In the story it means *the height of immaturity* or *childishness.* One says exasperated: **¡Esto es el colmo!** *That's the last straw!*

9. (124:106) *subjunctive* + **lo que** + *subjunctive* *whatever* + *verb* or *no matter what* + *verb.* This construction is similar to that in no. 4 above, except that here we are dealing with verbs rather than adjectives. There is a wide variety of renditions in English. The verb can be in the past subjunctive as in the story: **costara lo que costase** *whatever the cost, no matter how much it cost,* or the present subjunctive: **venga lo que venga** *come what may, no matter what comes,* **sea lo que sea** *be that as it may, no matter what it turns out to be.*

10. (124:108) **correr** *to slide, move over:* **Corrí un biombo.** *I slid a folding screen over.* It can also be used in the reflexive intransitively: **Córrete un poco.** *Move (slide, scoot) over a little.*

11. (125:114) **dejarse** + *infinitive   to allow, let oneself be* + *past participle*   This construction has a passive meaning in the sense that the reflexive object of the verb **dejar,** as in **Se dejó convencer,** is also the object of the next infinitive, producing the meaning of *She let herself be convinced* rather than *She let herself convince (someone else).*

12. (125:145) **el dorso de un leño** *the back* (or *top*) *of a log*   **Dorso** means the upper or opposite surface, as in **el dorso de la mano** *the back of my hand;* **espalda** is the *back* of a human being; **lomo** is the *back* of an animal; **respaldo** is the *back* of a chair; **fondo** is the *back* of a room.

13. (125:149) **producirse** *to happen:* **el milagro no se produjo** *the miracle did not happen.*

14. (126:152) **acordarse de** *to remember*

15. (126:155) **de** + *noun*   This construction indicates when something happens: **de niño** *when I was a child,* **de día** *during the day,* or *serving in the capacity of:* **Serví de intérprete** *I served as an interpreter,* **Trabaja de mozo** *He's working as a waiter.*

16. (127:202) *noun* or *pronoun* + **mismo**   *noun* or *pronoun* + *-self:* **tú misma** *you yourself,* **el jefe mismo lo dijo** *the boss himself said it.*

17. (127:207) **por más que** + *subjunctive   no matter how much* + *verb:* **por más que lo penetres y lo partas** *no matter how much you penetrate it and split it.* This construction can also be used in the past subjunctive: **por más que tratara** *no matter how much (hard) I tried.*

18. (127:226) **venir** + *present participle   to be (continue)* + *present participle*   This construction emphasizes the time that the action of the verb has been done: **Lo vengo esperando desde hace siglos.** *I have been waiting for him for centuries and centuries.* **Estas cartuchas de tinta me vienen durando meses enteros.** *These ink cartridges last me months and months.*

19. (128:239) **obligar** + *direct object* + **a** + *infinitive   to force one to* + *verb:* **La obligaban a danzar en sus hornillos diabólicos.** *They forced her to dance in their diabolical furnaces.*

20. (128:253) **moverse** *to move* (intransitive)   This verb expresses motion and is always reflexive when there is no object, as in the sentence cited here. The verb is used nonreflexively when there is an object: **Moví la mano.** *I moved my hand.* Remember also that *to move* in the sense of *to change residences* is **mudarse: Me mudo a fines de agosto.** *I'm moving at the end of August.*

Fósforos de madera

—Ah, son de madera —dije encendiendo el cigarrillo, mientras hacía pantalla con las manos a la trémula llama para protegerla del viento del río.

—Quédese con la caja, yo tengo otra —me respondió con
5 acento extraño el hombre al que pidiera[1] fuego, y desapareció antes de que pudiera darle las gracias.

Desapareció es la palabra exacta; pues fue como si se sumiera en las grandes manchas de tinta china con fondo celeste del nocturno portuario.

10 Le cubría el ancho pecho una tricota azul y la visera de hule de la gorra recortaba su media luna brillante[2] sobre los ojos grises del rostro descolorido con naciente barba rojiza. Era, a todas luces,[3] fogonero de un barco nórdico.

Subí la barranca con el fresco de la noche en la nuca, y por
15 las silenciosas recovas me encaminé al Retiro.[4] Vivía solo en la vieja quinta de Pacheco[5] que fue de mis padres, ahora en trance de remate por exigencias de la sucesión.[6]

Como aún faltaban veinte minutos para mi tren, el último, entré a la confitería de la estación y pedí un café. Después, como
20 es natural, saqué un cigarrillo y me dispuse a encenderlo, pero no lo hice, encendí el fósforo; atónito me quedé mirándolo arder hasta que me quemó los dedos. Dentro de la llamita había una figurilla de mujer. Estaba desnuda y, no obstante su pequeñez, todos los detalles del cuerpo de perfección estatuaria aparecían
25 nítidos y acusados, como los de las mujercitas de esmalte de las miniaturas que pueblan las tabaqueras del siglo XVIII. Su color era el blanquirosado de las figuras de Fragonard,[7] con ojos verdes y cabellos de cobre encendido, aunque por momentos tenía las tonalidades de la llama que la encerraba: rojo, amarillo y azulado.
30 Todo eso lo vi en el minuto escaso (el cálculo lo hice después) que tardó la llama en extinguirse.

Nada pensé durante largo rato, con el cabillo del fósforo apretado entre las yemas quemadas, mirando absorto la sutil

[1] *pidiera:* The imperfect subjunctive (*pidiera* here) is often used in literary or journalistic style for the past perfect (*había pedido*). This is similar, for example, to the literary English usage, *had I known,* instead of the more common *if I had known.*

[2] *la visera... brillante:* the oilcloth visor of his cap formed a brilliant semicircle

[3] *a todas luces:* to all appearances

[4] *recovas... Retiro:* The *recovas* are arched supports bordering the arcade that extends along Leandro N. Alem Street near the port of Buenos Aires. Retiro, as previously noted, is one of the major train stations of the city.

[5] *Pacheco:* a small town some thirteen miles west of Buenos Aires

[6] *en... sucesión:* in the process of being auctioned off owing to requirements of the estate

[7] *Fragonard:* Jean Honoré Fragonard (1732–1806), French Rococo painter and engraver, considered a superb colorist and noted for his erotic themes

columnilla de humo en que se había desvanecido la visión.
35 Cuando reaccioné a medias, mi tren estaba por salir y tuve que
correr para alcanzarlo.

Ya en el vagón solitario y traqueteante, traté de ordenar mis
pensamientos.

¿Se trataba de un sutil artificio pirotécnico rayando en la
40 hechicería? Deseché la idea. Una alucinación, tal vez... Nunca las
había tenido y mi equilibrio nervioso era perfecto. Quizá trasladé
la imagen de una mujer desnuda de las que adornan las paredes
de la confitería con fines publicitarios al corazón de la llama. Una
distracción profunda suele dar tales resultados por autohipnosis.
45 Algo así debió haber ocurrido, pero tales explicaciones no me
convencían por lógicas que fueran.

Saqué la caja de fósforos del fogonero y la estudié minu-
ciosamente. Era una caja común con papel de esmeril por ambos
costados y en la tapa una etiqueta amarilla que reproducía bur-
50 damente la imagen que vi en la llama. Decía en sueco (esto lo
averigüé más tarde con ayuda de un diccionario): «LA SALA-
MANDRA—50 fósforos de madera. Suecia». La marca echaba alguna luz sobre el caso, pero su claridad era más desconcertante
que las mismas tinieblas. La abrí y conté los fósforos; quedaban
55 siete. Eran unos fósforos de tamaño grande, de madera amarfilada
y con las cabezas de color violado.

¿Encendería otro? Lo encendí. Y la mujercita apareció en la
llama, exacta en un todo a la anterior. Más atento ahora, vi que
me sonreía, moviendo los labios como si hablara, pero si algo dijo
60 fue inaudible para mí con el traqueteo del viejo tren. Su voz debía estar en relación con su tamaño. Retrocedió un paso dentro de
la llama, como para tener espacio suficiente, y me tendió los brazos; la expresión de su bello rostro era ahora ansiosa y esperanzada.

—¿Qué, qué? —proferí en voz baja y apremiante. El hálito
65 de mi voz apagó el fósforo antes de que se consumiera totalmente.

El tren se detuvo. Ya estábamos en Pacheco. Recorrí en un
estado de ánimo difícil de precisar las siete cuadras por entre quin-
tas y descampados que separan la estación de mi casa.

Entré a tientas en el comedor familiar, con olor a polvo y a
70 encierro. Busqué en la cocina fósforos. Felizmente los encontré y
encendí la lámpara. Después la estufa de leña. Los troncos estaban húmedos y tardaban en arder; con grandes brazadas de ramas

secas de eucalipto conseguí calentar el ancho hogar y el fuego comenzó a crepitar y subir normalmente.

75   Me senté a la mesa con una taza de café humeante y la caja de fósforos de madera sobre la carpeta de felpa verde.

Mi propósito era meditar en calma sobre lo ocurrido y lo que podría ocurrir. No tenía miedo, aunque me sabía en el centro de un círculo mágico, ya que a aquella altura[8] buscar al prodigio una

80   explicación normal hubiera sido el colmo de la puerilidad. Me sentía en el límite que separa el mundo conocido de otro ignorado y lo verdaderamente realista era aceptarlo tal como se presentaba, y penetrar en él hasta donde me fuera dado.[9]

El reloj de péndulo, alto, oscuro y estrecho, dio gravemente

85   tres campanadas. Salvo el intermitente chisporrotear del fuego, ningún ruido en la noche.

Abrí la caja y encendí otro fósforo. Por tercera vez apareció la visión. Sus labios se movieron; fijó los ojos verdes en los míos con expresión implorante, retorciéndose las manos en un gesto

90   de dolor e impotencia. Acerqué el fósforo al oído, mirando a la mujercita de reojo; se aproximó cuanto pudo[10] al límite de la llama y oí claramente, pero viniendo de una gran lejanía, estas palabras.

—¡Sálvame, sálvame!

—¡Sí, sí, quiero salvarte! Pero ¿de qué y cómo?

95   Iba a contestarme, pero su voz se apagó con la llama. Debo aclarar que su voz, aunque apenas audible, era una voz plena, de mujer, que no recordaba su tamaño; no era ni una vocecita infantil ni una voz de muñeca, como pudiera suponerse.[11]

Precipitadamente encendí otro fósforo. Pero mal manejado

100   por mi creciente nerviosidad se me cayó de los dedos y se apagó sobre la felpa verde sin darme tiempo a verla y menos a reanudar el diálogo.

Sólo me quedaban tres fósforos, tres minutos escasos para desentrañar un misterio que presentía cargado de siglos. Además,

105   el grito de socorro de la mujercita era tan angustioso que sacudió hondamente mi compasión. Tenía que salvarla, costara lo que costase.[12] Pero, ¿cómo?

Tomé todas las precauciones posibles, corrí un biombo frente a la ventana para evitar la sorpresa de un aire colado. Esperé que

110   el fuego de la chimenea entrara en un período de calma, sin crepitaciones ni chisporroteos, y dominando mis nervios raspé

[8] *a aquella altura:* at that point
[9] *hasta... dado:* to wherever it led me
[10] *cuanto pudo:* as much as she could
[11] *como pudiera suponerse:* as one might suppose
[12] *costara... costase:* whatever the cost. *Costase* is a past subjunctive used mainly in written Spanish and is the equivalent of *costara*. Here it is used just for variety of expression.

en el esmeril otra de aquellas varitas mágicas con remate violáceo
y, cautamente, pero sin pérdida de tiempo, lo llevé al oído. La voz
de la mujercita se dejó oír ahora más segura, más cercana y alta;
115 escuché conteniendo la respiración.

    —Si quieres salvarme tienes que encender un gran fuego con
uno de estos fósforos. Pero un fuego en el que no entren más que
leños y hojas naturales, ninguna madera trabajada por el hombre,
ningún papel; bastaría un pedacito o una hilacha enredada a los
120 troncos para que todo se perdiera, entonces...

    Me estaba quemando los dedos, pero no lo sentía; en la
llamita decreciente sólo se veía su busto y la voz se apagó.

    No tenía ya más que dos fósforos.

    Una hora empleé en apagar el fuego y limpiar la chimenea.
125 Con las uñas arranqué de las junturas de las piedras aún calientes
toda partícula sospechosa; la froté con un cepillo de paja. Cuando
quedó limpia, fui al cobertizo de la leña y en varios viajes la traje
toda y la apilé junto a la chimenea. Era mucha, y ahora tenía que
revisarla cuidadosamente. Tronco por tronco la limpié mirándola
130 a la luz de la lámpara. Sobre una brazada de hojas de eucalipto la
acomodé en el hogar con mi mejor técnica.

    Me senté en una silla y sequé el sudor que me corría abun-
dante por la frente. El comedor estaba otra vez helado. No quedaban más que dos fósforos en la caja. Me arrodillé frente al hogar
135 y con mano trémula encendí la hojarasca. Ardió en una alta llamarada clara, con más de dorado que de rojo, que rápidamente se
propagó a los leños. Ahora había un fuego estable, por así decirlo,
que alzaba sus mansas alas rojas, amarillas y azuladas hacia el oscuro cañón de la chimenea.

140   Esperé largo rato, pero en contra de lo previsto,[13] la visión
no reapareció. ¿Habría cometido un error? ¿No habría entendido
bien sus explicaciones?[14] Estaba terriblemente desasosegado. ¡Qué
torpeza, Dios Santo, podía haber cometido!

    Miraba el fuego con fijeza hipnótica, hasta que algo me llamó
145 la atención: en el dorso de un leño, ya convertido en brasa, bri-
llaba un carbunclo pequeño, redondo y de color más vivo: la
cabeza de un clavo al rojo.[15] Sin duda aquél era el elemento extraño que impedía aparecer a la mujercita. Lo saqué con el atiza-
dor, pero el milagro no se produjo. Recomencé el trabajo de apagar
150 el fuego, limpiar la estufa y encenderla nuevamente.

[13] *en... previsto:* contrary to what I had expected

[14] *¿Habría cometido... explicaciones?* I wonder if I made (could I have made) a mistake? Is it possible I didn't understand her explanations correctly? In Spanish, the conditional can be used to express probability or conjecture in the past. It can be the simple conditional: *¿Quién sería? (I wonder who it was?)* or the conditional perfect with *haber + past participle* like the sentences in the text cited here.

[15] *un... rojo:* a red-hot nail

Al prender el último fósforo y arrimarlo a las hojas secas, me acordé del pasaje de «La isla misteriosa»[16] en que el marinero Pencrof, rodeado por el grupo expectante de sus compañeros de naufragio, frota la última pajuela que producirá el ansiado mila-
155 gro del fuego, y que, de niño, no podía leer sin contener yo también el aliento. En fin, entre sudores y angustias, el fuego ardió y en la primera llamarada de oro chisporroteante surgió la mujercita del fósforo, más grande ahora y sonriente.

La boca de la chimenea era muy grande, un metro veinte de
160 ancho por uno de alto,[17] y una mansa cascada de fuego invertida subía hacia las tinieblas del cañón. La mujer de pie alcanzaba la altura de una niña de seis años.

—¿Quién eres? —le pregunté.

—¿Todavía no has comprendido? Soy la Salamandra.

165 —¡Una salamandra!

—No, la Salamandra, no hay más que una. Nunca hubo más que una desde que el primer hombre ahuyentó las tinieblas originarias despertando el primer fuego.

—Pero, ¿y las otras?, ¿las que murieron con la luz de los
170 fósforos?

—Era siempre yo.

Se había sentado en el piso de la chimenea de perfil, con una pierna extendida y la otra flexionada, sujeta por las manos, pensativa. Así, su estatura era aproximadamente la mía.

175 La contemplaba embargado por un nuevo sentimiento; recién ahora tenía la sensación de estar ante una mujer, todo lo fantástica que se quisiera,[18] pero una mujer. La otra, la pequeña, resultaba por razones oscuras pero fácilmente comprensibles, a pesar de su singular belleza, un poco monstruosa. Lo excesiva-
180 mente pequeño, como lo excesivamente grande, puede ser atrayente, pero es siempre antinatural. Dentro de la llama del fósforo se me aparecía con la nitidez, pero también con la dureza de un esmalte. Ahora, a través de la ondulante cortina flamígera, sentía que no participaba del calor del fuego, que su piel era fresca y sus
185 labios húmedos.

—Los griegos presentaban a la salamandra como una pequeña lagartija, generalmente roja —musité.

—¡Oh, los griegos! —respondió e hizo un mohín de contrariedad. —Raza de charlatanes fantaseosos que no podían tomar
190 la simple realidad sin deformarla. Mitómanos, maniáticos mi-

[16] *«La isla misteriosa»:* a translation of the popular novel by Jules Verne
[17] *un... alto:* approximately four-feet wide by three-feet high
[18] *todo... quisiera:* as fantastic as anyone would want

tómanos es lo que eran. Los que mejor me vieron, aunque sin comprenderme, fueron algunos inquisidores medioevales. Al entreverme en las llamas de las hogueras purificadoras pensaron que era el alma condenada de las hechiceras que volaba al infierno
195 transformada en belleza simbólica.

    —¿Qué hacías en esas hogueras?

    —No lo sé. Renazco en los fuegos.

    —¿En todos los fuegos?

    —No, en algunos sí y en otros no.
200   —¿Y por qué?

    —¿Cómo puedo yo saberlo? Es un misterio.

    —Pero tú misma, en tantos siglos, debes haber encontrado alguna explicación, una hipótesis por lo menos.

    Después, una sonrisa burlona, de antigua sabiduría, entrea-
205 brió sus labios y me dijo:

    —Confundes un misterio con un acertijo. El verdadero misterio es como un diamante, por más que lo penetres y lo partas siempre encontrarás diamante.

    —Esos fósforos...
210   —No sé nada. Aparecí en sus luces como he aparecido en muchas otras, desde que el mundo es mundo.

    Se desperezó graciosamente y dijo con un suspiro:

    —¡Qué bien se está en tu casa! [19]

    Echó una mirada al montón de leña que yo había acumu-
215 lado, y comentó tristemente:

    —Lástima que esa leña no durará eternamente.

    La llama comenzaba a decrecer y me dispuse a alimentarla.

    —Deja, yo me arreglaré. Necesitaba que me vieras de tamaño humano, y ya me has visto...
220   —¡Y te quiero! —murmuré ahogadamente, completando su pensamiento.

    —Yo también te amo. —Había un toque de emoción en su voz.

    Sonreí escéptico.
225   —Te amo porque eres el primer hombre que me lo ha dicho, y lo vengo esperando desde hace siglos. Sólo el amor puede salvarme.

    —¿Rescatarte del fuego?

    —Sí, y redimirme del dolor y del terror ajenos que llevo en
230 el alma, en el alma que antes no tenía. Soy un espíritu elemental,

[19] *¡Qué... casa!* Oh, I feel so much at home in your house!

anterior al soplo divino que a los hombres anima, y durante siglos y siglos floté irresponsable y feliz en el fuego. Pero el dolor y la angustia de los incendios, de los autos de fe[20] y de cosas todavía peores, me fueron lentamente conformando un alma.[21] Imagínate

235 si habré visto sufrir,[22] impotente para ayudar a nadie. Fue una crueldad dejar ese hueco en mi ser para que fuera tan amargamente colmado.

—¿Y nadie quiso salvarte antes de ahora?

—Oh, sí, los hechiceros que me obligaban a danzar en la

240 llama azul de sus hornillos diabólicos. Pero ninguno me amó; unas veces era el deseo anormal y otras la codicia de los secretos de que me creían dueña. También quisieron salvarme desprevenidos bomberos, pero al tomarme en sus brazos...

—¿Morían? —pregunté y sentí un estremecimiento de

245 aprensión.

—Como yo no puedo salir del fuego, morían abrazados a mí. Aprendí a huir de llama en llama, desoyendo sus llamadas, hundiéndome en las profundidades del fuego.

—¿Qué pasaría si salieras de él?

250 —Mira —dijo extendiendo un brazo fuera de la llama, y apareció mutilada como una estatua antigua. Lo recogió sobre el pecho y volvió a verse[23] en toda su belleza.

En el fuego amortiguado se movía con gracia de danzarina, siguiendo las llamas más altas; yo la veía como una niña, ya como

255 una muñeca, ya pequeñita como en los fósforos.

Con voz apenas audible, desde una llamita azul y tenue, me interrogó temerosa:

—¿Me quieres bastante, tienes valor?

Por nada del mundo la hubiera dejado desaparecer con el úl-

260 timo leño.

—Yo, nada puedo prometerte, no sé lo que pasará —agregó.

Sin responderle, corrí la alfombra que cubría el piso de baldosas frente a la chimenea y comencé a amontonar leña ante la boca. De tanto en tanto[24] echaba un tronco al hogar para que ella

265 tuviera cómo sustentarse. Dispuesta ya la enorme pira, tomé un leño llameante como una antorcha y la encendí. Los troncos y las ramas ardieron rápidamente; pronto fue un gran cono flamígero cuya punta llegaba casi a las negras vigas del techo. El fuego de la chimenea y el de mi hoguera se comunicaban. Y la salamandra

270 apareció en el centro de la pira, encuadrada por el triángulo de

[20] *los... fe:* public ceremonies declaring the judgement of accused heretics by the Spanish Inquisition, usually culminating in the heretics' being burned at the stake
[21] *me... alma:* gradually gave me a soul
[22] *Imagínate... sufrir:* Imagine how much suffering I must have seen. *Habré visto* is the future perfect also used to express probability in the past. (See note 14 for an explanation of the use of the conditional to express probability. In those sentences, however, the conditional replaces the imperfect, *había*, where here *habré visto* replaces the preterit *vi*.)
[23] *volvió a verse:* you could see it again
[24] *De... tanto:* Every now and then

fuego de colores cambiantes. Era tan alta como yo, y nunca la había visto más bella. Sonreía triste y esperanzada. La claridad de sus ojos verdes aparecía empañada por un velo de lágrimas; me tendía los brazos, las puntas de sus afilados dedos rozaban el borde
275 de la llama.

Entré serenamente. Lo último que sentí fue la frescura de sus brazos alrededor de mi cuello y la suavidad de sus labios.

Me encontraron carbonizado frente a la chimenea, bajo los restos de mi casa incendiada.

280 Nadie vio —no tenían por qué verlas[25]— las huellas de un pie de mujer sobre las frías cenizas, que se perdía, cada vez más borroso, en la puerta que daba al jardín.

[25] *no... verlas:* they had no reason to see

Exercises

A. *Questions and Opinions*

1. ¿Quién obsequió al narrador la caja de fósforos de madera?

2. ¿Por qué se dirigió después a la estación Retiro?

3. ¿Qué cosa curiosa vio el hombre cuando encendió un fósforo en la estación?

4. ¿Qué explicación de este extraño fenómeno le ocurre al hombre?

5. Una vez llegado a casa, ¿cómo hace el hombre para comunicarse con la misteriosa visión?

6. Cuando reapareció la mujer en el segundo fuego estable, ¿de qué tamaño era?

7. ¿Dónde ha aparecido siempre la Salamandra, desde que el mundo es mundo?

8. ¿Qué pasaría si ella saliera del fuego?

9. ¿Qué le propone la Salamandra al hombre?

10. ¿Qué hizo el hombre para aceptar su invitación fatal?

• 11. ¿Cree Ud. que el hombre murió o es que se escapó al lado de la extraña Salamandra?

• 12. ¿Considera Ud. que hay personas que prefirieran una muerte repentina y misteriosa a la vida real de todos los días?

B. Verb Practice Use each of the following verbal expressions in an original sentence in Spanish, either based on the story or of your own design. Be prepared to explain the meaning of your sentences.

1. **quedarse con**
2. **faltar**
3. **estar por**
4. **correr**
5. **dejarse**
6. **producirse**
7. **acordarse de**
8. **venir**
9. **obligar**
10. **moverse**

C. Vocabulary Practice Complete the sentences below, matching the expressions on the right with the italicized words in English on the left. Be sure to use the correct form of each verb. Then use each expression in an original sentence in Spanish and indicate in English what your sentence means.

1. Él escribió el nombre de la chica en *the back* de su cuaderno.

2. Él no tenía la costumbre de salir *at* noche.

3. Sus repetidas ausencias eran *the last straw.*

4. *No matter how much* insistes, nadie te creerá.

5. Elena, Ud. *yourself* me dijo que viniera.

6. Era *as if* no hubiera pasado nada.

7. Diga Ud. *whatever* diga, no me va a convencer.

8. *What had* acontecido afectó a todo el mundo.

9. Su pañuelo tenía *the smell of* violetas.

10. *No matter how much* el muchacho protestaba, nadie le hacía caso.

por... que

como si

olor a

lo + *past participle*

el colmo

subjunctive + **lo que** + *subjunctive*

el dorso

de + *noun*

mismo

por más que

D. Communication Practice

1. Tell José that he may keep the disks.
2. Indicate that you're already about to leave.
3. Say that you never remember that actor's name.
4. Tell Marta and Rolando to move over a bit.
5. Say it's twenty-five minutes to twelve.

El hombre que robó a Borges

Rubén Loza Aguerreberre

RUBÉN LOZA AGUERREBERRE (1945–   ) was born in Minas, Uruguay, but for many years has been living in Montevideo, where he has worked as a journalist and literary critic for two important publications there, *El País* and *Mundocolor.* He has also attained distinction as a short-story writer. Most of his tales have been collected in *La espera* (1973), *La casa del atardecer* (1977), *El hombre que robó a Borges* (1977), *Pasado en limpio* (1984), and *Coto de caza y otros cuentos* (1993).

Loza was a personal friend of the late Jorge Luis Borges, whose brief parable, "Los dos reyes y los dos laberintos", opens the present volume. It seems appropriate, therefore, that we should end with a story in which Borges himself figures as a character. This tale, as you will discover, has a curious structure, a feature that Loza doubtlessly has drawn from his readings of Borges's prose and poetry. Be prepared, then, to have the conventional boundaries between reality and fantasy—between life and literature—perhaps slightly blurred. Such, indeed, is the effect produced by many of Borges's own writings. Loza's story, an homage of sorts to Borges, makes Bernardo Arévalo's fate a most strange and unsettling one.

A PRELIMINARY LOOK AT KEY EXPRESSIONS

Be sure to study these expressions before you read the story.

1. (135:8) **atravesar** *to cross*

2. (135:22) **acabar** + *present participle to end up (by)* + *present participle* This expression has the same meaning as **acabar por** + *infinitive*. Thus **Acababa llevándose el Quijote** is the same as **Acababa por llevarse el Quijote.**

3. (135:25) **cualquiera** *any one* This word ends in **-a** when not used directly before a noun: **cualquiera de los libros; Dame cualquiera.** The **-a** has nothing to do with gender. The word is shortened to **cualquier** immediately before a masculine or feminine singular noun: **cualquier libro, cualquier mesa.** Neither word has a plural.

4. (135:27) **cansarse** *to get tired*

5. (135:30) **rumbo a** *bound, headed for, in the direction of*

6. (135:30) **tener... años** *to be . . . years old*

7. (135:34) **junto a** *next to* Since this is a preposition, it is invariable in form: **Las máquinas estaban junto a la ventana.**

8. (136:37) **ingresar** *to enter* This verb is used for joining a company or enrolling in a school. **Entrar** is *to walk, go, come in,* as into a room, for example.

9. (136:53) **mareado** *lightheaded* This word has a wide range of meanings: *seasick, nauseated, dizzy, lightheaded, dazzled, overwhelmed,* etc. Only context can reveal which is meant.

10. (136:56) **dar cuerda a** *to wind* (a timepiece)

11. (136:60) **desvelado** *wide awake, not sleepy* This adjective comes from **desvelar** *to keep awake* and **desvelarse** *not to be able to sleep.*

12. (136:66) **de un tirón** *straight through, without a break, without stopping, all at once*

13. (136:66) **madrugada** *early morning* This noun refers to the "wee hours" of the morning when people are normally sleeping—from midnight to six or so. After that it is **mañana.**

14. (136:67) **soñar con** *to dream of, about*

15. (136:69) **imaginarse** *to imagine* This verb rarely occurs in any but the reflexive form.

16. (137:73) **poder más** *to win out, get the better (of one), be stronger* This expression also occurs on p. 137, line 109.

17. (137:102) **irse** *to leave, go away*   English speakers often use **salir** incorrectly for **irse. Salir** is *to leave* in the sense of *go* or *come out;* **irse** is *to leave* in the sense of *to go away* or *depart.*

18. (137:106) **hacérsele tarde a uno** *to get late*   In Spanish, the person who thinks it's late or needs to watch the time is the indirect object.

19. (138:117) **trago** *sip, swallow*   This noun has become synonymous with an alcoholic drink, as in **echar un trago** *to have a drink* (literally, "to toss a swallow").

20. (138:129) **tropezar (con)** *to trip, stumble*

El hombre que robó a Borges

El destino dibuja curiosos malentendidos.[1] La verdadera historia de Bernardo Arévalo me fue revelada mucho antes de que él traspusiera el umbral de mi casa, cuando ya mis ojos no veían el trazado de sus facciones,[2] la tarde del 24 de diciembre.

5   Bernardo Arévalo, hombre pequeño de mejillas con tintes rosa siempre bien afeitadas, azules los ojos y muy pulcro en todos los detalles de su vestimenta, que completaba con un infaltable portafolios en la mano derecha, atravesaba la plaza a las ocho menos cuarto y de pie ante el mostrador bebía un café, pagaba
10 con monedas justas,[3] hacía una pequeña reverencia en la puerta a quien allí estuviera,[4] y continuaba su camino. Cinco minutos antes de las ocho resonaban sus tacos en el largo corredor de la Biblioteca Municipal. Saludaba a su compañero de labor y se sentaba a leer los diarios, aguardando a que alguien (generalmente
15 jubilados o estudiantes, algunos jóvenes también) requiriera sus servicios. En esos momentos era un hombre feliz; brindaba sin retaceos cuanto estaba al alcance de su memoria,[5] que era casi prodigiosa, con una sonrisa permanente en sus labios finos. Había leído muchos libros; su cabeza era un ordenado fichero de títulos
20 y autores de las más variadas materias. También tenía arraigadas preferencias; si alguien le solicitaba orientación literaria, invariablemente acababa llevándose bajo el brazo el tomo I del *Quijote*,[6] el *Esquema del porvenir* de H.G. Wells,[7] *Los siete pilares de la sabiduría* de T.E. Lawrence,[8] en las viejas ediciones de Ercilla[9] o, de lo
25 contrario, cualquiera de los libros de Borges, en especial sus *Ficciones*.[10] Y él volvía a la penumbra de aquella sala silenciosa y solitaria, y sus ojos se cansaban descifrando pequeñas letras sobre hojas amarillecidas.

Bernardo Arévalo vivía con su madre. Su padre salió una mañana de invierno rumbo a la sastrería y no volvió nunca. Tenía
30 cinco años, Bernardo, cuando ello sucedió. Su madre no derramó una sola lágrima. Vendió a quienes lo tenían arrendado un campito[11] que había heredado de su abuela y se dedicó a pedalear una grande, oscura y pesada máquina de coser, día y noche, junto a la

[1] *El destino... malentendidos:* Fate produces some strange misunderstandings.
[2] *mis ojos... facciones:* The supposed narrator of this story is the great contemporary Argentine writer, Jorge Luis Borges (1899–1986), the actual author of the first story in the present collection. Borges had been partially blind for years before his death.
[3] *monedas justas:* exact change
[4] *a... estuviera:* to anyone who happened to be there
[5] *brindaba... memoria:* he offered freely everything within his memory
[6] *tomo I del Quijote:* Volume I of *Don Quijote* (1605), the novel written by the Spaniard Miguel de Cervantes (1547–1616)
[7] *Esquema... Wells:* *The Shape of Things to Come* (1933), a work written by British novelist and historian H.G. Wells (1866–1946)
[8] *Los siete... Lawrence:* *The Seven Pillars of Wisdom* (1926), written by British soldier and writer, Thomas E. Lawrence (Shaw) (1888–1935), better known as Lawrence of Arabia
[9] *Ercilla:* a Chilean publishing house

35 ventana que daba al patio. Luego agregó la luz macilenta de una
lamparita.

Pasaron años. Bernardo ingresó como mandadero en la Biblioteca Municipal.[12] Todas las Nochebuenas llegaban a su casa
los tíos, desde el campo, y poco después de la medianoche se
40 iban. Entre sus manos grandes tomaban la cabeza del niño y la
besaban sonoramente y sonreían con cierta nostalgia antes de
alejarse, entre los estruendos de los cohetes y los fuegos artificiales. Cuando Bernardo cumplió 41 años murió Ema, su madre.
Era, para decirlo de una vez, un hombre solitario de vida clara;[13]
45 quedó más solo aún. La muerte de Ema alteró su ritmo, que recuperó poco después, sintiéndose liberado de toda congoja, situación que por las noches le sumía en penosas introspecciones. Pero
acababa invariablemente releyendo algunas páginas de sus libros
de cabecera: *Los siete pilares de la sabiduría, El Aleph*[14] *y Ficciones.*
50 Lo peor eran los crepúsculos que se prolongaban más que
en las pasadas primaveras. Bernardo salía de la Biblioteca con sol
alto y las horas permanecían quietas. Una tardecita, al abrir la
ventana que daba al patio, mareado por el dulce olor de los jazmines, vio o creyó ver a su madre, a Ema, cortando unas flores
55 cerca del limonero.

¿Qué hacer? Bernardo llegaba y, luego de[15] bañarse, daba
cuerda al reloj de péndulo de la sala, con el secreto deseo de que
el tiempo transcurriera.

Una larguísima madrugada de finales de noviembre, Ber-
60 nardo Arévalo, desvelado, imaginó un plan para su cercana licencia. Solo, ahora, podía arriesgarse a pasar unos días fuera de la
ciudad; quizá fuera del país; podría llegar hasta Buenos Aires. ¿Por
qué no? y ver a Borges, claro.

Se sentó en la cama y diagramó sus pasos, día a día y hora a
65 hora. Durante semanas—desde aquella noche durmió sin sobresaltos, de un tirón, salvo una madrugada de domingo cuando
soñó con unos tigres o pumas, que le perseguían—no dejó de
pensar en ello; en cada momento libre releía la poesía de Borges,
que conocía menos, preparándose para su encuentro. Se imaginó
70 a ambos, en la calle, posando para una fotografía, mientras la
gente pasaba junto a ellos y los miraba.

Tuvo algunos contratiempos con su licencia, que se postergó por algunos días. Pudo más la ansiedad[16] y el 21 de diciembre viajó a Buenos Aires. En el bolsillo interior del saco llevaba
75 una tarjeta que un escritor de su ciudad, visitante de la Biblioteca,

[10] *Ficciones:* a collection of short stories (1944), written by Borges. A common theme in these stories and others by Borges is the shifting nature of roles or identities between the main characters.
[11] *Vendió... campito:* She sold a small piece of land to the people who were renting it from her
[12] *la Biblioteca Municipal:* The Municipal Library (of Uruguay, located in Montevideo). Borges was for many years the Director of the Argentine *Biblioteca Nacional,* an institution on the scale of our Library of Congress.
[13] *vida clara:* plain, simple life
[14] *El Aleph:* another collection of short stories (1949) written by Borges
[15] *luego de:* after
[16] *Pudo... ansiedad:* His impatience got the better of him

le dirigía a Ulyses Petit de Murat,[17] para que éste le hiciera accesible el camino hasta Borges.

La tarde del 24 de diciembre fue recibido por Borges en persona. «Si es oriental[18] es bienvenido», le dijo el escritor, ofreciéndole una temblorosa mano. Bernardo Arévalo jamás se había sentido tan emocionado. «Ulyses me habló de usted esta mañana», agregó el escritor mientras retornaba a la sala, sin el bastón.[19] Se orientaba sin problemas; a Bernardo le costaba creer[20] que no viera nada.

Se sentaron. Conversaron unos diez minutos; Borges recordó algunas imágenes del Uruguay que estaban en su memoria: un arco iris en el paso Molino,[21] los zaguanes de Montevideo y el agua clara del río Arapey,[22] donde se bañaron una mañana de verano con Enrique Amorín.[23] El monólogo de Borges fue interrumpido por dos periodistas de la televisión que querían un mensaje navideño del escritor. Con su voz apagada e impersonal, el escritor dijo dos o tres cosas que Bernardo juzgó geniales, y accedió a asomarse al balcón para una filmación final con la extendida ciudad como telón.

Tardaban. Entre los libros, a la derecha de Bernardo, asomaban unas hojas pálidas que, como si robara dinero, tomó temblorosamente. Miró unos párrafos; reconoció la pequeña letra de Borges. Sintió escalofríos.

Cuando retornaron—antes que ellos, le llegó el aviso de sus voces,[24]—Bernardo Arévalo se guardó los papeles en el bolsillo. Temblaba como una hoja al viento cuando lo vio entrar. Los periodistas se despidieron; Bernardo también: «Yo me voy, maestro».[25] Buscando el brazo del sillón con la mano abierta, Borges le preguntó si no quería un té. Bernardo le tomó la mano y, reteniéndola en la suya, le dijo: «Maestro, yo bajo con los señores. Se me hace tarde y hoy vuelvo a Uruguay. Ha sido un privilegio conocerlo y estrechar la mano con la cual escribe».

«Uruguay...» repitió Borges; luego recitó unos versos de Emilio Oribe.[26] «Buen viaje» le dijo, ya en la puerta. Pudo más la sonrisa que los ojos ciegos del viejo escritor, e iluminó su rostro.

En su casa, en su dormitorio, a la noche siguiente, Bernardo Arévalo leyó el manuscrito de Borges. Necesitó de[27] la soledad y de las sombras para hacerlo.

Al principio le costó descifrar la esmerada caligrafía, llena de palitos en las «p» y en las «f», del escritor casi ciego; descubría palabras sueltas, al margen de su significado y su correlación.[28] Hizo

[17] *Ulyses Petit de Murat* (1907–1985): an Argentine writer, who was for many years a close friend of Borges
[18] *oriental:* This is a colloquial term for *Uruguayan.* It comes from the name given to Uruguay during colonial days, *la Banda Oriental* (*the Eastern Strip*).
[19] *sin el bastón:* without his cane (Remember that Borges was partially blind.)
[20] *a... creer:* Bernardo had a hard time believing
[21] *paso Molino:* a suburb of Montevideo, capital of Uruguay
[22] *río Arapey:* one of the main rivers of Uruguay
[23] *Enrique Amorín:* Enrique Amorim (1900–1960) was an Uruguayan novelist and a relative by marriage of Borges. The spelling **Amorín** represents exactly how this name is pronounced in Spanish.
[24] *le... voces:* their voices announced to him that they were on their way back
[25] *maestro:* literally, *master,* a term of respect used by a disciple or student with his teacher
[26] *Emilio Oribe:* Oribe (1893–1975) was an Uruguayan doctor and poet.
[27] *Necesitó de:* He needed some
[28] *descubría... correlación:* he was able to make out words here and there, although he wasn't sure of their meaning or how they fit into the text

una pausa para beberse unos tragos del whisky que había traído de Buenos Aires, antes de aplicarse a la lectura. Sentado en la cama, muy cerca de la alta portátil,[29] leyó las primeras frases: «El destino
120 dibuja curiosos malentendidos. La verdadera historia de Bernardo Arévalo me fue revelada mucho antes de que él traspusiera el umbral de mi casa, cuando ya mis ojos no veían el trazado de sus facciones...»

      Con la frente bañada en sudor leyó las cuatro carillas. El
125 cuento del ladrón soñado por Borges estaba inconcluso. Las últimas palabras del manuscrito eran éstas: «Borracho, salió al patio de su casa, bajo el cielo estrellado. Se sentía tranquilo y feliz: hacía años que no lo estaba. Bebió un trago, el último y arrojó lejos la botella vacía. Tropezando, entre los canteros, recogió la
130 cuerda de colgar la ropa y la fue anudando,[30] mientras sus ojos buscaban la gruesa rama alta del limonero»...

[29] *la alta portátil:* the tall floor lamp
[30] *la fue anudando:* slowly tied a knot in it

Exercises

A. Questions and Opinions

1. ¿Por qué no podía el narrador ver las facciones de Bernardo Arévalo?

2. ¿Dónde trabajaba Arévalo y qué hacía?

3. ¿Cómo era la vida familiar de él?

4. ¿Quién era el autor predilecto de Arévalo?

5. ¿Dónde pensaba pasar Arévalo su cercana licencia?

6. ¿Quiénes interrumpieron su conversación con Borges?

7. ¿Qué hizo Arévalo con las hojas manuscritas de Borges?

8. ¿Cuándo se puso Arévalo a leer el manuscrito?

9. ¿De qué se dio cuenta Arévalo cuando terminó la lectura de las hojas?

10. ¿Qué cosas buscó Arévalo del manuscrito cuando salió al patio?

• 11. ¿Cree Ud. que Bernardo Arévalo iba a suicidarse? ¿Por qué?

• 12. ¿Qué interpretación le daría Ud. a este cuento?

B. Verb Practice Use each of the following verbal phrases in an original sentence in Spanish, either based on the story or of your own design. Be prepared to explain the meaning of your sentences.

1. **atravesar**
2. **acabar** + *present participle*
3. **cansarse**
4. **tener... años**
5. **ingresar**
6. **soñar con**
7. **imaginarse**
8. **irse**
9. **hacérsele tarde a uno**
10. **tropezar**

C. Vocabulary Practice Complete the sentences below, matching the expressions on the right with the English words on the left. Be sure to use the correct form of each verb. Then use each expression in an original Spanish sentence and indicate in English what your sentence means.

1. Su devoción *got the best of him* y le escribió a Borges una larga carta de admiración.
2. El empleado no llegó a casa hasta *the small hours of the night*.
3. Vamos a tomar un *drink* juntos cuando terminemos.
4. No importa, dame *any one*.
5. Me sentí algo *dizzy,* y me recosté.
6. Yo siempre prefiero leer una novela policial *straight through*.
7. Partieron ayer *bound for* Montevideo.
8. Él estuvo *wide awake* toda la noche, haciendo sus planes para la licencia.
9. Yo los vi conversando *next to* la entrada.
10. *I wound* el reloj y me fui a la cama.

cualquiera
rumbo a
junto a
mareado
dar cuerda a
desvelado
de un tirón
la madrugada
poder más
trago

D. Communication Practice

1. Say that you have always dreamed of being a writer.

2. Tell your friend that you had to leave because it was getting late.

3. Ask Sara how old Marta's sister is.

4. Say that you ended up buying the car.

5. Indicate that you get tired when there's nothing to do.

Vocabulary

The following types of words have been omitted: (1) most easily recognizable cognates; (2) obviously derived words, such as diminutives, superlatives, and **-mente** adverbs if the adjective is listed; (3) high-frequency structure words, such as articles, prepositions and pronouns; (4) past participles of listed infinitives unless they have a different meaning as nouns or adjectives; (5) individual verb forms with a few low frequency exceptions, such as **hubo** from **haber;** (6) well-known proper nouns and cultural, historical, and geographical items explained in footnotes; (7) words that an average student of intermediate Spanish would be expected to know.

The gender of masculine nouns ending in **-o** is not listed, nor of feminine nouns ending in **-a, -ción, -d,** and **-z.** Radical stem changes and some verb irregularities are indicated in parentheses after the infinitive. When there is one change, it is for the present tense: **volver (ue).** When there are two, the first is for the present tense and the second for the preterit: **seguir (i, i).** Also, **aislar (í),** for example, indicates **aíslo, aísla,** etc. Prepositional usage is given after verbs—without parentheses if the verb is commonly used with the preposition and a following element: **dirigirse a** — and with parentheses if the verb can be used alone: **acordarse (de).** Most multiword expressions are cross-listed for each important word, with (—) representing the alphabetized word. For example, **manera: de otra** — *otherwise* and also **otro: de —a manera** *otherwise.* Many of the above criteria were not applied in an absolute fashion; we included any term that we felt might not be known by an average intermediate student.

Following what is becoming common practice in lexical listings in Hispanic publications, the letters **ch** and **ll** are no longer treated separately, but rather are listed in their proper order in the **c**'s and **l**'s, respectively.

ABBREVIATIONS

adj.	adjective	*imperf.*	imperfect	*part.*	participle
adv.	adverb	*ind.*	indicative	*pers.*	person
Arg.	Argentine	*inf.*	infinitive	*pl.*	plural
aug.	augmentative	*intrans.*	intransitive	*pr.*	present
aux.	auxiliary	*Lat.*	Latin	*prep.*	preposition
coll.	colloquial	*lit.*	literally	*pret.*	preterit
dim.	diminutive	*m.*	masculine	*sent.*	sentence
e.g.	for example	*Mex.*	Mexican	*sing.*	singular
expl.	expletive	*n.*	noun	*subj.*	subjunctive
f.	feminine	*opp.*	opposite	*trans.*	transitive
imp.	imperative	*p.*	past	*v.*	verb

A

abajo down, under, below; **de arriba —** up and down; **para —** downward; **río —** downstream

abalanzarse to rush

abanicar to fan

abatir to depress; to knock down; to humble, humiliate, discourage; **—se** to be disheartened

abeja bee

abertura opening

abismo abyss

ablandar to soften

abochornarse to be embarrassed

abofetear to punch, slap

abolido annulled

abominar to hate

aborrecer to hate

abrasar to burn

abrazar to embrace

abrigar to keep warm

abrigo shelter, cover, blanket; coat

abrir to open; **— paso** to clear the way

abrumado oppressed

absoluto: en — (not) at all

abstraído absorbed

aburrido boring

acabar to finish, end; **— de** + *inf.* to have just + *p. part.;* **—** (*in pret.*) **de** + *inf.* to finish + *pr. part.* (e.g., **Acabó de es- cribir** He finished writing); **— por** to finish (end) up by

acaecer to happen

acallar to silence, shush

acangrejado crab-shaped

acariciador *adj.* caressing

acariciar to cherish; to caress, pet, fondle

acaso maybe, perhaps; **por si —** just in case

acceder to grant, give in to, agree, consent

acceso attack

acechante lying in wait

acechar to spy on

aceitar to oil

aceite *m.* oil

acera sidewalk

acerca de about, with regard to

acercarse (a) to approach, go (come) up (to), go (come) closer (to)

acero steel

acertar (ie) a + *inf.* to happen to, chance to + *v.;* to succeed in + *pr. part.*

acertijo riddle

acicalado neat, clean

acodado leaning over on one's elbows

acodarse to merge; to abut; to lean on one's elbows

acogedor friendly, hospitable

acolchado quilted

acólito assistant

acometer to attack, come on; to under- take, attempt

acomodar to place, arrange; **—se** to settle oneself, settle down; to get a "soft" job; to marry into money

acompañante *m.* companion

acompasado measured, rhythmic, slow

acongojado afflicted, grieved

aconitina aconitine (*a poison made from the roots of certain plants*)

aconsejar to advise

acontecer to happen, befall

acontecimiento event, happening

acordar (ue) to decide, agree; to grant; **—se (de)** to remember

acorrer to help, aid

acosado beset, harassed

acostar (ue) to put to bed; **—se** to lie down, go to bed

acostumbrar + *inf.* to be in the habit of + *pr. part.;* **—se a** to get used to

acre sour

acribillar to riddle, mark

acto continuo immediately afterwards

actual present, present-day

acuarela watercolor

acudir to come, appear, run up; to come to the rescue; to hurry, rush

acuerdo agreement, accord; **de — a, con** in accordance with, according to; **de —** agreed, in agreement; **ponerse de —** to come to an agreement

acurrucado huddled

acusado sharp, clear

adecuado adequate

adelantar to advance; **—se (a)** to excel, outdo; to take the lead, get ahead (of)

adelante forward, onward, ahead; **de hoy en —** from now on; **en —** from then (now) on

ademán *m.* gesture, movement of the hand

adentro inward, inside; *n.* inside; **para mis —s** to myself

aderezado set (*places at a table*)

aderezar to straighten

adherido pressed, held against

adinerado well-to-do, wealthy

adivinar to guess, figure out, divine, prophesy

adjudicar to award

admirable excellent, admirable

admirado amazed, surprised, astounded

adornado decorated

adornito knickknack

adosado stuck, fastened

aduanero *adj.* customs

adueñarse de to take possession of, take charge of, take over

adusto stern, sullen

advertir (ie, i) to notify; to warn, inform; to notice, observe

afable affable, warm, friendly, easy to talk to

afamado noted, famous

afán *m.* eagerness

afanosamente laboriously, painstakingly

afecto fondness, affection; feeling

afeitar to shave

afianzar to support, back (up)

afilado sharp, tapering; slender

afilar to sharpen, hone

afinar to refine, sharpen, polish

afirmar to assert; to rest, secure

afligir to afflict, sadden

aflorar to crop out, appear on the surface

afónico mute

afrentado insulted, ashamed

afrontar to face, put up with

agachar (*trans.*) to bend down, lower; **—se** (*intrans.*) to crouch, bend, stoop down

agarrado holding on

agarrar to catch, grab; to head, set out for

agazapado hidden, crouched down

agazaparse to crouch, duck down

agitar to wave, agitate, move, stir; **—se** to move about

aglomeración crowd, mass of people

agonizante dying

agonizar to die slowly, be dying

agotado exhausted, worn out

agotarse to be exhausted; to run out (*material, food, etc.*)

agradar to please

agradecer to thank, be grateful for

agradecido grateful

agradecimiento gratitude

agrandar to enlarge

agregar to add

agriarse to sour

aguas arriba upstream

aguamanil *m.* washstand

aguantar to endure, bear, suffer, stand; to wait

aguardar to wait (for)

agudo sharp

aguja needle

agujerito *dim. of* **agujero** hole

ahito gorged, stuffed

ahogado stifled, muffled, unclear

ahogar to drown (out), stifle; **—se** to drown

ahora (bien) well now (then); **— mismo** right now

ahorrar to save

ahorro saving

ahuyentar to drive away, frighten off; **—se** to run away

aire: — colado draft of air; **al — libre** outside

aislar (í) to isolate, put apart, separate

ajado wrinkled

ajedrez *m.* chess

ajeno alien, of others; foreign, inappropriate

al + *inf.* (up)on + *pr. part.* (e.g., **al levantarse** on getting up)

ala wing

Alá Allah

alabado praised

alambrado wire fence

alambre *m.* wire

álamo poplar tree

alardear to boast

alargado slender, long

alargar to extend, draw out, lengthen

alarido howl, scream, cry

alarmante alarming

alba dawn

albergado lodged

alborotar to make noise

alboroto disturbance, row, brawl

alcaide *m.* special guard

alcance *m.* reach

alcanzar to reach, gain; **— a** + *inf.* to succeed in + *pr. part.*, get + *inf.*

alcoba bedroom

aldaba door knocker

aldea village

alegrar to make happy, gladden; **—se (de)** to be happy, glad (about)

alegre happy

alegría happiness

alejar to take farther away; **—se (de)** to leave, go (move, draw) away, walk off

alelado stupefied, bewildered

alentar (ie) to encourage

aleta wing, small wing

aletargado lethargic, drowsy, groggy

alfiler *m.* pin

alfombra rug, carpet

algazara din, clamor

algo: servir de — to do any good

algodón *m.* cotton

alguna: — parte somewhere; **— vez** ever, sometime

alhajar to adorn

alharaca clamor

aliento breath

alimentar to feed, nourish; to nurture; to harbor

alimento food

alineado lined up

alisar to smooth down, smooth out

aliviado relieved

alivio relief

allá there; **— arriba** up there; **más —** far away, farther on; **más — de** beyond; **el más —** *m. n.* the great beyond

alma soul, "heart"

almohada pillow

almuerzo lunch

alocado wild, crazed

alojamiento lodging, room

alojarse to stay, take lodging

alpestre Alpine

alquilar to rent

alquiler *m.* rent

alrededor *m. n.:* **a su —** around him (her, etc.); *pl.* surroundings, outskirts; **— de** around

alteración unevenness

alterado upset

altivez haughtiness

alto high; tall; **lo —** high up; *pl. n.* upstairs; **pasar por —** to overlook, pass over

altura height

alucinación hallucination

alumbrar to light, illuminate

alvéolo cell, compartment

alzar to lift, raise; **—se** to rise, go higher

ama housekeeper

amamantar to nurse (*an infant*)

amanecer *m. n.* dawn; *v.* to dawn; to wake up

amante *m., f.* lover

amarfilado ivory-colored

amargo bitter

amargura bitterness

amarillecido yellowed

amarillento yellowish

amarillo yellow

amarrar to tie, fasten, moor

ambicionar to aspire to, seek

ambos both

amenazar to threaten

amistad friendship

amistoso friendly

amoldar to mold, fashion, figure

amonedar to coin

amonestador admonishing, reproving

amontonar to pile up, gather together

amoratado livid

amortajar to wrap in a shroud

amortiguar to muffle, deaden, dampen

amotinado in a mob, milling about

amparado protected

ampararse to take refuge; to have recourse

amparo protection

amueblado furnished

analfabeto illiterate

anaranjado *adj.* orange

anca rump (*of a horse*)

ancho *adj.* wide; *n.* width

anclar to anchor

andar to walk; to go; **con el — del tiempo** with the passing of time

andrajoso ragged

andén *m.* platform (*railroad station*)

anegar (ie) to overwhelm

angosto narrow

angustia anguish

angustioso anguished

anhelado longed for

anhelo desire, longing

anheloso longing for

anidar to nest

animal de presa predatory animal

animalejo odd-looking creature, nasty animal

animar to encourage; **—se** to get lively, excited; **—se** (**a** + *inf.*) to get up the energy, have the courage (+ *inf.*)

ánimo courage, fortitude, strength; mind, soul, spirit

aniquilar to destroy, wipe out, crush

anochecer *m.* nightfall

anonadado annihilated, crushed

anotación note

ansia eagerness; anxiety, fear; **con —s de** anxious to

ansiado anxious; long-awaited, eagerly awaited

ansiedad anxiety, impatience

ansioso anxious
antaño long ago, "yesteryear"
Antárdida Antarctica
antebrazo forearm
antecámara anteroom
antecomedor *m.* small serving room (*adjacent to a dining room*)
antemano: de — beforehand, in advance
antes: cuanto — without delay, as soon as possible, immediately
anticipo advance (*money*)
antojar: —sele a uno to take a fancy, have a whim
antojo fancy, whim
antorcha torch
anudar to tie, bind, knot
anular to eliminate, overcome; to annul
añadido addition
añadir to add
añicos *pl.* bits, fragments, pieces of broken glass
año: cumplir ... —s to be . . . years old
añorar to reminisce
apacible peaceful
apaciguador comforting, pacifying
apaciguar to soften, soothe, pacify, calm, alleviate; **—se** to calm, settle down
apagado subdued
apagar to put, turn out, extinguish; to muffle; **—se** to go out, die out, be extinguished
aparador *m.* sideboard, china cabinet
aparecer to appear, show up
aparentar to feign, pretend
apariencia appearance, illusion
apartado isolated, retired
apartar to spread, separate, take away, push away; **—se** to move away (back)
aparte *adv.* aside
apellidarse ... to have . . . as a last name

apellido surname, last name
apenas scarcely, barely, hardly; just as soon as
apercibirse (para) to prepare (for)
apilarse to pile up
aplacar to placate, soothe
aplastar to crush, smash, flatten; to stick (against)
aplaudidor *m.* admirer, applauder
apoderamiento seizure of power
apoderarse de to overcome, take possession of, seize
apodo nickname
apogeo apogee, height, crowning moment
apolillado moth-eaten
apoltronado lounging
apostura good looks
apoyar to support, lean
apoyo support
apreciar to perceive; to appreciate; to value
aprehendido arrested
apremiante urgent, pressing
aprendizaje *m.* apprenticeship; learning
apresuramiento hurry, haste
apresurar to hasten, quicken (*trans.*); **—se** to hurry (*intrans.*)
apretado clenched
apretar (ie) to press, squeeze, pinch, grasp, clench
aprobar (ue) to approve
aprontarse to prepare
aprovechar to take advantage of, make use of
aproximarse to approach, come closer
apuesta bet
apunte *m.* note
apuñalar to stab
apuro difficulty, "tight spot"
aquél the former (*lit.* that one)

B

baba drool

baboso drooling

badajo bell clapper

bagaje *m.* beast of burden

bailarina dancer

baja discharge (*from service, hospital*); **dar de —** to discharge

bajar to go (come) down; to get out (*of a vehicle*)

bajo under

bala bullet

baladí trivial

balanza scale

balazo shot; bullet wound

balbucear to babble, stammer, stutter

balde: en — in vain

baldosa paving stone; floor tile

balido bleat(ing)

ballena whale

bananal *m.* banana plantation; banana tree area

bancarrota bankruptcy

banco bench

bandada flock

bandeja tray

baño bath

barajar to shuffle; to pass around, back and forth

barato cheap

barba beard

barbudo bearded

barco boat

barraca (*slang*) "boxcars" (*12 in dice games*)

barranca gully, ravine

barrer to sweep

barrera barrier

barriada district, quarter (*of a city*)

barriga belly

barrio district, neighborhood

barro clay, mud

barroso muddy

barrote *m.* rung, bar

bastar to be enough, suffice; **¡Basta! Enough!; — con** + *inf.* to be enough + *inf.*

bastardo hybrid, mixed, vile

bastón *m.* cane, stick

basura garbage, trash

bata housecoat, dressing gown

beato devout, pious

bebida drink, beverage

belleza beauty

bendición blessing

bendito blessed one; **dormir como un —** to sleep like a baby

bermejo vermillion

berrear to bellow, howl

besar to kiss

beso kiss

bestia beast

bicho bug, insect

bien: — mirado carefully considered; **— que** although; **ahora —** well now (then); **de —** honest; **más —** rather, more; **pues —** well then; *m. n.* good, benefit; **tener a —** to see fit, find convenient; «**No hay mal que por — no venga**» "Everything turns out for the best," "Every cloud has a silver lining"; *m. pl. n.* property, estate

bienaventuranza bliss

bienvenido welcome

bigote *m.* whisker, moustache

billete *m.* bill (*money*)

biombo folding screen

bioquímica biochemistry
bisabuelo great-grandfather; *pl.* great-grandparents
bisturí *m.* scalpel
bizcocho pastry; cupcake
blando soft
blandura tenderness, softness
blanqueado whitewashed
blanquear to whiten
blanquirosado pinkish-white
bloqueado blocked (off)
boato luxury, pomp, pageantry
boca mouth; entrance, opening
bocacalle *f.* intersection
bocado mouthful, bite
bocal *m.* jar
bocanada whiff, breath, gasp; puff of smoke
bofetada slap
boga style, vogue; **en** — popular
bola ball
boleta report, document, draft
boleto ticket; — **de ida** one-way ticket
boliche *m.* general store
bolsillo pocket
bolsita *dim. of* **bolsa** bag
bolso purse, bag
bombero firefighter
bombita *dim. of* **bomba** light bulb
bombón *m.* candy, sweet stuff; "honey" (*term of endearment*)
bondad kindness, goodness
bondadoso kind
borde *m.* edge, border
bordo: a — **de** aboard
borrachera drunkenness, drunken state
borracho drunk, drunken
borrar to erase, remove
borroso blurry
bosque *m.* woods

bota boot; leather wine bottle
botella bottle
botica medicine shop, pharmacy
botín *m.* booty, loot
brasa burning ember
bravío wild, fierce
bravo wild, savage; mad, angry; rough, rugged
brazada armful
brazo arm
brea tar
brillante *m.* diamond
brillar to shine, gleam
brillo shine, gleam
brincar to caper, frisk, leap, jump
brinco leap, jump; **dar un** — to jump, take a jump; **de un** — with a leap; **pegar un** — to jump
brindar to offer, present; to toast
brisa breeze
broma joke, joking around
bromear to jest
bronco solid, hard, rough
brotar to spring forth, sprout, appear suddenly, flow
bruma fog, mist
brusco sudden, abrupt
bucle *m.* curl, lock (*of hair*)
buche *m.* craw (*of a bird*)
bueno: de —**a gana** willingly; **de una** —**a vez** once and for all, finally
buhardilla garret
bullicio uproar
bullir to bubble, boil
bulto package, bundle
burbuja bubble
burdo coarse
burla scorn, jest, mockery, taunt; **hacer** — **de** to mock
burlarse de to make fun of, mock, scorn

burlesco ludicrous
burlón *adj.* mocking, teasing, scornful
butaca easy chair
buzo underwater diver

C

cabal: a carta — through and through, in every respect
cabalgar to ride on horseback
caballero gentleman
cabecera head (*of a bed*)
cabellera head of hair
cabello hair, lock
caber to fit, be contained
cabestro halter
cabezal *m.* small pillow
cabillo stem, stalk; match stub
cabo end, handle; **al fin y al —** after all
cabrita kid (*goat*)
caburé *m.* pygmy owl (*bird of prey native to southern South America*)
cachas *pl.* handle, butt (*of a gun*)
cachete *m.* (fat) cheek
cachorro cub; young (*of various animals*)
cachucha cap
cada each, every; **— cual** each one; **— vez más** more and more
cadeneta chain stitch
caer to fall; **dejar —** to drop; **—se** to fall down
cafetera coffee pot
cafetería coffee house, coffee shop
caída fall
caja box, case; main part of telephone; **— fuerte** safe, strongbox
cajero cashier
cajón *m.* drawer; big box, case
calafate *m.* caulking

calafatear to caulk
calavera skull
calcomanía decal, transfer
calefacción heat
calentar (ie) to heat
cálido hot
caligrafía penmanship, calligraphy
cáliz *m.* center of a flower (*within the petals*)
callado silent
callar to silence; **—(se)** to be silent, shut up
calleja side street, alley
callejón *m.* alley
callejuela narrow street, alley
calorcillo extreme heat; nice warmth
calorífico burner, stove, hot plate
caluroso hot, warm (*weather*)
calvo bald
calza cord, fetter (*used on animals*)
calzado footwear; *p. part.* **— con** wearing (*on one's feet*)
calzar to wedge; **—se** to put on shoes, gloves
camarero waiter
cambiación change
cambiar to change, exchange
cambio change; **a — de** in exchange for; **en —** on the other hand, on the contrary
camello camel
caminar to walk, go, travel
caminata long walk, hike
camino way, road; trip; **— de** on the road to, in the direction of
camiseta undershirt, T-shirt
campanada peal, ring(ing) of a bell
campanilla *dim. of* **campana** bell
campaña campaign
camposanto cemetery
canal *m.* channel

canalizar to channel
canastilla *dim. of* **canasta** basket
canelas: capuera de — grove of cinnamon trees
canoso gray-haired
cansancio fatigue
cantaleta noisy ridicule
cántaro pitcher
cantero flowerbed
canto song, chant
caña reed, cane
cañaveral *m.* cane field
caño pipe, tube
cañón *m.* flue, shaft, stack (*of a chimney*)
capa layer, coating, covering
capacitar to prepare, qualify
capataz *m.* **de servicio** head waiter
capaz capable
capilar: vasito — capillary
capilla chapel
capitalino *adj.* from the capital
capricho caprice, whim
capuera de canelas grove of cinnamon trees
cara face
caramelo hard candy
carbonero coal peddler
carbonizado charred
carbunclo burning coal; ruby
carcajada burst of laughter, guffaw
cárcel *f.* jail, prison
carcelario *adj.* jail, prison
cárdeno livid, purple, violet
cardo thistle
carecer de to lack
carga charge, load; **de —s** loading
cargar to carry, transport; **— (de)** to load, burden (with); **— con** to carry, haul; **—se** to become charged
cargo charge; **a — de** in charge of
caricia caress

carilla page (*of a manuscript*)
cariño affection, fondness, love
cariñoso affectionate, loving
caritativo charitable
carne *f.* flesh; *pl.* flesh, fat (*on human body*)
carnicero *n.* butcher; *adj.* bloodthirsty, carnivorous
caro dear; expensive
carpeta table cover; manilla folder, file
carrera course; career; race; **a la —** hastily
carrero wagon driver
carreta cart, wagon
carretero driver (*of a cart*)
carretilla wheelbarrow
carroza carriage, coach
carta: a — cabal through and through, in every respect
cartel *m.* poster
cartera briefcase, portfolio; purse; wallet
cartucho cartridge, bullet
casarse to get married
cascada cascade
cáscara bark
casco helmet
casero *adj.* home(made), domestic
caserón *m.* large, ramshackle house
casilla cage; booth
caso incident, fact; case; **darse el —** to happen; **hacer — (de)** to pay attention (to), listen (to), heed; **poner... por —** to take . . . as an example (e.g., **Pongamos a mi jefe por caso.** Let's take my boss as an example.)
casta breed
castaña chestnut
castillo castle; **— de artificio** artificial castle
casualidad chance, chance event, coincidence
casualmente by chance, coincidentally

catarata waterfall, cataract
caterva throng, crowd
cauda train, tail
caudal *m.* fortune, wealth, property
caudaloso of great volume, carrying a lot of water
caudillo boss, strong man, leader, dictator
causa: a — de because of
cautela caution
cauteloso cautious
cautivador captivating, charming
cautivo captive
cauto cautious
cavilación doubts, second thoughts, deep thoughts, penetrating thoughts, consideration
cavilar to ponder, consider, think over
caza hunt, pursuit; **dar —** to hunt, pursue
cazador *adj.* hunting
cazar to hunt, catch, chase, pursue
cebar to brew, make
ceder to yield, give (up), give way; **— la plaza** to give up
cedro cedar
cegado stopped up
ceja eyebrow
celda cell
celeste celestial, heavenly; blue
celo zeal
cena supper
cenar to eat supper
ceniciento ash-colored
ceniza ash
centella flash
centenar *m. n.* hundred; **a —es** by the hundreds
centésimo hundredth
ceñir (i, i) to go, fit around
ceño brow
cepillo brush
cera wax

cercanía nearness
cercano *adj.* near, nearby, close
cercar to enclose, encircle, surround
cercenar to cut, lop off; to pare, trim
cerciorarse (de) to find out (about); to make sure (of)
cerco wall, fence
cerdo pig
cerebro brain
cernirse (ie) to spread against; to sift; to hover, soar
cerrada: noche — completely dark
cerradura lock
cerrar (ie) to close; **— el paso** to block the way
cerro hill
cerrojo bolt, latch
certidumbre *f.* certainty
cesar to stop, cease
césped *m.* lawn, grass
cesta basket
cetrino yellow-skinned
chacal *m.* jackal
chaleco vest, waistcoat
chapita small metal plate
chapotear to splash
chapucero clumsy, bungling, amateurish
chaqueta jacket, coat
charco puddle
charlar to chat
charlatán *m.* charlatan, con man
charol *m.* patent leather
chasqueado disappointed
chasquear to snap, crack; to disappoint
chicotazo strike, blow; shot (*from a gun*)
chicuelo *dim. of* **chico** boy, lad, kid
chichón *m.* bump
chillar to scream, shriek
chimenea fireplace; chimney
chino: tinta —a India ink (*permanent black ink*)

chiquilín *dim. of* **chico** boy, lad, kid
chiquillo *dim. of* **chico** boy, lad, kid
chirca *type of wild fruit tree*
chiribitil *m.* shack, hovel
chirigota joke
chirrido squeaking
chispa spark
chisporroteante hissing, sputtering
chisporrotear to spark; to hiss, sputter
chisporroteo sizzling, sputtering, crackling
chiste *m.* joke, funny story
chivos *pl.* (*slang*) dice
chocar (con, contra) to bump, crash, run (into), hit
chocarrero coarse, vulgar
chocolatín *m.* piece of chocolate candy
cholo biracial (*Indian and white*); dark-skinned person
chorro stream, spurt
choza hut
chúcaro wild, untamed
chucho chill; fright
cianuro de potasio potassium cyanide
cicatriz scar
cicatrizar to heal over
cicuta hemlock
ciego blind; sluggish
cielo: — raso ceiling; **¡Cielos!** Good heavens!
ciénaga marsh, swamp
cieno mire, slime
cifra sum total, number
cigarra locust (*insect*)
cinta tape; ribbon
cinto belt; sash
cintura waist
cinturón *m.* belt
circundar to circle
circunvecino neighboring, surrounding, nearby

cirio candle
cirujano surgeon
cisco coal dust, small pieces of coal
citarse to make an appointment (date)
ciudadano citizen
clamar to cry out
claridad light, brightness
clarividencia clairvoyance, intuition, ESP
claro light (*colored*); of course
clausura closing
clavada (*slang*) a losing roll (*in dice games*)
clavar to fix, nail; to stick in, pierce, prick, thrust with sharp instrument
clave *f.* key (*metaphorical*)
clavo nail, spike
cliente *m., f.* client; customer
clientela clientele
coartada alibi
cobayo guinea pig
cobertizo covering; shed
cobertor *m.* bedspread
cobrador *m.* bill collector
cobrar to charge (for), collect, take in (*money*); to get paid; to settle (*account*)
cobre *m.* copper
cochero driver
cocimiento concoction
cocina kitchen; cooking
cocinera cook
codicia fervent desire; envy, greed, covetousness
codicilo document, codicil
código code, key
cofradía religious brotherhood
cofre *m.* box, chest
coger to catch, grab; to pick up
cogote *m.* back of the neck
cohete *m.* rocket
cohetón *m. aug. of* cohete
coima "rakeoff," "take" (*for the operator of an illegal establishment*)

cojear to limp

cola tail

colado: aire — draft of air

colarse (ue) to pass (steal) through, slip (sneak) in

colateral *m. a relative not in one's "direct" line, such as an aunt, uncle, nephew, cousin, etc.*

colchón *m.* mattress

colear to pull an animal's tail

colegio secondary school

cólera rage

colgante hanging (down)

colgar (ue) to hang (up); **cuerda de — la ropa** clothesline

colmar to fulfill, satisfy, fill

colmena hive

colmenar *m.* apiary (*group of beehives*)

colmo height, summit, limit

colocar to place, set, put

colorado red

comadrear to gossip

comadrería gossip

comarca territory, region, district, neighborhood

comedor *m.* dining room

comer: dar de — to feed

comerciante *m., f.* businessman, businesswoman

comercio business

comestible *adj.* edible

cometer to commit

comida food

comisario commissioner

comisura corner (*of the mouth*)

como: — para as if to; **hacer — que +** *ind.* to pretend + *inf.;* **tal —** just as; **tanto ... — ...** both . . . and . . .

cómoda dresser

cómodo comfortable

compadecer to pity

compadecido showing pity, sympathetic

compañero friend, companion, "mate" (*as in roommate, classmate, etc.*)

compañía: hacerle — a uno to keep someone company

compartir to share

compás *m.* compass; beat, rhythm

complacencia pleasure, satisfaction

complacer to please; **—se (en)** to take pleasure (in), be pleased (with)

complaciente agreeable, kind

cómplice *m., f. n.* accomplice; *adj.* helping, protective

componer to fix, adjust, repair

compra purchase

comprensivo understanding

comprobar (ue) to verify, confirm, substantiate, prove

comprometedor compromising

comprometer to compromise; **—se** to become engaged; to commit oneself

comprovinciano *person from the same province*

compuesto *p. part. of* **componer;** dressed up, made up; tidy

con que so (*sent. introducer*)

concertar (ie) una entrevista to arrange, set up an interview

concienzudamente conscientiously

concluir to finish, end; **— de +** *inf.* to finish + *pr. part.* (e.g., **Concluyó de comer.** She finished eating.)

concordar (ue) to agree, tally

concurrir (a) to attend, show up (at), go (to)

concurso aid, assistance

condiscípulo classmate

conducir to lead, direct, take, conduct; to carry, drive

conductor *m.* driver; conductor (*Mex.*)

conejo rabbit

confabularse to plot, scheme
conferencia speech, lecture
confesionario confessional
confianza trust, reliability, familiarity, "closeness"
confianzudo confident, trusting
confiar (í) to confide, trust; **—se** to trust, entrust
confitería cafe; snack bar
conformarse (con) to make do (with); to go along (with); to decide (to), agree (to), resign oneself (to)
conforme agreed; as soon as; according to the way, accordingly; **— a** in accordance with
confundir to confuse, mix (up)
congestionado congested, flushed
congoja grief, affliction, distress
congregar to gather together (*trans.*); **—se** to gather together, congregate (*intrans.*)
conjunto combination
cono de hormigas ant hill
conocedor *adj.* expert, competent (*as a connoisseur*)
conocer to know, be acquainted with; **dar a —** to make known
conocido acquaintance, friend
conocimiento knowledge
consabido well-known
consagrar to consecrate, dedicate
consecución acquisition, attainment
conseguir (i, i) to obtain, get, gain; **— +** *inf.* to get to, be able to, manage to + *v.*
consejo piece, bit, word of advice; *pl.* advice
conservar to retain, keep
consiguiente resulting
constancia record, account, proof, evidence
constar de to consist of, be composed of

consuelo consolation, comfort
contabilidad bookkeeping, accounting
contador bookkeeper, accountant
contaduría accounting office, department
contar (ue) to tell, relate; to count
contener (ie) to hold, contain
contenido *n.* contents; *adj.* prudent, careful, restrained, controlled, moderate
contestar to answer
contiguo adjoining
continuación: a — next, following
continuo: acto — immediately afterward
contoneo swaying
contorno vicinity; outline, form
contra: a la — against it; **dar —** to hit against; **en — de** contrary to
contraer to contract
contrariar (í) to upset, annoy
contrariedad annoyance
contrario adverse, contrary; **por el —** on the other hand; **todo lo —** just the opposite
contrasentido contradiction
contratar to engage, rent
contratiempo snag, problem
contraveneno antidote
contundente forceful
conveniente desirable, suitable, fitting, proper; **—mente** *adv.* in the right way, as one is supposed to
convenir (ie) to be desirable, suitable, fitting, proper; to agree
conventillo tenement house, slum dwelling
convento monastery
convertir (ie, i) to turn into (*trans.*); **—se en** to turn into, become
convivir to coexist
copa drink (*alcoholic*); wine glass

copera waitress, bar maid
copetudo high, lofty
copudo thick-topped (*tree*)
corazón *m.* heart
cordón *m.* cord; curb
corista chorus girl, dancing girl
coro chorus, choir; **a (en) —** in chorus (unison)
corola corolla, petals
corona ring; crown
coronar to crown, top
corporeidad body weight
correaje *m.* leather strap
corredizo *adj.* moving, sliding
corredor *m.* front porch
corregir (i, i) to correct
correntón *m.* gust
correr to run; to pursue, chase; to go through, over; to undergo; to slide, move over (*trans.*); **—se** to slide, move over (*intrans.*)
corriente *f.* current; **darle la — a uno** to humor someone; **llevarla la — a uno** to let someone have his own way; *adv.* **—mente** in the usual way
cortadera *type of sharp-bladed grass*
cortajeado scuffed
cortante cutting
cortapapeles *m. sing.* letter opener
cortaplumas *m. sing.* penknife
cortar to cut (off); to hang up (*telephone*)
corte *m.* cut, cutting; *f.* court
cortejar to court, woo
cortésmente courteously
corteza bark (*tree*)
cortina curtain; **— metálica** steel shutter (*rolled down over store fronts at night*)
cosa thing; **— de** a matter of; about, more or less; **— de pensarlo** something to think about; **gran —** much, very much

coser to sew
costado side; **de —** on one's side
costar (ue) to cost; to be hard, difficult; **— poco** to be easy
costear to go along the edge of, pass close to; to go along the coast
costilla rib
costoso expensive, costly
costumbre *f.* custom; **de —** usual
cráneo skull, head
crecer to grow, increase (*intrans.*)
crecido large
creciente growing, increasing
crédito belief, faith
creencia belief
creer: ¡Ya lo creo! Of course!, Yes, indeed!
crepitaciones *pl.* crackling
crepitar to crackle
crepuscular *adj.* twilight
criado servant
crianza breeding
criar (í) to raise, bring up
crin *f.* mane
criollita *dim. of* **criolla** *f. creole (woman of European descent born in Spanish America)*
crispado curled, contracted, twisted
cristal *m.* glass, crystal
criterio judgment, discernment
cromo picture
crónica chronicle
crujido rustle; creak
crujiente *adj.* rustling; creaking, crackling
cruz cross; withers (*highest part of horse's back at base of neck*); **— gamada** swastika
cruzar to cross
cuadernillo open envelope or folder to hold tickets
cuadra city block

cuadrante *m.* dial

cuadrilla crew, gang (*of workers*)

cuadro square; **a —s** checkered

cuajado ornately decorated; encrusted

cual: cada — each one; **tal o —** such-and-such, so-and-so

cuan how (*used only before adj. and adv.*)

cuando: — menos at least; **de — en —** from time to time; **de vez en —** from time to time, now and then

cuanto all that, everything that, as much as; **— antes** without delay, as soon as possible, immediately; **en —** as soon as; **unos —s** a few, some

cubierto *p. part. of* **cubrir: a —** protected

cubilete *m.* cup (*for rolling dice*)

cuchichear to whisper

cuchillero thug, street brawler

cuchillo knife

cuchufleta joke, wisecrack

cuello neck

cuenta bill, account; **a — de** through the fault of; **cobrar una —** to settle an account; **dar — (de)** to give an account (of), relate; **darse — (de)** to realize, become aware of; **por su —** on one's own; **tomar en —** to take into account

cuentagotas *m. sing.* medicine dropper

cuento story, tale

cuerda rope, string; **— de colgar la ropa** clothesline; **dar — a** to wind (*a timepiece*)

cuero leather

cuerpo body; **— de policía** police force

cuervo crow

cueva cave, opening

cuidado care; be careful; **— con** watch out for, careful with

cuidadosamente carefully

cuidar to care for; **—(se) de** + *inf.* to take care (be careful) to + *v.;* **— de** + *n.* to take care of + *n.*

cuitado unfortunate

culata end of the bolt chamber of a gun

culpa blame, guilt; **tener la —** to be to blame

culpable blameworthy, guilty

culpar to blame

cultivo cultivated field

cumbre *f.* peak

cumplimiento fulfillment; performance; compliance

cumplir to fulfill, carry out, keep, observe; comply with; to keep one's word; **— ... años** to be . . . years old

cuna family, lineage; cradle

cundir to grow, flourish, expand

cuñada sister-in-law

cuota dues

curarse to get well

curiosear to look around

curtiembre *f.* tannery

cúspide *f.* tip, point

cutis *f.* skin, complexion

cuyo whose

D

dado que given the fact that, since

dado die; *pl.* dice

daga dagger

dama lady; queen (*chess*)

damnificado injured party

dañino harmful

daño harm, damage, injury; **hacerle — a uno** to hurt someone

dar to give; to strike (*the hour*) (e.g., **Dieron las cinco.** The clock struck five.); **— a** to face; **— a conocer** to

make known; — **a entender** to lead
to believe, imply, insinuate; — **caza**
to hunt, pursue; — **con** to come across;
— **contra** to hit against; — **cuenta**
(de) to give an account (of), relate;
— **cuerda a** to wind (*a timepiece*); — **de**
baja to discharge; — **de comer** to
feed; — **de mamar** to nurse (*an infant*);
— **en** to take to, get into the habit of;
— **la vuelta (a)** to go around; — **las**
buenas noches to say goodnight;
— **que hablar** to give occasion for talk,
comment; — **razón a** to confirm;
— **sobre** to fall (hit) on; — **un brinco**
(salto) to jump, take a jump; — **una**
mirada to take a glance, look; — **un**
paso to take a step; — **una vuelta** to
take a walk, turn; — **voces de socorro**
to call for help; — **vuelta** to turn
around; — **vueltas** to walk around;
—**le a uno por** + *inf.* to take a notion +
inf.; —**le la corriente a uno** to humor
someone; —**le la gana a uno** for someone to feel like; —**se a** + *inf.* to devote
oneself to, take to, up + *pr. part.;* —**se**
cuenta (de) to realize, become aware
of; —**se el caso** to happen; —**se por**
satisfecho to be satisfied; —**se prisa**
to hurry; —**se una vuelta** to turn
around

dársena dock, wharf

dato fact; *pl.* information, data

deber *m. n.* duty, obligation; homework
assignment; *v.* to owe; to be supposed
to, should, ought to, must; — **(de)** *used*
to express conjecture, probability (e.g.,
Deben (de) ser las ocho. *It must be [is*
probably] eight o'clock.); —**se** to be due

debidamente duly, in the proper fashion

debido due

débil weak

debilidad weakness

decible utterable

decir (i): — **entre dientes** to mutter; **a**
— **verdad** to tell the truth; **es** — that is
to say; **oír** — to hear, hear it said; **por**
así —**lo** to put it one way, in a manner
of speaking; **querer** — to mean

declinación fall, end

decreciente declining, decreasing

dedicar to devote, dedicate

dedo finger, toe

definitivamente finally

defunción death, decease (*legal*)

deglutir to swallow

degollar (üe) to cut a person's throat

dejar to let, allow, permit; to leave;
— **caer** to drop; —**(se) de** + *inf.* to
stop + *pr. part.* (e.g., **Dejó de escribir.**
He stopped writing.); **no** — **de** + *inf.*
not to fail, be sure + *inf.* (e.g., **No deje**
de llamarla. Don't fail [be sure] to
call her.)

delantal *m.* apron

delantero *adj.* front

delatar to give away, betray

delator *m.* informer, stool pigeon; *adj.*
accusing, betraying

deleite *m.* delight

deletrear to spell

deleznable fragile, insubstantial

delgado slender, thin

delicadeza daintiness, tenderness

delicioso delightful

delirio delirium, ravings

delito crime

demacrado emaciated

demanda: en — **de** asking for

demás *pl.* rest, other(s)

demoler (ue) to demolish, tear down

¡Demonios! The devil!
demora delay
demorar to delay
denostar (ue) to condemn
deporte *m.* sport
deportivo *adj.* sport(s)
depósito depot, warehouse
derecho *n.* right, privilege; *adj.*
   right(-hand)
derramar to pour, spill; to shed
derribar to destroy, raze, knock down
derroche *m.* flood, proliferation; squan-
   dering, waste
derrota defeat
derrotar to defeat
desafiante defiant
desafiar (í) to challenge
desafinado out of tune
desafío challenge
desaforado outrageous, wild, extraordi-
   nary, crazy
desagradecido ungrateful
desagrado displeasure
desalentado out of breath
desaliento dejection, dismay
desamargar to make less bitter
desamparado unprotected, abandoned
desangrar to drain the blood
desapacible harsh, unpleasant
desarmar to take apart
desarrapado ragged
desarrollar to develop, carry out
desasosegado uneasy, anxious
desatar to untie
desayunar to eat breakfast
desayuno breakfast
desazón *f.* annoyance, displeasure
desbande *m.* rush of people trying to get
   out of the way or to go somewhere
desbocado runaway (*horse*)

desbordante overflowing
desbordarse to come out of, overflow
descalabrarse to fracture one's skull
descalzo barefoot
descampado open fields
descansar to rest
descanso rest
descartado discarded, pushed aside
descascarado peeled, with the bark
   stripped off
descendiente *m.* descendant
descolgar (ue) to unhook, take down; to
   lift, pick up (*telephone receiver*)
descolorido faded, pale
descomponerse to separate, come apart,
   break down
descompostura disorder, upset
descompuesto broken, upset
desconcierto uneasiness, uncertainty
desconocido unknown, strange;
   n. stranger
desconocimiento ignorance, lack of
   familiarity
descosido stitches that have come out
descoyuntar to dislocate
descubrimiento discovery
descubrir to uncover, discover
descuento discount
descuidado careless
descuidar to overlook, neglect, disregard
desde from, since; **— luego** of course;
   — hace *shows lapse of time* (e.g., **Vivo
   aquí desde hace cinco años.** I've
   been living here for five years.)
desdecirse (i) to retract
desdeñar to disdain, scorn; **—se de** to
   disdain, scorn
desdeñoso disdainful
desdichado unhappy, unfortunate
desear to desire; to wish

desechar to discard, cast off

desembocar to come into, flow into

desempedrar to tear up

desempeñar to perform, discharge; to redeem, take out of pawn

desenfado ease, naturalness

desenfrenado unrestrained

desenfundar to take out of a holster

desengañado disillusioned, disappointment

desenlace *m.* conclusion (*of the plot of a story*)

desentenderse (ie) to feign ignorance, pay no attention

desentendido: hacerse el — to play dumb

desentonado discordant, out of tune

desentrañar to unravel, get to the bottom of

desenvainar to unsheathe

desenvoltura ease, freedom, confidence, poise

desenvuelto free, confident, open

deseo wish, desire

deseoso desirous

desequilibrado mentally unbalanced

desesperación desperation, despair

desesperado desperate

desesperante maddening, desperate

desesperanza desperation

desesperar(se) to lose hope

desfile *m.* parade

desfondado with the bottom out

desgarradura break, tear

desgarrar to tear, claw

desgraciado unfortunate

desgranar to spell out

deshacer to destroy, cut to pieces; **—se** to be overwhelmed, overcome; to come apart, fall off; **—se de** to get rid of

deshilachado shabby, worn, frayed

desierto desert

designio plan

desistir to stop, cease

deslizar to slip, slide; **—se** to slip, slide, slither, glide

deslumbrado puzzled, bewildered

desmayado in a faint, unconscious

desmayarse to faint

desmoronarse to crumble, fall apart

desnucarse to break one's neck

desnudo naked, bare

desocupado idle; free, vacant

desoír to ignore, turn a deaf ear to

desorbitado disproportionate, excessive

desordenado wild, irregular

despachar to deal with, attend to; to take care of; to dismiss, put away, send away

despacho office

despacito very slowly, very softly; *dim. of* **despacio**

desparpajo ease, self-confidence

despatarrado stupified, motionless, dumbfounded

despavorido terrified

despecho scorn

despectivamente contemptuously

despedazado ruined, broken, crumbled

despedida farewell

despedir (i, i) to dismiss, fire, discharge; **—se (de)** to say good-by (to), take leave (of)

despegar to unglue, separate, detach, remove

despejar to clear

desperezarse to stretch (*with arms up in the air*)

despertar (ie) to wake up (*trans.*); **—(se)** to wake up (*intrans.*)

despilchado poorly dressed (*Arg. slang*)

despistar to throw off the track

desplegado unfolded, opened up

despoblado deserted

despojado free, stripped

despojar to strip, deprive, divest, denude

despojo loot, war trophy; *pl.* spoils, ruins

despotismo tyranny, despotism

despreciar to scorn

desprecio scorn, contempt

desprender to remove, detach; —**se** to come (peel) off, come loose, separate, detach

desprendido detached

despreocupar to put someone's mind at ease; —**se** to become at ease, indifferent

desprevenido unready, unwarned, unwary

desprolijo untidy

desprovisto (de) bare, lacking, deprived (of)

desquiciarse to become unhinged, disordered

destacarse to stand out, be prominent

destartalado poorly furnished

destejer to undo, unravel knitting

destello flash

destemplado out of tune

desteñido faded

destiempo: a — at the wrong time

destreza skill, agility

destrozado ruined, destroyed

destrozar to ruin, destroy

desvalido helpless

desvanecerse to vanish; to fade, melt away

desvanecido vanished, out of sight, disappearing from sight; in a faint

desvanecimiento dizzy spell

desvelar(se) to stay awake, not to be sleepy

desvestir (i, i) to undress

desviar (í) to deflect, warn off; —**se** to stray, deviate, get sidetracked

detención stopping, halt

detener (ie) to stop, hold back; to arrest, detain; —**se** to stop

detenido slow, careful, thorough

detenimiento care, thoroughness

detonador *m.* detonator

devastar to destroy, ruin

devolución return

devolver (ue) to return, give back

di *imp. familiar of* **decir**

día: al otro — on the next day

diablo devil

diafanidad transparency, translucency

diáfano translucent; of very light texture

diariamente on a daily basis

diario *n.* daily newspaper; *adj.* daily

diarista *m., f.* writer for a daily newspaper

dibujar to draw, sketch; —**se** to stand out, be seen, displayed, outlined

dicha happiness, good fortune

dicho *p. part. of* **decir**; — **y hecho** no sooner said than done; **lo —** as I (you, he, etc.) have said; *n.* saying, proverb; **mejor —** rather, better said, I mean to say, more precisely

dichoso happy, fortunate

diente *m.* tooth; **decir entre —s** to mutter

diestro right-handed

digitado with fingers

digno worthy; — **de fe** trustworthy

dilatar to stretch out, lengthen, widen

diluir to dilute

diminuto tiny, minute

dique *m.* dike

directorio board of directors

dirigible blimp, dirigible

dirigir to direct; to send; **—se a** to turn to, go up to, go toward; to address, speak to

díscolo unruly

disculpa apology

disculparse to apologize

discurrir to pass, flow by

discurso speech

discutir to argue; to discuss

disecado stuffed, mounted

disfrazar to disguise

disfrutar (de) to enjoy, benefit (from)

disfrute *m.* enjoyment

disgustado displeased

disgusto displeasure, disagreement, unpleasant occurrence

disimulado feigned, fake

disimular to hide, disguise; to pretend

disminución loss, decrease

disminuir to lessen, diminish

disolverse (ue) (de) to disappear; to dissolve

disparar to shoot, fire

disparate *m.* nonsense

dispensar to excuse

displicencia disagreeableness, displeasure

disponer to order, command; **— de** to have available; **—se a** + *inf.* to get ready to + *v.*

dispositivo device, contrivance

dispuesto *p. part. of* **disponer** ready, inclined, disposed

distinguir to make (pick) out, distinguish

distraer to distract

divagación digression; *pl.* wandering, rambling

divagar to roam

divertido enjoyable, amusing

divertir (ie, i) to amuse; **—se** to enjoy oneself, have a good time

divisar to sight, see, perceive at a distance, spot, make out

doblar to bend (over), fold, flex; to turn

dócil docile, meek

dolencia illness, ailment

doler (ue) to hurt, pain

dolor *m.* pain

dolorcillo little pain, twinge

dolorido sore, painful

dolorosamente painfully

dominar + *language* to speak + *language* + fluently

don *m.* gift, talent

dorado golden

dormir (ue, u) to sleep; **— como un bendito** to sleep like a baby; **—se** to go to sleep, fall asleep

dormitorio bedroom

dorso back

dosis *f. sing.* dose

dotar to give (*as a gift*)

dote *f.* dowry

duda doubt

dudar to doubt

duende *m.* goblin, elf

dueño owner

dulce *m. n.* piece of candy; *adj.* sweet

dulzura sweetness, softness

durar to last

dureza hardness

durmiente *m.* railroad tie

duro *n.* dollar, peso; *adj.* hard, tough; **a —as penas** with great difficulty

E

echado lying, stretched out

echar to stick out; to throw, toss; to put; to pour; to mail; **— a** + *inf.* to begin to

+ *v.;* — **a perder** to spoil, ruin; — **de menos** to miss; — **llave** to lock; — **mano de** to make use of; — **una ojeada** to take a quick look, glance

edad age

editorial *f.* publishing house

educación upbringing, training, breeding

educar to raise, bring up, train

efectivamente really, actually, as a matter of fact, in effect

efecto: en — as a matter of fact, in fact, in effect, indeed

eficacia efficacy, worth, effectiveness

eficaz efficatious, effective

efímero fleeting, ephemeral

eje *m.* axle

ejecutar to carry out

ejercer to exercise

ejercitar to exercise

ejército army

elaborar to make, manufacture, work out

eléctrico: linterna —a flashlight

elegir (i, i) to elect, choose

elevarse to rise

emanación glow

embalar to wrap

embalsamado embalmed

embanderar to decorate with banners or flags

embarcar to board (*a ship*), embark

embargado *p. part. of* **embargar** to impede, hinder

embargo: sin — however, nevertheless

embaucar to deceive, trick

embelesado charmed, delighted, enraptured

embobado fascinated

embolsar to pocket

emborracharse to get drunk

emboscada ambush

embotamiento dullness

embriagador intoxicating

embrujado bewitched, haunted

embrutecido depraved

embutir to imbed, force into

empalme *m.* road junction, freeway exit or entrance

empañado tarnished, sullied, cloudy, dim, misty, faint, dull

empapar to soak

empaque *m.* look, appearance

empeñar to pawn; **—se (en)** to insist (on), persist (in)

empeño effort

empero nevertheless

empezar (ie) (a + *inf.*) to begin (+ *inf.*)

empinarse to rise up

emplasto poultice

emplazar to summon

empleado employee

emplear to employ; to use

empleo employment; use

emponchado with a poncho on

emponzoñado poisoned

emprender to undertake

empresa company, firm; enterprise, undertaking

empresario *adj.* business

empujar to push

empujón *m.* push, shove

empuñadura hilt, handle, grip (*knife*)

empuñar to clutch, grab, grip

en: — **cuanto** as soon as; — **eso** just then, at that moment; — **fin** anyway

enaltecer to ennoble

enamorarse (de) to fall in love (with)

encaminarse a to set out, head for

encantador charming, delightful, enchanting

encantar to charm, delight, enchant

encanto charm, delight, enchantment, magic

encaramarse to climb (up)
encarar to face, confront
encarcelar to jail, imprison, incarcerate
encarecer to promote, favor
encargado person in charge
encargar to order, assign; **—se de** to take charge of
encargo charge, order
encarnar to embody, personify
enceguecido blinded, enraged
enceguedor blinding
encender (ie) to light; to turn on
encendido bright, lit, burning
encerado waxed
encerrar (ie) to enclose; to shut (lock) up
encía gum (*mouth*)
encierro confinement, being closed up
encima (de) on top (of), over; on one's person; **por — de** on top of
encogerse to shrink; **— de hombros** to shrug one's shoulders
encogido huddled
encomendar (ie) to commend, entrust, put in the hands of
encomienda parcel
encontrar (ue) to find, meet; **—se con** to meet, run into; **—se en falta** to be mistaken
encorvado curved
encrespado curled up
encristalado *adj.* glass
encuadrar to frame; **—se** to fit
encuentro meeting; **al — de** to meet (e.g., **Salió al encuentro de su amigo.** He went out to meet his friend.)
endeble feeble, frail
endemoniado demoniacal, devilish
enderezar to go straight; to straighten out
enebro juniper
enérgico energetic

enfadarse to get angry
enfermedad illness, sickness
enfermería infirmary
enfermizo sickly
enfrentar to face
enfrente *adv.* across the street
enfriamiento chill, chilling
enfundado encased, in a holster
enfurecerse to get furious
enfurecido furious
engañar to fool, cheat, deceive
engarzado joined, set in
engendro monster
engolfar to engulf, plunge
engorroso bothersome, trying
enharinado whitened with flour
enjambre *m.* swarm
enjugar to wipe dry
enlazar to join, unite, link, bind
enloquecer to drive crazy, madden
enmascarado masked
enmohecerse to get rusty
enmohecido rusty
enmudecer to become silent
ennegrecido blackened
ennoblecer to ennoble, embellish
enojarse to get annoyed, angry
enorgullecerse to become proud
enredadera vine
enredado tangled, caught
enrojecido reddened, reddish
ensangrentado bloody
ensayar to test, try (out); to rehearse; **—se** to try
enseñanza teaching, education
enseñar to teach; **— a** + *inf.* to show how + *inf.*
ensillar to saddle
ensombrecido shaded, in shadow
ensueño illusion, fantasy, daydream
entablado herded (*Arg.*)

entablar to initiate, start, begin

ente *m.* being, entity

entender (ie) to understand; **—se** to imagine, understand; **—se con** to handle; to get along with; **dar a —** to lead to believe, imply, insinuate

entendimiento understanding, knowledge

enterarse (de) to find out (about), be informed (of)

entero entire, full

enterrar (ie) to bury

entidad entity, organization

entonar to sing, intone

entonces: en ese — at that time

entornado ajar, half-open

entorpecerse to slow down, be delayed

entorpecimiento delay, slowdown

entrada entrance; admission ticket; **de —** right away, from the start

entrañable strong, deep; intense

entrañas *pl.* innards, intestines, entrails

entreabrir to open half-way, part-way

entrecejo brow

entrecerrado half-open

entrecruzar to crisscross, interlace

entrega delivery

entregar to give up, surrender, hand over; to deliver; **—se a** to give oneself over to, lose oneself in

entrelazado intertwined

entrelazar to intertwine

entrenamiento training

entretanto meanwhile

entretener (ie) to entertain

entrever to glimpse, just make out, catch a glimpse of

entrevista: concertar una — to arrange, set up an interview

entristecer to sadden

entrometerse to intrude, interfere, butt in

entusiasmado enthusiastic

envenenar to poison

enviar (í) to send

envidiar to envy

envidioso envious, jealous

envoltura covering, wrapping, "skin"

envolver (ue) to wrap

envuelto *p. part. of* **envolver**

equivaler (a) to be equivalent (to), be worth the same

equivocar to mistake; **—se** to make a mistake

érase (*imperf. of* **ser** + **se**) once upon a time there was (*used to begin a story*)

erguido upright

erguirse (ye, i) to straighten up

erigir to erect

erizado raised

errante *adj.* wandering

errar (ye) to miss, err; to wander

es decir that is to say

esbelto slender, well-built

escala stop, stopping place; scale

escalera stairway

escalerilla boarding steps

escalinata set of steps

escalofrío chill

escalón *m.* step

escándalo tumult, improper conduct; scandal

escaparate *m.* store display window

escarmentar (ie) to take warning, learn one's lesson

escasear to be scarce

escaso scarce, scanty

escena scene

escéptico skeptical

escogido elite, classy

escolar *m. n.* schoolboy; *adj.* school, academic

escombros *pl.* rubble, debris

escribir: máquina de — typewriter

esforzarse (ue) por + *inf.* to make an effort + *inf.*

esfuerzo effort

esfumar to soften, blur; **—se** to disappear, vanish, melt away

esguince *m.* slight movement, jerk

eslabón *m.* link (*of a chain*)

esmaltado enameled

esmalte *m.* enamel

esmerado careful, neat, fastidious

esmeralda emerald

esmeril *m.* emery

eso that; **— sí** that's for sure; **en —** just then, at that moment; **por —** therefore

espada sword

espalda back (*of a human*); **de —s** on one's back; with one's back toward

espantar to frighten, terrify; to shoo off

espanto fright, terror

espantoso frightful, dreadful

esparcirse to spread

especie *f.* kind, type

espejismo mirage, illusion

esperanza hope

esperanzado hopeful

espeso thick (*nonsolid substance*)

espetar to quiz, grill

espía *m.* spy

espina fishbone; thorn

espinazo spinal column

esposas *pl.* handcuffs

espuma foam

espumarajo froth (*at the mouth*)

espumoso foamy

esquila bell

esquina corner (*outside*)

esquinado sharp corner

esquivo aloof, unsociable, shy

estación season; station

estada stay, sojourn

estadística statistics

estallar to explode, break out (*war*)

estallido explosion

estampa picture

estampido crack, report of a gun

estante *m.* shelf

estar: — de vuelta to be back, return; **— para (por)** + *inf.* to be about (ready) + *inf.;* **—se** to be, stay, remain

estatura figure; height

estatuario statuesque

éste the latter (*lit.* this one)

estelar stellar

estilo: de — usual, customary; **por el —** like that

estirar to stretch

esto: en — just then

estoico stoic

estómago stomach

estorbar to disturb, get in the way

estrado stage platform, dais

estragar to despoil, ruin

estrago havoc, ruin

estrechar to shake (*one's hand*)

estrechez austerity, poverty

estrecho narrow, close

estrella star

estrellado starry

estremecer(se) to shake, tremble, shudder, shiver

estremecimiento shudder, shiver; thrill

estrépito noise, ruckus

estrepitosamente noisily

estriado grooved, striated

estridente harsh, strident

estropear to injure, cripple

estruendo noise, racket, din
estrujar to wring, squeeze
estrujón *m.* squeezing, pressing
estuario estuary, meeting of the mouth of a river and the sea's tides
estuche *m.* box, case
estufa stove
estupefacto stupified
estupidez stupidity
etéreo ethereal, delicate, airy
eterno eternal
etiqueta label
evasiva evasion
evitar to avoid
exangüe bloodless, anemic
exánime lifeless
exigencia demand, need, exigency
exigente demanding
exigir to demand
éxito success
expectativa expectation
expedición sale
expediente *m.* means, resource, device
expedir (i, i) to order, issue
expender to sell
experiencia experiment; experience
explicar to explain; —**se** to understand, see
expuesto *p. part. of* **exponer**; liable, exposed
expulsar to expel, get rid of
extender (ie) to draw up (*document*)
extenuarse (ú) to languish
extirpar to eradicate, root out
extorsionar to extort
extranjero foreign; **al** — abroad
extrañar to surprise, seem strange; to miss
extrañeza strangeness, oddness; surprise
extraño *adj.* strange; *n.* "outsider"

extraviar (í) to lose, misplace; —**se** to get lost, misplaced
extremo: en — a great deal
exvoto votive offering

F

fabricación manufacture
fabricar to make
fabril *adj.* manufacturing
facción feature; *pl.* face
fachada façade, front
facultad college, school (*of a university*)
falacia fallacy, myth, false notion
falange *m.* bone of the finger
falda slope; skirt
falla defect, failure, handicap
fallar to fail
fallecer to pass away, succumb
fallecimiento death
fallo mistake
falsa: llave — passkey
falta lack, need; error, mistake; **encontrarse en** — to be mistaken; **hacer** — to be necessary, needed
faltar to be lacking, missing, needed; — **(a)** to be absent (from), miss
fama fame
fanfarrón *m.* boaster, loudmouth
fango mud
fantasear to fantasize
fantaseoso fantasizing, given to fantasy
fantasma *m.* ghost, spirit, phantom
farol *m.* streetlight, lamp
fastidio arrogance, nuisance
fastidioso annoying, bothersome
fastuoso pompous, lavish
fatiga fatigue, weariness

fatigar to fill (*figurative*)

fatigoso tiresome; **— amente** laboriously

fauna the animals from a given region

favor: a — de with the help of; **por —** please

faz face

fe *f.* trust, faith, credence; **digno de —** trustworthy

fechar to date (*mark with the date*)

fecundo fertile, fruitful

felizmente happily

felpa plush, felt (*material*)

feo ugly

feria fair, festival

ferrocarril *m.* railroad, railway

ferrocarrilero *adj.* railroad

ferroviario *adj.* railroad

festejar to celebrate; to admire, praise

feúcho ugly, homely

fiambre *m.* cold food (*as cold cuts*)

fichero file (*for records*)

fidedigno trustworthy, creditable

fiebre *f.* fever

fiel faithful

fiera beast, wild animal

figa fig

figurar to have the shape of; **—se** to imagine

figurilla *dim. of* **figura** shape, form, figure

fijamente steadily, unwaveringly

fijar to fix, establish; **—se (en)** to notice, observe

fijeza firmness, fixity, fixedness

fijo fixed

fila row, line

filiación description

filial *f.* subsidiary, branch

filo line; edge of a blade

fin: al — finally, after all; **al — y al cabo** after all; **en —** anyway; **por —** finally, at last

finca farm

fingir to feign, simulate, pretend

finura refinement

firmar to sign

firulete *m.* contorsion, quick circular movement

fiscal *m.* prosecuting attorney

fisgón *m.* snooper

fisonomía face

fláccido soft, flabby

flaco thin, skinny

flamante brand new; bright, polished

flamear to flutter

flamígero flaming

flanco side, flank

flanqueado flanked, standing beside

flaqueza weakness

flecha arrow

flexionado bent

flor *f.* flower

florecer to blossom, flower; to flourish

florero flower vase

florido flowery, showy

florón *m.* big flower

fluctuante floating, fluctuating

fogonero fireman, stoker (*on a ship*)

follaje *m.* foliage

fonda inn

fondo bottom, depth; background; back, rear (*of a house, room, etc.*); **telón de —** backdrop

forastero stranger (*from another city or town*)

forense *m.* coroner

forjado wrought, built, constructed

fornido husky

forrado lined
fortuna: por — fortunately
forzado compelled, forced
forzar (ue) to break open
fosa grave, hole, ditch
fósforo match
fracaso failure, "flop"
fracasar to fail
fraile *m.* friar, monk
franquear to open, clear, pass, get through
frasco bottle, flask
frenar to check, restrain
frenesí *m.* frenzy
frenético frenzied
freno brake
frente *f.* forehead; *m.* front; **— a** opposite; in front of, facing; **al —** opposite, across the street; **en —** opposite, in front
fresco *n.* cool, coolness; **tomar el —** to get some fresh air; *adj.* fresh, cool; ruddy, healthy
frescura coolness; freshness
fresquito very fresh *dim. of* **fresco**
frialdad coldness
frotar to rub
fruncido wrinkled
fruncir to pleat, gather
fuego fire
fuente *f.* fountain, stream; large serving dish
fuera away; off (with); **— (de)** outside (of), out (of)
fuerte: caja — safe, strongbox
fuertemente tightly
fuerza(s) force, strength; **a la —** by force, against one's will, under pressure; **por —** necessarily, compulsively, against one's will; **sin —** exhausted
fuga flight

fugaz fleeting
fulgor *m.* brilliance
fulgurar to flash
fullero "shady," dishonest
fumar to smoke
funda slipcover, cover; case
funesto fatal, disastrous
furor *m.* rage, fury
fusil *m.* rifle
fútbol *m.* soccer

G

galantear to court, pay attention to
galería hall
gallardo gallant, proud, dashing
gallina hen
galpón *m.* shed
gamada: cruz — swastika
gana desire, whim; **darle la — a uno** for someone to feel like; **de buena —** willingly; **de mala —** unwillingly; **tener —s (de)** to feel like
ganar to gain; to earn; to win; to get to, reach; **—se el pan** to earn a living
gangoso twangy, nasal
gansa female goose
garabatear to scribble, scrawl
garbo jauntiness, grace
garboso jaunty, graceful
garganta throat
gargantillo *South American songbird*
garra claw, talon
garrafal enormous, monumental
gas lacrimógeno tear gas
gastar to waste, spend; to wear out (*trans.*); **—se** to wear out (*intrans.*)
gasto expense
gaveta small drawer

gemido moan, cry, groan
gemir (i, i) to moan
genial brilliant
genio genius
germencito seed
gesto face, expression; gesture
gira trip, visit
girar to spin, turn, swing, rotate; **— en redondo** to spin, turn around
globo balloon
glutinoso gluey, sticky
gobernar (ie) to rule, direct
goce *m.* joy
golosina, sweet, "goody"
goloso greedy, "sweet-toothed," glutton
golpe *m.* blow; **de —** suddenly
golpear to hit, knock, strike, beat
golpecito tap, rap
golpeo beating
gota drop
gotera leak
goterón *m.* large drop, glob
gozar (de, con) to enjoy
grabadora tape recorder
gracia: hacer — to be funny
gracioso funny
gradas *pl.* gallery (*of an amphitheater*)
grado degree (*of temperature*)
gramilla grass
granate *adj.* garnet, deep red
gran cosa much, very much
grandullón *m.* big brute
grasoso greasy
gresca uproar, row
griego Greek
gris gray
gritar to cry out, shout, scream
gritería shouting
grito cry, shout, scream
gritón loud-mouthed

grosería rudeness, boorishness; coarse word, action
grosero rude, crude, boorish, coarse, rough
grúa crane, derrick
grueso thick, heavy
gruñir to growl
gruta cavern, grotto
guante *m.* glove
guapo *adj.* good-looking; tough
guardar to keep; to put away
guarida lair, den
guía guide, guidebook, directory, telephone book
guiar (í) to guide, lead
guijarro pebble, stone
guiñapo tattered rag
guiño wink
guisar to cook
guiso stew, cooked dish
gula gluttony, greed
gusano worm
gusto pleasure; taste

H

haber to have *aux.;* **— de** to be supposed to, be to, have to; **— que** to be necessary to
habilitación backing (*business*)
habitación room
habituarse (ú) (a) to become accustomed (to)
hablar: dar que — to give occasion for talk, comment
hacendado rancher, landowner
hacer to do, make; **desde —** shows lapse of time (e.g., **Vivo aquí desde hace cinco años** or **Hace cinco años que**

vivo aquí I've been living here for five years; **Llegué hace pocos días** I arrived a few days ago); expresses weather (e.g., **Hace calor.** It's hot.); — **burla de** to mock; — **caso (de)** to pay attention (to), listen (to), heed; — **como que** + *ind.* to pretend + *inf.*; —**le compañía a uno** to keep someone company; —**le daño a uno** to hurt someone; — **falta** to be necessary, needed; — **gracia** to be funny; — **llegar** to convey, send; — **saber** to inform, notify; —**se** to "play," pretend (e.g., **No se haga el tonto.** Don't play dumb.); to become; —**se el desentendido** to play dumb; —**se el sordo** to turn a deaf ear

hacha axe

hachar to chop

hachazo blow with an axe

hacia toward

hacienda estate, ranch

hada fairy

hálito breath

hallar to find; —**se** to be, be found

hallazgo find, discovery

hambre *f.* hunger

hambriento hungry

hartarse to get one's fill, be satisfied

harto full, fed up

hastío weariness, tedium

hazaña feat, deed

hebra string, thread (*of yarn*)

hechicera witch, sorceress

hechicería witchcraft, sorcery

hechicero wizard, sorcerer

hecho *p. part. of* **hacer; dicho y** — no sooner said than done; **lo** — that which was done; *n.* fact, deed; — **de sangre** crime, bloody deed

helado *adj.* frozen, ice cold, icy; *m. n.* ice cream

helarse (ie) to freeze

hembra female

hendija crack

herboristería herb shop

heredar to inherit

herencia heredity

herida wound, injury

herido wounded, injured, struck

herir (ie, i) to wound

hermanar to harmonize

herramienta tool

herrumbrar to rust

hervir (ie, i) to boil, seethe

hiato hiatus, gap, interval

hidalgo nobleman, gentleman

hiel *f.* gall

hielo ice

hierro iron, piece of iron

higo fig

hilacha fiber, shred; "true colors"

hilarse (por) to filter (through)

hilera file, row

hilo thread, thin wire

hinchado swollen

hinchar to swell (up)

hipócrita: a —s hypocritical(ly)

hipotensión low blood pressure

historieta comic strip

hito: de — en — from head (top) to foot (bottom)

hogar *m.* fireplace, hearth; home

hoguera fire, bonfire

hoja leaf; page, sheet; blade

hojarasca dead leaves and twigs

hojear to leaf through, turn the pages

holgazán *m.* idler, loafer

holgazanería idleness, laziness

hollar (ue) to tread, trample

hombro shoulder; **encogerse de —s** to shrug one's shoulders

homicida *n., f.* murderess

hondo deep, profound
hongo mushroom
honradez honesty
honrado honest
horizonte *m.* horizon, skyline
hormiga ant; **cono de —s** anthill
hormigón *m.* concrete
hormiguear to swarm
hormigueo itching, tingling
hornillo *dim. of* **horno**
horno oven
hosco sullen, grumpy
hoy: de — en adelante from now on
hoyuelo little hole; dimple
hubo *3rd pers. pret. of* **haber** there was (were)
hueco *n.* hole, hollow, open space; *adj.* hollow; **a —as** hollow(-sounding)
huella track, trace; footprint; print
huérfano orphan
huerto orchard
hueso bone
huésped *m.* guest; host
huida flight
huir to flee
hule *m.* oilcloth; rubber
humeante steaming; smoking
humear to smoke (*intrans.*)
humedecer to wet, moisten
humedad humidity, dampness
húmedo humid, damp, wet
humilde humble
humildoso excessively humble
humillar to humiliate
humo smoke
humor *m.* mood; humor
hundir(se) to sink
húngaro Hungarian
hurgar to poke, jab, stab; to handle, move, agitate
hurto theft

I

ida: — y vuelta round trip; **boleto de —** one-way ticket
idear to conceive the idea of
idilio idyll
idioma *m.* language
ignorar not to know, to be ignorant of
igual: por — equally
igualado equalized, the same
ilimitado unlimited
ilusionista *m.* magician
imagen *f.* statue, image
imborrable indelible, unremovable
impar odd, unequal
impedir (i, i) to prevent, keep from, impede
imperioso overbearing, haughty; urgent, overriding
impermeabilizar to make waterproof
impermeable *m.* raincoat
implacable inexorable, unbending, relentless
imponente impressive
imponer to impose
impracticable rough, impassable
imprecisable unforeseeable
impreso printed
imprimir to print
impropio inappropriate, unsuited
imprudencia indiscretion
inadvertencia accident, oversight
inadvertido unnoticed
inapelable inevitable, not open to appeal
inapreciable invaluable, inestimable
inaudito unheard of, inconceivable
incapaz incapable
incendiar to set fire to
incendio fire, blaze
incipientemente just beginning
inclinado bowed, tipped

incluso even, including
inconsciente unaware, unconscious
inconveniente *m.* objection; disadvantage, obstacle, difficulty, problem; **tener — (en)** to mind, object (to)
incorporarse to sit up
incorpóreo bodiless, intangible
increpar to rebuke, chide
inculcar to inculcate, ingrain
indagar to ascertain
indecible inexpressible, indescribable
indefenso defenseless
indemnizar to pay for, compensate (*damages*)
índice *m.* index finger
indicio hint, clue
indigesto undigested
indistintamente indifferently, without distinction
ineludiblemente unavoidably, inescapably
inerte paralyzed
infaltable everpresent, unfailing
infamación infamy
infamar to dishonor, slander, defame
infamia disgrace, insult
infausto unlucky, ill-starred
infeliz unhappy
ínfimo low, vile, mean
informe *adj.* formless; *m. pl. n.* information
infortunio misfortune, bad luck
infranqueable impassable
infundir to infuse
ingeniero engineer
ingenio talent, skill, cleverness
ingenuo candid, ingenuous
ingestión *f.* eating
inglés: pase — craps (*dice game*)
ingrato unpleasant

ingravidez lightness, weightlessness
ingresar to enter, enroll
iniciar to begin, initiate
injuria insult, slander
inmóvil motionless
inmovilidad motionlessness
inmutarse to become disturbed, lose one's composure
inopinado unexpected
inquietar to make uneasy; **—se** to worry, become nervous, restless, uneasy
inquieto restless, anxious, uneasy
inquietud restlessness, uneasiness
inquilino tenant
inquina ill will
insano unhealthy
insidia snare, trap; sneakiness, treachery
insobornable incorruptible
insoportable insufferable, unbearable
instante: por —s continuously
íntegro whole, complete
intemperie *f.* bad weather
intempestivo sudden, unexpected, inopportune
intentar to try
intercalar to insert
interlocutor *m.* interlocutor (*one who takes part in a conversation*)
internarse to go into
interponer to interpose, place between
interrogante *m.* question
interrogatorio interrogation, questioning, grilling
intimar to order, require
intransitable impassable
inútil useless, unnecessary; **—mente** *adv.* in vain
inutilizar to disable, render useless
inverosímil unlikely, implausible
inversión *f.* investment

invierno winter
inyectar to inject
ir to go; **¡Vaya!** *imp.* Well! (*to express surprise or strong approval*); — + *pr. part.* to be gradually + *pr. part.*
iris: arco — rainbow
irremisiblemente irretrievably
irrumpir (en) to burst (into)
isla island
itinerario schedule, timetable
izquierdo *adj.* left

J

jactarse to brag, boast
jadear to pant, gasp
jadeo panting, heavy breathing
jamás never
jaque mate checkmate (*chess*)
jaqueca severe headache
jardín *m.* yard; garden
jaula cage
jazmín *m.* jasmine (*shrub with fragrant flowers*)
jefatura police station
jerárquico hierarchical
jinete *m.* rider (*horseback*), cavalryman
jirón *m.* shred, piece, wisp
joya jewel
jubilación retirement
jubilarse to retire
juego game
jugada move (*chess*), play; trick
jugar (ue) to play; **— sucio** to cheat; **—se** to gamble, risk
juguete *m.* toy, plaything
juguetear to frolic, cavort
juicio senses, judgment; **poner en tela de —** to question

juicioso wise, prudent
juncal *m.* field of reeds, rushes
juntar to gather, join
junto together; **— a** next to, against
juntura joint
jurar to swear, take an oath
justamente just, exactly, right; to be precise
justicieramente fairly, justly
justipreciar to evaluate
justo exact
juzgar to judge

L

laberinto labyrinth
labio lip; **sellar los —s** to silence
labrador *m.* farmer
lacrimógeno: gas — tear gas
ladear to tilt, tip
ladino sly, crafty
lado side
ladrar to bark
ladrillo brick
ladrón *m.* thief, crook
lagartija small lizard
lago lake
lágrima tear (*teardrop*)
laja rock protruding out of the water
lamentarse (de) to be sorry (about)
lamento wail, lament
lámina sheet, layer, plate
lámpara lamp
lana wool
lancha launch
languidecer to be weak, languish
lanzallamas *m. sing.* flame thrower
lanzar to launch, fling, throw; to issue, let out, emit

lápida gravestone
lares *m. pl.* home
largar to release, launch; to cast, throw
largo *n.* length; *adj.* long; **a lo — de**
lengthwise, along (the length of)
lástima pity, sympathy, sorrow; **tener —
de, a** to feel sorry for
lastimosamente painfully
lastre *m.* steadiness, good sense; ballast
lateral *adj.* side
latigazo crack, blow of a whip
látigo whip, lash
latir to beat, pulsate
lavandera laundress
lavar to wash
lavatorio lotion; lavatory
lazo tie, band, bond
lecho bed
lechoso milky
lectura reading
legista: médico — criminal pathologist
legua league (*distance of about three miles*);
a la — a mile away
legumbre *f.* vegetable
lejanía distance
lejano distant, far
lejos: a lo — in the distance
lengua language; tongue
lente *m.* lens; **—s** eyeglasses
lentitud slowness
lento slow
leña firewood
leño log; timber, piece of wood
leonado tawny
lesionado injured
letanía litany
letargo lethargy
letra letter (*of the alphabet*); handwriting
letrero sign

levantar to raise, lift; **—se** to stand up;
— vuelo to take off (*as a bird or plane*)
leve light (*in weight*), slight
levedad lightness; levity, lack of
importance
levitar to float
ley *f.* law
libar to sip
librarse (de) to be free (from), get rid of
libre: al aire — outside
librería bookstore
libreta memorandum book, notebook
licencia leave, vacation
licenciar to license; to confer a degree (on)
ligado bound, fastened
ligadura bond, tie
ligar to tie, join
ligero quick, fast; light (*in weight*)
lijado ground, worn down
lila lilac
limitar to border, bound
limonero lemon tree
limpiar to clean
limpidez cleanness, purity
limpieza cleaning, cleanliness
limpio clean, neat; **sacar en —** to
gather, conclude
lindar con to border on
linde *f.* border, edge
lineaje *m.* lineage
linfa stream
linterna lantern; **— eléctrica** flashlight
liquidación sale
lirio lily
liso smooth, flat
lisonjero flattering
listo ready
liviandad lewd, immoral behavior
liviano, light (*in weight*)

llaga wound
llama flame
llamada call
llamarada flare-up, sudden blaze, burst of flame
llameante flaming, on fire
llanos *pl.* plains, flatland
llanura flatland
llave *f.* key, electric switch; **— falsa** passkey; **echar — a** to lock
llegada arrival
llegar (a) to arrive, get (to); **— a** + *inf.* to manage (get) + *inf.;* **hacer —** to convey, send
llenar (de) to fill (with)
lleno full
llevadero bearable
llevar to carry, take; to lead; **—** + *time* + *pr. part.* to be + *pr. part.* + for + *time* (e.g., **Lleva dos años trabajando aquí** He's been working here for two years); **—le la corriente a uno** to let someone have his own way; **—se** to take away, carry off; **—se con** to get along with; **—se una sorpresa** to be surprised
llorar to cry, weep
lluvia rain
lobo wolf
lóbrego gloomy, somber, dark
locura madness, insanity
lodo mud
lograr to win, succeed; **—** + *inf.* to manage (get) + *inf.*
loro parrot
losa stone, flagstone
lote *m.* lot, group
loza china
lucecita *dim. of* **luz** light
lucha fight, battle, struggle

luchar to fight
luciérnaga firefly
lucir to shine
ludión *m.* Cartesian devil (*device used in physics*)
luego then; later; immediately, soon afterward, right away; **— de** after; **desde —** of course
lugar *m.* place; village
lugarteniente *m.* lieutenant
lúgubre mournful, gloomy
lujo luxury
lujoso luxurious, lavish, fancy
luna moon
lustro period of five years
luto: de — (dressed) in mourning
luz *f.* light

M

macilento pale, dim
macizo *n.* flower bed; *adj.* solid, massive
madeja skein (*of yarn*)
madera wood
maderero lumberman
madriguera den
madrugada dawn, early morning (*between midnight and daylight*); **muy de —** at daybreak
maduro grown-up, mature
magia magic
mágico magician
mago magician, sorcerer
majadería nonsense
mal *m.* sickness; evil, wrong; «**No hay — que por bien no venga**» "Everything turns out for the best", "Every cloud has a silver lining"; *adv.* badly, poorly; **sen-**

tarle — a uno to disagree with one, not suit one

malacara *adj.* (*Arg.*) describing a reddish-brown horse with a white forehead

maldad evil

maldecir (i) to curse, damn

maldición curse

maldito *p. part. of* **maldecir** cursed, damned

malear to spoil, sour, corrupt

malecón *m.* pier, jetty, sea wall

maleficio curse, spell

malentendido misunderstanding

malevito (*Arg.*) tough guy, criminal

malgastar to waste, squander

malo: de —a gana unwillingly

maltrecho battered

malva mallow (*type of wildflower*)

malvado evil, wicked

mamar: dar de — to nurse (*an infant*)

mamarracho grotesque figure

mamífero mammal

mamotreto huge, imposing book or volume (*slang*)

mancebo young man

mancha stain, spot

manchar to stain

manchón *m.* large stain, spot

manco one-handed; crippled in one hand or arm

mandadero errand boy, office boy

mandar to send; to command, order

manejar to drive (*vehicle*); to manage, handle

manejo use, handling

manera: de — que in such a way that, so; **de otra —** otherwise; **de todas —s** anyway

manga sleeve

mango handle

maniatar to tie one's hands

maniático fanatical, eccentric; maniacal, crazy

manicura manicurist

manifestar (ie) to declare, reveal, show, make clear, indicate; **—se** to appear

maniobra maneuver

manipuleo handling

manivela crank

mano *f.* hand; **— de pintura** coat of paint; **echar — de** to make use of; **untar la —** to grease the palm, bribe

manosear to paw, handle

manotada blow with the paw, hand

manotazo blow with the hand

manotear to cuff, flail

manotón *m.* slap with the paw

manso tame, mild, meek

manta blanket; poncho (*Chile*); **a —s** by the dozen, in abundance

mantenerse (ie) to stay, continue

manuscrito handwritten

maña skill, art

mañana: — mismo tomorrow at the latest; **pasado —** day after tomorrow

mañanita bed jacket

máquina machine; car; **— de escribir** typewriter

maquinalmente automatically, mechanically

maquinaria machinery

mar *m. f.* sea, ocean

maraña trick, ruse

maravilla wonder; marvel

maravillado in wonderment, marveled, amazed

maravillar to amaze, surprise

marca brand

marcha motion, walk, course, way, journey, route, advance; **en —** moving, going; **poner en —** to start (*a vehicle or machine*)

marchar to go; to march; **—se** to leave, go away

marco picture frame, window case

mareado dizzy, slightly nauseated, airsick, seasick; dazzled

marfil *m.* ivory

marginado outcast

marido husband

marinero sailor, seaman

marino *adj.* sea

mármol *m.* marble

martillar to hammer

martirizar to torture, torment

mas but (*literary*)

más: — allá far away, farther on; **— allá** *m. n.* great beyond; **— allá de** beyond; **— bien** rather, more; **a — de** besides; **no — que** only; **no poder —** not to be able to go on (stand) anymore, to be tired (worn) out, to be "all in"; **poder —** to win out, overcome; **quien — quien menos** everyone more or less; **sin —** without further ado; **valer —** to be better

máscara mask

mascullar to mumble

matadero slaughterhouse

matasellos *m. sing.* cancellation stamp

mate dark, dull; **jaque —** checkmate (*chess*)

matinal *adj.* morning

matiz *m.* shade, nuance

matizado colored, tinged

matrimonio married couple

matutino *adj.* morning

mayólica plaster wall decorations; china covered with metal

mayor *m. n.* adult; *adj.* older, oldest; greater, greatest; **persona —** adult

mayordomo butler

mecha wick, fuse

mediado halfway through

mediano average

medias *pl.* stockings; *adv.* **a —** part way, slightly, half-heartedly

médico legista criminal pathologist

medida: a — que as, while, at the same time as

medio *n.* way, manner; middle; *adj.* half; **a —as** halfway, partway

medir (i, i) to measure

medrar to thrive, prosper

mejilla cheek

mejor better, best; **— dicho** rather, better said, I mean to say, more precisely; **a lo —** when least expected; probably, as likely as not

mejorar(se) to improve, get better

melífluamente sweetly, like honey

membrete *m.* letterhead

memoria: de — by heart

mendicante *m.* beggar

menos less, least; **a — que** unless; **cuando —** at least; **echar de —** to miss; **no poder — de** + *inf.* not to be able to help but + *v.* (e.g., **No se podía menos de imaginarlos.** One could not help but imagine them.); **por lo —** at least; **quien más quien —** everyone more or less

menosprecio scorn

mensaje *m.* message

mensajero messenger

mensualidad monthly payment, pension

mentecato idiot

mentir (ie, i) to lie (*tell a falsehood*)

mentira lie (*falsehood*)

menudo small; **a —** often

mercachifle *m.* small-time dealer, huckster

mercado market

merced favor, benefit

mercería dry goods store

merecedor deserving

merecer to deserve

merienda luncheon, light meal (*taken in the afternoon*)

metálica: cortina — steel shutter (*rolled down over store fronts at night*)

meter to insert, put into; **— la pata** to butt in; to stick one's foot in it, "goof"; **—se** to enter, slip into

meticulosidad meticulous care

metro meter (*39.37 inches*)

mezcla mixture

mezclar to mix up (*trans.*); **—se** to be mixed together

mezquite *m.* cactuslike shrub

miaja bit

miedo fear; **tener — (de)** to be afraid (of)

miel *f.* honey

mientras while; **— tanto** meanwhile

milagrero miracle maker

milagro miracle

milagroso miraculous

milico soldier; policeman

millar *m.* thousand

mimar to spoil, indulge

mimbre *m.* wicker

mimo spoiling, pampering

mimosidad indulgence, solicitousness

minar to sap, weaken

minúsculo small

mío: a pesar — against my better judgment

miope nearsighted

mira sight (*of a gun*)

mirada look, glance, gaze; **— de reojo** side glance, a look out of the corner of one's eye; **dar una —** to take a glance, look

mirado: bien — carefully considered

mirón *m.* onlooker, observer

misa mass (*church service*)

misántropo misanthrope, hater of mankind

misericordia pity, mercy

mísero miserable

mismo same; -self; very; **ahora —** right now; **el rey —** the king himself; **mañana —** tomorrow at the latest; **por lo —** by the same token; **yo —** I myself; **el agua —a** the very water

misto *South American songbird*

mitad half, middle

mito myth

mitómano myth maker; one who exaggerates, liar

mobiliario furniture

mocasín *m.* loafer (*shoe*)

mocedades *pl.* youth, younger days

mocetón *m.* lad

mocoso brat

modales *m. pl.* manners

modo way, manner; **a — de** in the manner of, like; **de — que** so, so then; **de (tal) — que** in such a way that, so; **de todos —s** anyway, at any rate

mohín *m.* grimace, "face," pout

mohíno peeved

mojar to wet; **—se** to get wet

mole *f.* mass, bulk (*of buildings*)

moler (ue) to grind; **— a palos** to give a severe beating

molestar to annoy, bother; **—se (en +** *inf.***)** to bother, take the trouble (+ *inf.*)

molestia bother, trouble

molesto annoying, bothersome, bothered

momento: al — at once; **de —** for a (the) moment

moneda coin

monja nun

mono monkey, ape

monstruo monster

montar to assemble, put together; to ride (*horseback*)

monte *m.* woods, uncultivated fields, wilderness, countryside; hill, mountain

montón *m.* pile

moño topknot, crest

morada abode, dwelling

morder (ue) to bite, gnaw

mordida payoff (*lit.,* "bite")

moreno dark (*skin or hair*)

morfología structure, morphology

moribundo dying

morir(se) (ue, u) to die

morisco Moorish

mortífero deadly, lethal

mortuorio funereal, having to do with death

mosca fly

mosquitero mosquito netting

mostrador *m.* counter, bar

mostrar (ue) to show; **—se +** *adj.* to appear, look + *adj.*

mote *m.* nickname

motivo reason, motive; occasion

movedizo shifting, moving

moverse (ue) to move (*intrans.*)

movimiento motion

mozo boy, lad; waiter

mucama maid (*Arg.*)

muchachada group of children

muchacherío group of children

muchedumbre *f.* crowd, multitude

mudar to change

mudo mute, silent

mueble *m.* piece of furniture; *pl.* furniture

mueca grimace, grin, "face"

muelle *m.* wharf, pier

muerte *f.* death

muestra example, sign; sample

mugir to moo, bellow

mugre *f.* dirt, filth, grease, grime

mugriento dirty, grimy

multa fine (*traffic*)

mundo world; **todo el —** everyone

muñeca doll; wrist

muñeco mannequin, dummy (*store window*)

muralla wall

murmullo murmur

murmurar to gossip; to murmur

muro wall

muslo thigh

mustio withered

N

naciente growing; new

nacimiento birth

nadar to swim

naftalina naphthalene (*a crystalline substance obtained from coal tar*)

naranja orange

nariz nose; nostril

naturaleza nature

náufrago castaway, shipwrecked person

naufragio shipwreck
navideño *adj.* Christmas
neblina fog, mist
neblinoso foggy, misty
necesitado needy person
necio stupid, silly
negar (ie) to refuse, deny; **—se (a** + *inf.*) to decline, refuse (+ *inf.*)
negocio business establishment; business deal, transaction; *pl.* business, commercial affairs
negrura black(-ness)
nexo connection, link
ni siquiera not even
niágara stream (*poetic*)
nido nest
niebla fog, mist
nieto grandson
niquelado nickel-plated
nitidez brightness, clarity, sharpness
nítido neat, clean, clear, spotless
no obstante nevertheless
nobleza nobility
noche: — cerrada completely dark; **de —** at night
Nochebuena Christmas Eve
nocturno *n.* evening; *adj.* evening, night(ly)
nombre: poner un — to name
nórdico Nordic (Germanic or Scandinavian)
noticias *pl.* news; **recibir — (de)** to hear (from)
novedad something new
noveno ninth
novia bride; girlfriend, fiancée
novio groom; boyfriend, fiancé
nube *f.* cloud
nubecilla *dim. of* **nube**
nublado cloudy

nuca back of the neck
nudo knot
nuevamente again
nuevas *pl.* news
nuevo: de — again
numen *m.* deity
nupcias *pl.* wedding
nutrirse to be nourished

O

o sea that is, I mean to say, "like"
oblicuamente slanting, obliquely
obra work, deed
obrar to work, operate; to behave
obrero *n.* worker; *adj.* working, labor
obsecuente humble, obsequious
obstante: no — nonetheless, nevertheless
ocasional incidental
ocaso setting sun, sunset
occidente *m.* west
ocultar to hide (*trans.*); **—se** to hide (*intrans.*)
oculto hidden
ocuparse de to take care of, pay attention to; to bother, take the trouble + *inf.*
ocurrencia witticism
ocurrir (a) to have recourse (to), apply (to); **—sele a uno** to get an idea
odiar to hate
odio hate, hatred
odioso hated, hateful
oeste *m.* west
ofrecer to offer
oído ear (*inner*)
¡oiga! *imp. of* **oír** Hey!, Listen!
oír decir to hear, hear it said
ojalá may, I hope, God grant (e.g., **Ojalá**

que te acompañe siempre. May he always be with you.)

ojeada glance; **echar una —** to take a quick look, glance

ojeroso having circles under the eyes

ola wave

óleo oil; oil painting

oler (hue) to smell (*trans. and intrans.*)

olfatear to smell (*trans.*)

olor *m.* smell, odor

olvidarse (de) to forget

olvido forgetfulness, oblivion

onda ripple, wave

ondulante wavy; swaying

opaco opaque

opinar to have an opinion, judge

oponerse (a) to oppose

oportuno opportune, timely

oprimir to press down; to oppress

optar por + *inf.* to choose + *inf.*

orar to pray

orbe *m.* earth

orden *f.* order, command; **a sus —es** at your service; *m.* order (*arrangement*)

ordenadamente in an orderly manner

oreja ear (*outer*)

orgullo pride

orgulloso proud

orificio orifice, small hole

orilla shore, bank, edge

oro gold

orondo smug; serene (*Arg.*)

osar to dare

o(b)scurecer to get dark

oscuras: a — in the dark

oso bear

otoño autumn, fall

otorgar to grant, give, authorize

otro: —a parte elsewhere; **—a vez** again; **al — día** on the next day;

de **—a manera** otherwise; **por —a parte** on the other hand; **unos a —s** each other, one another

ovillo ball of wool, string

oyente *m., f.* listener

P

pábulo food

pacífico peaceful

padecer to suffer

padrino godfather

página page

paisaje *m.* landscape, view

paja straw

pajarera bird cage

pájaro bird

pajuela match

paladear to savor

palanquita *dim. of* **palanca** lever

palidecer to turn pale

palidez paleness, pallor

pálido pale

palito stray mark (*in handwriting*)

palma palm tree, palm

palmada pat with the hand

palmera palm tree

palmotear to clap, slap

palo stick; **moler (ue) a —s** to give a severe beating

palpar to feel (*touch*)

palúdico noxious, malarial

pan bread; **ganarse el —** to earn a living; **—es de tierra** strips, pieces, clumps of sod

panal *m.* honeycomb

pandilla gang

pantalla lamp shade; screen (*movies, TV*)

pantalón *m.* pair of pants

pantera panther

pantuflas *pl.* slippers

paño cloth, rag

pañoleta woman's triangular shawl

pañuelo handkerchief

papagayo parrot

papel *m.* **de plata** tinfoil

papeleta ticket, slip of paper

par *m.* pair, couple, few; *f.* par; **a la — de** even with; *adj.* even (*numbers*)

para: — abajo downward; **— arriba** upward; **— que** so that; **— siempre** forever; **como —** as if to; **estar —** to be about (ready) to

parada stop

parado stopped; standing

paraguas *m. sing.* umbrella

pararse to stand up; to stop (*intrans.*)

parcela piece, section

parecer to seem, look like, appear; **—se** to look alike; **—se a** to look like, resemble; **al —** apparently

parecido similar

pared wall

paredón *m.* thick wall

pareja couple

pariente *m.* relative

parpadear to flicker, blink

párpado eyelid

párrafo paragraph

parroquiano customer; parishioner

parsimoniosamente carefully, unhurriedly

parte: alguna — somewhere; **de — de** on the side of; **otra —** elsewhere; **por otra —** on the other hand; **todas —s** everywhere

particular private (*as opposed to public*)

partida game, match; departure; shipment; group, party

partidario de *adj.* favoring, partial to

partir to break, split, divide, share; to leave, depart

parvada flock

pasada pacing

pasadizo passageway, corridor

pasado mañana day after tomorrow

pasador *m.* bolt

pasajero passenger

pasamano *m.* railing

pasar to spend (*time*); to pass, happen; to enter, come (go); to swallow; **— por alto** to overlook, pass over

Pascua Easter; *any one of several important Church holidays*

pase *m.* pass, nonlosing throw (*in dice games*); **— inglés** craps (*dice game*)

paseante *m.* stroller, passerby

pasear to walk, stroll; to pass; to go on a pleasure trip

paseo walk, stroll, outing; wide street, boulevard, avenue

pasillo hall

pasmo wonder, astonishment

paso passage, passing, way, crossing, path; step, footstep; **abrir —** to clear the way; **cerrar el —** to block the way; **dar un —** to take a step; **de —** in passing, incidentally, by the way; **vedar el —** to block the way

paspado chapped

pasto fodder; grass

pastoso thick, mellow; pasty

pata paw, foot, leg (*animal*); **meter la —** to butt in; to stick one's foot in it, "goof"

patalear to kick, thrash around

patente obvious, evident

patitieso stupefied

patito duckling

patraña story, hoax

patria country, homeland
patrimonio heritage, legacy, birthright
patrón *m.* boss
paupérrimo very poor
pausadamente slowly, deliberately
pavor *m.* fear, terror
paz *f.* peace; **en —** alone
pebete *m.* fuse
pecado sin
pechera breast, front
pecho chest; breast
pedacito *dim. of* **pedazo** piece
pedido request; order
pedir (i, i) to order, request; to ask for
pedrada stoning, blow from a stone
pedregullo crushed stone
pegado attached, stuck
pegar to stick, attach, glue; to hit, strike, beat; **— un brinco** to jump; **—le un tiro a uno** to shoot someone
pelea fight, quarrel
pelear to fight, quarrel
peligro danger
peligroso dangerous
pellejo skin, "neck"
pellizcar to pinch
pelo hair
pelota ball
peludo hairy, furry
pena pain, sorrow; **a duras —s** with great difficulty; **valer la —** to be worthwhile
penacho crest
pender to hang
pendiente hanging; pending; waiting
penetrar to enter, get in
penoso painful
pensamiento thought
pensar: cosa de —lo something to think about

pensativo thoughtful
pensión *f.* boarding house, rooming house; pension, retirement
penumbra semidarkness, shadows
penumbroso shadowy
peón *m.* farm worker
pequeñez small size
percance *m.* misfortune, mishap
percatarse (de) to be aware (of), to notice (take note of)
percha hat rack
perdedor *m.* loser
perder (ie) to lose; to waste; to miss; **— de vista** to lose sight of; **— pie** to lose one's footing; **echar a —** to spoil, ruin; **—se** to lose one's way, get lost; to disappear, end
pérdida loss, waste
perdonar to excuse; to forgive
perecer to perish
peregrinación pilgrimage
perfil *m.* profile, outline
periodismo journalism
periodista journalist
perito expert
perjudicado damaged, injured
perjudicar to damage, harm
perjuicio damage, harm, financial loss
permanecer to stay, remain
pernoctar to spend the night
perplejo perplexing
persa Persian
persecución pursuit
perseguir (i, i) to chase, pursue
persiana slatted shutter; **—s** Venetian blinds
persona mayor adult
personaje *m.* person, character
personal *m.* personnel
perspicacia shrewdness

pertenecer to belong
pesadilla nightmare
pesado heavy, weighty
pesadumbre *f.* grief, sorrow
pesar to weigh, have weight; *m. n.* grief, sorrow; **a — de** in spite of; **a — mío** against my better judgment
pesaroso sorrowful, sad
pescado fish (*after it is caught*)
pescante *m.* driver's seat
pescar to fish
pescuezo neck (*animal*)
pese a despite
peso weight; peso
petirrojo robin
pétreo stony
pez *m.* fish (*before it is caught*)
piadoso pious, merciful
pica lance
picado perforated
picaflor *m.* hummingbird
picardía: con — roguishly
pico beak
pie: de — standing, on one's feet; **perder —** to lose one's footing; **ponerse en (de) —** to stand up; **puntas de —** tiptoes
piedad pity, mercy
piedra stone
piel *f.* skin
pierna leg
pieza room; piece, part (*of a machine*)
pila heap, pile
pillar to catch, grab
pillo rogue, scoundrel
pinchar to prick, puncture, pierce
pino steep
pintoresco picturesque
pintura paint; **mano** *f.* **de —** coat of paint

pira pyre
piringundín *m.* cheap bar
piropeador *m.* admirer (*man who makes complimentary or flirtatious remarks to passing women*)
pirotécnico *adj.* fireworks, pyrotechnic
pirueta pirouette (*a whirl on the toe while dancing*)
pisada footstep
pisapapeles *m. sing.* paperweight
pisar to step on; to set foot on
piso floor
pisotear to trample
pistolero gunman
placa plaque, sign
placenteramente pleasantly, agreeably
placer *m.* pleasure
plano *n.* plan, blueprint, map; *adj.* flat; **de —** flat
planta sole (*foot*)
plata silver; money, "dough"; **papel** *m.* **de —** tinfoil
platanar *m.* group of banana trees
plateado silvered, silver(y)
playa beach
plazo term, period of time
plazuela *dim. of* **plaza**
plegada fold
plegar (ie) to fold, bend
plegaria prayer
pleito lawsuit; **poner un —** to sue
pleno full, complete; **de — derecho** completely; **en —a selva** right in the middle of the jungle
pliego sheet of paper
pliegue *m.* fold, crease, line
plomo lead (*metal*)
pluma feather; pen
población town, population

poblar (ue) to populate, inhabit
pocillo demitasse
poco: a — in a little while; **costar(ue) —** not to be easy
poder *m.* power; *v.* **— más** to win out, overcome; **no — más** not to be able to go on (stand) anymore; to be tired (worn) out, to be "all in"; **no — menos de** + *inf.* not to be able to help but + *v.* (e.g., **No se podía menos de imaginarlos.** One could not help but imagine them.); **puede que** maybe
poderío power
poderoso powerful, mighty
podrido rotten
policía: cuerpo de — police force
polvo dust
pólvora powder
polvoriento dusty
pomada ointment
pomo fist (*figurative*)
poner to put, place, set; **— ... por caso** to take . . . as an example (e.g., **Pongamos a mi jefe por caso.** Let's take my boss as an example.); **— a prueba** to put to the test; **— en marcha** to start (*a vehicle or machine*); **— en tela de juicio** to question; **— reparos (a)** to find fault (with); **— un nombre** to name; **— un pleito** to sue; **—se** + *adj.* to get, become + *adj.;* **—se** + *article of clothing* to put on + *article of clothing;* **—se a** + *inf.* to begin + *inf.;* **—se de acuerdo** to come to an agreement; **—se en (de) pie** to stand up; **—se en ridículo** to look ridiculous, make a fool of oneself
por for, through; **— así decirlo** to put it one way, in a manner of speaking; **— el**

contrario on the other hand; **— eso** therefore; **— fin** finally, at last; **— favor** please; **— fuerza** necessarily, compulsively, against one's will; **— lo visto** apparently; **— otra parte** on the other hand; **— si acaso** just in case; **— su cuenta** on one's own; **estar —** + *inf.* to be about (ready) to + *v.*
porfía persistence, stubbornness
porquería cheap, unsavory food
portador *m.* bearer
portal *m.* doorway
portarse to behave
portátil portable
portazo door slam
portentoso prodigious, marvelous
portezuela small door (*often in a vehicle*)
pórtico hall, portico
portón *m.* gate
portoncito little door
portuario *adj.* port
porvenir *m.* future
posarse to land, (a)light
postergar to delay, postpone
postizo artificial
postre: a la — at last
postrero last, final
potasio: cianuro de — potassium cyanide
potrero pasture, paddock, field
potro colt
poyo stone seat
pozo well, pit
precipitado hurried, hasty, wild
precipitar to hasten; **—se** to rush, race, charge
precisar to determine exactly, pin down
preciso necessary
predilecto favorite

prefijar to determine beforehand
preguntar to ask; **—se** to wonder
premiar to reward
premio prize
prenda article, garment
prendarse (de) to become attracted (to),
  fond (of)
prendedor *m.* pin, brooch
prender to light; to attach
prendido (de) grasping, holding on (to)
prensa press
preocupar to worry (*trans.*)
prerrogativa right, prerogative,
  privilege
presa capture, catch, prey; prisoner, captive; **animal de —** predatory animal
presagiar to foretell
prescindir de to do without, do away
  with
prescribir to indicate
presenciar to witness
presentarse to show up
presentir (ie, i) to sense, have a
  premonition
presidio prison
presión *f.* pressure
preso prisoner
préstamo loan
prestar to lend; to pay (*attention*); to
  provide
pretender to claim; **— +** *inf.* to try + *inf.*
pretendiente *m.* suitor
preterido left out, ignored
prevalecer to prevail
prevenir (ie) to warn, caution
prever to foresee, anticipate, expect
previsible foreseeable
previsión *f.* foresight
previsor foresighted
previsto *p. part. of* **prever**

primogénito first-born
primor *m.* beauty, elegance
principiante *m., f.* beginner
principiar to begin
principio: al — at first
prisa hurry, haste; **darse —** to hurry;
  de — hurriedly; **tener —** to be in a
  hurry
privar to deprive
proa prow, bow (*ship*)
probar (ue) to prove; to try out, test
proceder (de) to come (from), origi-
  nate (in)
procurar + *inf.* to try + *inf.*
prodigar to lavish
prodigio wonder, marvel, prodigy
producirse to happen, occur, take place
proferir (ie, i) to utter, speak
prófugo fugitive, escapee
profundidad depth
progresista progressive
prolijamente excessively, meticulously
prometer to promise
pronto soon; ready; **de —** suddenly; **por
  de —** in the meantime; **por lo —**
  meanwhile, for the present
propaganda advertising, promotion;
  propaganda
propagarse to spread
propicio favorable, right, propitious
propiedad: con — properly
propietario owner
propio own; characteristic; -self (e.g., **la
  propia botella** the bottle itself)
proponer to propose; **—se** to plan,
  intend
proporcionar to furnish, provide
propósito purpose, end; **a —** on purpose
proseguir (i, i) to go on, continue
prospecto brochure, pamphlet

prosternarse to prostrate oneself

protegido protected

provisto (de) provided (with)

prueba proof, test, trial; **poner a —** to put to the test; **viaje de —** trial run; *pl.* evidence

púa barb, sharp tip

¡puaf! bah! (*or any similar exclamation of exasperation*)

puchuela trifle, insignificant sum

pueblecito little village

puente *m.* bridge

puerilidad childishness, immaturity

puerto waterfront

pues well (*expl.*); since, because; **— bien** well then

puesta de sol sunset

puesto *p. part. of* **poner**; on (wearing, *as with clothing*); **— que** since; *n.* post, position, job; place-setting; stand (*in market*)

pulcro neat, clean

pulgar *m.* thumb

pulido polished

pulmón *m.* lung

pulsar to feel one's pulse

pulsera bracelet; **reloj** *m.* **de —** wristwatch

punta tip, end, point; **—s de pie** tiptoes

puntapié *m.* kick

puntería marksmanship, aim

punto dot, point; popular song; stitch; **al —** at once, instantly

puñado handful; **a —s** by the handful

puñal *m.* dagger

puñalada stab

puño fist; handle, grip (*knife*)

puro pure (*when after the noun*); nothing but, only (*when before the noun; e.g.,* **puras tonterías** nothing but foolishness)

Q

quebrado weak, trembling, shaky

quebrarse to break (*intrans.*)

quedar to stay, remain, be left; **— en** to agree to, on; **—se** to stay, remain

quedo quiet, still

quehacer *m.* task, chore

queja complaint

quejarse (de) to complain (about)

quejido moan, groan

quejumbroso plaintive

quemadura burn

quemar to burn (*trans.*)

querella quarrel

querer (ie) to want, wish, try; to love, like; **— decir** to mean; **sin —** unintentionally

querida mistress

querido dear, beloved

quiebra bankruptcy

quien más quien menos everybody more or less

quieto still, motionless

quimera chimera (*unreal creature of the imagination*)

quimérico fanciful, hopeless

quinta country house, villa, small estate on outskirts of town; farm

quitar to take off, away; **—se** + *article of clothing* to take off + *article of clothing*

quizá perhaps, maybe

R

rabia rage, fury

rabiosamente furiously

racha gust; streak; run of good (or bad) luck

ráfaga small cloud, a gust of wind
raicilla little root
rajar to cleave, slit
raleado sparse, thinned out
rama branch
ramalazo gust; lash
ramo bouquet; bunch
rancio stale, musty
rapaz *m.* lad; bird of prey
rápido express train
rapiña: ave *f.* **de —** bird of prey
rapto impulse
raro strange
rascacielos *m. sing.* skyscraper
rascar to scratch, scrape
rasgar to tear; to slash
rasgo feature
raso satin; **cielo —** ceiling
raspar to scratch, scrape
rastro trace, track
rata *m.* thief, "punk"
rato time, while; **al —** in a little while
raudamente rapidly
raya line, streak, stripe
rayado lined, striped
rayar to emit rays; **— en** to border, verge on
rayo streak of lightning
raza race
razón *f.* reason; **dar — a** to confirm; **en — de** with regard to, as regards to, due to; **tener —** to be right
razonamiento reasoning
reacio opposed, reluctant
real real; royal
realizar to carry out, make, do
reanudar to resume
rebatir to refute
rebote *m.* bounce, rebound
rebozo shawl

rebullir to stir, move about
rebuscar to search carefully
recargo extra charge, new charge
receloso suspicious
recepción lobby, outer office
receso recess
receta prescription; recipe
recibir noticias (de) to hear (from)
recién recently, just a minute (while) ago
recinto enclosure, place
recio tough, robust
reclamación claim, demand
reclamar claim, demand
recobrar to recover; **—se** to recover, recuperate
recoger to gather, take in, collect, pick up; **—se** to crouch
recogido drawn up
recogimiento withdrawal, quietness
recomenzar (ie) to begin again
recompensa reward
recóndito obscure, profound
reconocer to recognize
reconquistado regained
reconvenir (ie) to reproach, reprimand
recordar (ue) to remind (of); to remember
recorrer to travel (go) through (over, across)
recorrido search, check; journey, route, course
recortado outlined
recostado reclining
recostarse (ue) to lie down, recline, lean back
recova street market; arcade
recreo play, recreation
recruzar to recross
recto straight
recuerdo memory

recuperar to recover, regain
recurrir a to resort to
recurso means, resort, recourse
rechazar to turn away, down, to reject, refuse
red net, network, system
redacción composition
redactor *m.* editor
redondel *m.* circular area
redondelito little circle, ring, disk
redondo round: **girar en —** to spin, turn around
redundar to redound, result, accrue, reflect
reencender (ie) to rekindle
referir (ie, i) to relate, tell; **—se a** to refer to
reflejo reflection
reflexionar to reflect
refrán *m.* proverb
refuerzo reinforcement
refugiarse to take refuge, shelter
refunfuñar to growl, mutter
regalar to present, give as a gift
regaño scolding, reprimand
regazo lap
registrar to search
registro record
regla rule; **en —** in order, in proper form
regocijo joy, elation
regresar to return
regreso return
reguero trickle, stream of drops, line left by liquid
rehuir to shun, avoid
rehusar (ú) to refuse
reina queen
reino kingdom
reírse (i, i) (de) to laugh (at)
reiterado repeated

reja grill, bars
relamer to lick
relámpago lightning, flash of lightning
relato story, narrative
relieve *m.* importance
rellano landing (*of a stairway*)
relleno stuffed
reloj *m.* **de pulsera** wristwatch
reluciente glittering, gleaming
relucir to glitter, glisten
remanso quiet place, haven, oasis
rematar to finish off, end, top off; to sell cheaply
remate *m.* auction, house sale; tip, point
remedio solution, remedy, choice
remendar (ie) to patch, repair, fix up
remero boatman
remolino swirl
remordimiento remorse
removerse (ue) to move around
remudar to change
renacer to be reborn
rencor *m.* ill will, resentment, rancor
rendija crack
rendir (i, i) to produce, achieve, give to; **—se** to give up, surrender
renegrido very black
renguear to limp
renovarse (ue) to be renewed
renuevo shoot (*plant*)
reojo: de — suspiciously; **mirada de —** side glance, a look out of the corner of one's eye
reparar (en) to notice; to repair
reparos: poner — (a) to find fault (with)
repartir to divide, distribute
reparto distribution
repasar to go over, through
repaso review
repechar to go uphill

repente: de — suddenly
repentino sudden
repicar to ring out, resound
repique *m.* peal, ringing
repleto crowded, fall
replicar to reply
reponer to reply; to replace, pay (for the replacement of)
reposado relaxed, rested
reposición recovery, recuperation
reprobar (ue) to blame, condemn
resabio bad taste
resbalar(se) to slip, slide
rescatar to rescue
resecar to dry thoroughly
resentir (ie, i) to weaken, damage
resolver (ue) to solve, resolve
resonar (ue) to sound, resonate, echo, ring
resoplar to snort, pant
resorte *m.* spring (*metal*)
respirar to breathe
resplandecer to gleam, shine
resplandeciente shiny, luminous
resplandor *m.* glow
respuesta reply, answer, response
resquebrajado cracked, split
resquicio crack
restablecido recovered, recuperated
restante remaining
restar to subtract
restos *pl.* remains
resuelto *p. part. of* **resolver;** determined, prompt, resolute
resultado result
resultar to be, turn out (to be), end in
resultas: de — as a consequence
retaceo misgiving, hesitation
retintín *m.* sarcastic tone
retirado remote, withdrawn

retirar to take away (out); **—se** to go away, withdraw, "get out of the picture"
retocar to adjust
retomar to take again, regain, go back to
retorcer (ue) to wring, twist; **—se** to twist, writhe, squirm
retozar to frolic, caper
retrato portrait
retroceder to retreat, move backward, back up
reunir (ú) to gather, collect
revelar to reveal; to develop (*film*)
reventar (ie) to burst
reverencia bow; nod
revés *m.* reverse, back; **al —** in reverse, backward; **al — de** just the opposite from
revisar to look, check over, examine; to revise
revolcarse (ue) to roll about, turn over and over
revoloteo fluttering
revolver (ue) to rummage, go through, turn over; **—se** to move back and forth
revuelto *p. part. of* **revolver;** intricate, tangled, mussed up, topsy-turvy
rezar to pray; to grumble, growl, grouse
rezongar to grumble, growl, grouse
riachuelo stream
ribera bank (*river*)
ridículo: ponerse en — to look ridiculous, make a fool of oneself
riesgo risk
rincón *m.* corner
río: — abajo downstream; **— arriba** upstream
riqueza wealth
risa laugh, laughter
risita giggle

risotada loud laugh, guffaw
roble *m.* oak
robo robbery
roce *m.* poise, ability to get along with others; brushing, rubbing
rodar (ue) to roll, tumble; to travel
rodear to surround, circle, cover
rodeo: sin —s without "beating around the bush," straight to the point
rodilla knee
rogar (ue) to beg, request
rojizo reddish
rojo: al — red-hot
rollizo sturdy, stocky
rombo diamond-shaped parallelogram, rhombus
romper to break, tear; **— a** + *inf.* to begin + *inf.*
roncar to snore
ronco hoarse
ronda police patrol
rondar to patrol, prowl
ronronear to purr (also **runrunear**)
ronroneo purring, whirring, humming
ropa clothing; **cuerda de colgar la —** clothesline
ropero wardrobe
rosado pink, rose-colored
rosal *m.* rosebush
rostro face
rozado worn, partially nibbled away
rozar to rub, brush against
rubor *m.* blush, flush
ruborizado blushing
rudeza roughness
rudo hard, vigorous
rueda semicircle, ring, group of people; wheel
rugido roar
rugir to roar

rugoso wrinkled
ruido noise
ruidoso noisy
ruin weak, miserable
ruiseñor *m.* nightingale
rumbo course, destination, direction; "way out"; **— a** bound (headed) for, on the way to
rumor *m.* noise, sound
runrunear to purr (also **ronronear**)
rutilante sparkling

S

sábana sheet
sabandija nasty insect, vermin
saber to know; **— con** to have to do with; **hacer —** to inform, notify
sabiduría wisdom
sabio wise; *n.* wise man, sage
sabor *m.* flavor
saborear to relish, enjoy
sacar to take out; to get, roll (*with dice*); **— en limpio** to gather, conclude; **—se** to take off (*hat*)
sacerdote *m.* priest
saco suitcoat, sport jacket
sacristán *m.* sexton (*of a church*)
sacudida shake
sacudir to shake
sacudón *m.* violent jerk, shake
sagrado sacred
sal *f.* salt
salado salty
salamandra salamander
salida exit; departure, outing; an errand to run; **trampa de —** trapdoor
salitre *m.* saltpeter
salobre salty

salón *m.* room; living room, drawing room; theater

salpicado sprinkled

saltadura nick, chip

salto jump, leap; **dar un —** to jump, take a jump

salud health

saludar to greet, hail

saludo greeting

salvador *m.* savior

salvaje *m. n.; adj.* savage

salvar to save; to cross (*an obstacle*)

salvo except, save; **a —** safe, out of danger

sangrante bleeding

sangrar to bleed

sangre *f.* blood; **hecho de —** crime, bloody deed

sangriento bloody

sano sound, healthy, well; harmless

santiguarse to make the sign of the cross

santo *n.* saint; *adj.* holy, saintly, sainted

sañas *pl.* fury

sastrería tailor shop

Satanás Satan

satisfecho: darse por — to be satisfied

saya skirt

sea: o — that is, I mean to say, "like"

secar to dry

seco dry

secuestrar to kidnap

sed thirst

seda silk

seguida: en — right away, at once, immediately

seguido consecutive

seguir (i, i) to follow, continue, keep on

según according to; as, while

segunda: de — second class

seguridad safety

sellar to seal; **— los labios** to silence

sello stamp

selva jungle, forest; **en plena —** right in the middle of the jungle

semejante similar, such a

semilla seed

sencillo simple

sendero path

seno bosom, breast

sensato sensible

sensible sensitive

sentar (ie) to seat; **—le a uno** to look good on someone; to agree with; **—le mal a uno** to disagree with one, not suit one

sentenciar to pass judgment, decide

sentenciosamente sententiously, in a self-righteous manner

sentido meaning, sense

sentimiento feeling

sentir (ie, i) to feel, note, sense; to regret; **—se +** *adj.* to feel + *adj.*

señal *f.* signal, sign

señalar to show, point out

señas *pl.* distinguishing marks; **por más —** to be exact, more specific

señor mío my good man

señorío stateliness, elegance

separado: por — separately

sequedad dryness

sequía drought

ser: como es de imaginar as one might imagine; **así siendo** in that case; *m. n.* being

serenar to calm

sereno calm

seriedad seriousness

servicio: capataz de — headwaiter

servidumbre *f.* staff of servants

servir (i, i) to serve; **— de algo** to be any good; **— para** to be good for; **—se** to do business

sesgo direction, turn

sesos *pl.* brain

sí: volver(ue) en — to come to (*regain consciousness*)

siempre: para — forever

sien *f.* temple (*of the head*)

siendo: así — in that case

siervo slave

sigilo secrecy

sigilosamente secretly, stealthily

siglo century

significado meaning

signo sign

siguiente following, next

silbar to whistle

silbido whistle (*sound*)

silla chair

sillón *m.* chair, easy chair

simpatía kindness, "niceness"; liking, friendly feeling

sin: — embargo however, nevertheless; **— fuerzas** exhausted; **— más** without further ado; **— querer** unintentionally; **— rodeos** without "beating around the bush," straight to the point; **— tregua** unceasingly

síncope *f.* failure (*medical*)

sindical *adj. from* **sindicato** labor union

siniestro sinister; left (*opp. of right*)

sino but, except; **— que** but, rather

siquiera at least, even; **ni —** not even

sirviente, —a servant

sitio place, spot

sobrar to be more than enough, exceed, be left over

sobre *m.* envelope; *prep.* over, above, on; **— todo** above all, especially; **dar —** to fall (hit) on

sobrecoger to startle, take by surprise

sobrellevar to bear, endure

sobrenatural supernatural

sobrepasar to exceed, surpass

sobreponerse to recover

sobresaltar to startle, frighten, alarm; **—se** to be startled

sobresalto scare, shock, start, sudden fear

sobrevenir (ie) to take place, follow; to come along unexpectedly

sobrio plain, ordinary

sobrino nephew

socavar to undermine

socio member, partner

socorro help, aid; **dar voces de —** to call for help

sofocar to suffocate, stifle

soga rope

sol *m.* sun; **de — a —** from sunup to sundown; **puesta de —** sunset

solapa flap

solas: a — alone

solazo hot sun

soleado sunny

soledad solitude; lonely place

soler (ue) + *inf.* to be in the habit of + *pr. part.*, to be accustomed + *inf.*

solidez solidity, weight

solito *dim. of* **solo** all alone

sollozar to sob

sollozo sob

soltar (ue) to let go of, loosen, set free, release; **—se (de)** to let go (of), break away (from)

soltero unmarried

solterona "old maid"

solucionar to solve

sombra shadow, shade; **a la —** in the shadow

sombrío dark, shadowy, brooding, gloomy

someter to submit

son *m.* sound; **en — de** by way of

sonar (ue) to sound, ring

sonido sound

sonoramente loudly
sonreír(se) (i, i) to smile
sonriente smiling
sonrisa smile
sonrosado pink
sonsonete *m.* mocking sing-song
soñador dreamy
soñar (ue) (con) to dream (about)
sopa soup
soplar to blow
soplo breath, puff
soporífero boring, sleep-inducing
soportable bearable
soportar to stand, endure, bear
soporte *m.* support
sorber to sip
sordidez meanness, nastiness
sordina: a la — very quiet, muffled
sordo deaf; muffled, quiet, silent, dull;
　hacerse el — to turn a deaf ear
sorna sarcasm
sorprendente surprising
sorprender to surprise
sorpresa surprise; **llevarse una —** to be
　surprised
sorpresivamente surprisingly
sospecha suspicion
sospechoso suspicious
sostenerse (ie) to hold on, endure
sótano basement, underground level
suave soft
subalterno subordinate
subir to rise, go up; to raise; **— a** to get
　on (in) (*a vehicle*)
súbito sudden
subrayar to underline
subrepticio surreptitious
subsuelo area below the street level
subterráneo underground, below the
　street level; subway
subvenir (ie) to provide, supply

succionar to hold by suction
suceder to happen, occur; to turn out
sucesión inheritance, estate
suceso event
sucio dirty, filthy; **jugar(ue) —** to
　cheat
sudar to sweat
sudor *m.* sweat
sudoroso sweaty
Suecia Sweden
sueco Swedish
suela shoe
suelo ground, soil; floor
suelto *p. part. of* **soltar;** loose
sueño sleep, sleepiness; dream
suerte *f.* luck, fate, destiny; type, kind;
　way, manner, fashion; **de — que**
　so that; **por —** luckily, fortunately;
　tener (ie) — to be lucky
sugerir (ie, i) to suggest
suicida *m., f.* one who attempts or com-
　mits suicide
suizo Swiss
sujetar to hold (down, tight); **—se (de)**
　to hang on (to)
sumamente exceedingly, highly
sumar to add
sumergirse to sink
sumir(se) to sink
suncho (*also* **zuncho**) metal band, ring
superchería trick, fraud
superior upper
superpuesto superimposed
súplica entreaty, plea
suplicante pleading
suplicar to ask, beg, entreat, plead
suplicio torture, torment
suponer to suppose, assume
supuesto *p. part. of* **suponer;** supposed;
　por — of course
surco furrow, row

surgir to come into existence; to come out (forth)

surtir to supply

suscribir to sign

suspicacia suspicion, mistrust

suspirar to sigh

suspiro sigh

sustento livelihood

sustraerse to withdraw, elude

susurrar to whisper

susurro murmur, hum (*of voices*)

sutil subtle

sutileza subtlety

suyo: de — naturally; **los —s** the members of his family (*lit.* his)

T

tabaquera tobacco jar; snuff box; cigarette case

tablero chessboard; board, panel

tableteo tapping, clatter, rattle

taburete *m.* stool

tacha defect

tachito can, container

taconear to strut, put one's heels down hard

tahur *m.* gambler; cardsharp

tajear to slash

tal such, such a; **— como** just as; **— o cual** such-and-such, so-and-so; **— vez** perhaps; **de — modo que** in such a way that, so

taladrar to drill, bore into

talante *m.* will, mood

talismán *m.* amulet, charm

talón *m.* heel (*foot*)

tamaño size

tamarindo tamarind (*large tropical tree*)

tambaleante staggering

tambalear(se) to stagger

tamborilear to drum, pound

tangente bordering

tanque *m.* reservoir, tank

tantear to grope, feel around

tanto so much (many), as much (many); **— ... como ...** both . . . and . . . ; **de — en —** every so often; **en —** meanwhile; **en — que** while; **mientras —** meanwhile; **un —** somewhat

tapa cover, top

tapar to stop up, plug; to cover

tapia wall

tardanza slowness, delay

tardar to delay, be late; to last, take (time); **— en +** *inf.* to take time + *inf.* (e.g., **Tardó un día en terminar.** It took him a day to finish.)

tarde *f.* afternoon, evening

tarea job, task

tarifa fare

tarima low bench; platform

tarjeta card

tarlatán *m. shiny-surfaced thin cloth*

tartamudear to stammer, stutter

taza cup

techo roof; ceiling

tecla key (*piano, computer, tape recorder,* etc.)

teja roof tile

tejer to weave

tejido knitting

tela cloth, fabric; **poner en — de juicio** to question

telaraña spider web

telón *m.* **de fondo** backdrop

temblar (ie) to tremble, shake, shiver

temblor *m.* tremor

tembloroso trembling

temer to fear, be afraid

temerario reckless, bold

temeridad rashness, recklessness, folly

temeroso fearful

temor *m.* fear

tempestad storm

templar to harden; to temper, moderate

temporal temporary

tenaz tenacious

tender (ie) to spread (hold) out; to make (*bed*); to extend, lay down; **—se** to stretch out, lie down

tendero shopkeeper

tener (ie) to have, hold; be; to be wrong with one (e.g., **¿Qué tienes?** What's wrong with you?); **— a bien** to see fit, find convenient; **— ganas (de)** to feel like; **— inconveniente (en)** to mind, object (to); **— la culpa** to be to blame; **— lástima de, a** to feel sorry for; **— miedo (de)** to be afraid (of); **— prisa** to be in a hurry; **— que** to have to; **— que ver con** to have to do with; **— razón** to be right; **— suerte** to be lucky; **—... años** to be . . . years old

tentar (ie) to tempt

tentativa attempt, try, effort

tenue thin, light, delicate

teñir (i, i) to tinge, stain, darken, dye, tint

terminante final, decisive, definite

terminantemente unconditionally, without exception, absolutely, definitely, strictly

terminar (de + *inf.***)** to finish (+ *pr. participle*)

ternura tenderness

terraza terrace

terreno earthly, terrestrial; *n.* lot (property)

terrón *m.* clod (*of earth*)

tesoro treasure

testarudo stubborn

testigo witness

tez *f.* skin

tibio warm

tiempo: con el andar del — with the passing of time

tientas: a — feeling around, groping

tierno tender

tierra: panes de — strips, pieces, clumps of sod

tieso stiff

timbrazo ringing of a small bell or buzzer

timbre *m.* mark, tone, quality; bell, buzzer; stamp

tímpano eardrum

tinieblas *pl.* darkness

tinta ink; **— china** India ink (permanent black ink)

tinto stained

tiple *m. stringed instrument similar to guitar*

tipludo falsetto, sopranolike

tipo "guy"; type

tirador *m.* marksman

tirante tight, clutching

tirar to pull; to throw; to shoot

tiro shot; **pegarle un — a uno** to shoot someone

tirón pull, tug; **de un —** all at once, without a break, straight through

tiroteo shooting

titubear to hesitate

título: a — de by way of, in the capacity of

tiza chalk

tizne *m.* soot

tocadiscos *m. sing.* jukebox, record player

tocador *m.* dressing table

tocar to touch; to knock; to ring (*bell, buzzer*); to sound, play (*musical instrument*); **—le a uno** to be someone's turn (e.g., **Le toca a él.** It's his turn.)

todo: —as partes everywhere; **— el**

mundo everyone; **— lo contrario** just the opposite; **a — trance** at any cost; **de — as maneras** anyway; **de —s modos** anyway, at any rate; **del —** completely; **en un —** completely, in all its parts; **sobre —** above all, especially

todopoderoso all-powerful, omnipotent

tomar to take; to eat, drink; **— asiento** to be seated; **—el fresco** to get some fresh air; **— en cuenta** to take into account; **—lo a la tremenda** to be surprised, get excited; **—sela con** to have a grudge against, pick on, quarrel with

tomo volume

tonelada ton

tonito tone of voice

tontería foolishness, nonsense

toque *m.* touch

torcer(se) (ue) to twist

tordo thrush

tormenta storm

tornar to return; **— a** + *inf.* to do again; **—se** + *adj.* to turn, become + *adj.*

tornasolado iridescent

torno: en — de around

torpe clumsy, slow

torpeza clumsiness, slowness

torre *f.* tower; rook (*chess*)

torrentera ravine

torta loaf, cake

toser to cough

tozudo stubborn

trabajosamente with great effort

trabar to block, trip, tie (*the tongue*)

tráfago hustle-bustle

tragar(se) to swallow

trago swallow, gulp; drink (*alcoholic*)

traición betrayal

traicionar to betray

traicionero treacherous

traje *m.* suit; dress

trajeado well-clothed

trajinado well-traveled, knocked about

tramar to plot, scheme

tramitar to transact; to proceed with, carry out, take the necessary steps

tramo section, link, division

trampa to plot, scheme; **— de salida** trapdoor

trance *m.* juncture, moment; difficult moment, situation; **a todo —** at any cost

tranquear to bound, take long strides

transcurrir to pass, elapse, transpire

transeúnte *m.* passerby

transigir to compromise, give in

transitar to travel, pass through

tránsito passage, way; traffic

transitoriamente temporarily

translúcido translucent

transportarse to be carried away

transporte *m.* rapture, ecstasy; transportation

tranvía *m.* streetcar

trapo rag

traqueteante *adj.* rattling, clattering

traqueteo *n.* rattling, clattering

tras after, behind; **— de** behind

trasladar to translate, transfer, move

traslado act of moving

traslucir to show, reveal, betray

trasnochar to stay up (out) late

traspasar to transfix, penetrate, go through

traspirar to perspire

trasponer to go behind, over; to pull, go across, over

trastienda back room

trastornar to upset, confuse

trastorno upset, setback, disturbance, disorder

tratar to treat; to discuss, deal with;
tratar (de + *inf.***)** to try (+ *inf.*); **—se
de** to be a question (matter) of
través: a — de through, across
travieso mischievous
trazado outline, shape
trazar to draw, trace
trayecto section, stretch
trébol *m.* clover
trecho space, stretch, lapse
tregua: sin — unceasingly
tremendo terrible, tremendous (*with an
unfavorable connotation*); **tomarlo a
la —a** to be surprised, get excited
trémulo trembling
trepador *adj.* clinging, social climbing
trepar to climb
treta trick, ruse
tricota knit sweater
trigésimo thirtieth
tripas *pl.* "guts," insides
tripulante *m.* crew member
tristeza sadness
trocarse (ue) (en) to be transformed,
changed (into), be exchanged (for)
trompa proboscis (*of an insect*)
tronco trunk; piece of firewood
tropezar (ie) (con) to stumble (against,
over), trip (over), run into
tropilla herd
trozo piece
trueno thunder
tuerca nut (*metal*)
tufo bad odor
tugurio slum
turbación confusion
turbar to disturb, upset
turbio turbulent, muddy; misty, cloudy,
murky
tutear to speak to someone in the familiar **tú** form

U

u or
ubicar to locate
ufano conceited, haughty
últimamente lately
ultrajado outraged
umbral *m.* threshold
unir to join, unite (*trans.*); **—se** to join
(*intrans.*)
unísono: al — all together, as one
unos: — a otros each other, one another;
— cuantos a few, some
untar to grease, oil, smear; **— la mano**
to grease the palm, bribe
uña fingernail; claw
urbanidad politeness, manners
usurero money lender

V

vacante *f.* vacancy
vaciar (í) to empty
vacilación hesitation
vacilante hesitating, stumbling, hesitant
vacilar to hesitate
vacío empty, vapid
vagabundo vagrant
vagar to roam, wander
vago *n.* bum, tramp; *adj.* lazy, idle
vagón *m.* railroad car
vahido dizziness
valer to be worth, be of value; **— la pena**
to be worthwhile; **— más** to be better;
—se de to make use of
validez validity
valija suitcase, valise
valimiento benefit
valioso valuable
valla barrier

valor *m.* courage; worth, value

válvula valve

vanagloria excessive pride in one's accomplishments

vano empty

vapor *m.* steam

vaqueta *type of cow leather*

varilla stick, bar

varita little stick; wand

varón man, male

vasito capilar capillary

vaso glass (*container*)

vaya *imp. of* **ir** Well! (*to express surprise or strong approval*)

vecindad neighborhood, vicinity

vecino *n.* neighbor; *adj.* nearby, neighboring

vedar el paso to block the way

velador bed lamp

velar to stay awake, keep watch over

veleidad whimsy

vello fuzz, down, hair

velludo hairy

velo veil

veloz swift, fleet, rapid

venal venal, corrupt

venalidad corruptibility

vencer to conquer, defeat

venda bandage

vendedor *m.* clerk; salesperson

veneno poison

venenoso poisonous

venganza revenge

vengarse to take revenge, avenge

venida coming

venta sale

ventaja advantage

ventajoso advantageous

ventanal *m.* large window

ventanilla *dim. of* **ventana** window (*of a vehicle*)

ventura happiness

venturoso lucky, successful, prosperous

ver to see; **a —** let's see; **—se** to find oneself (*in a particular situation*); **—se con** to have it out with, have a talk with; **tener (ie) que — con** to have to do with

veras *pl.*; **de —** really

verdad truth, true; **¿—?** isn't it?, aren't they?, etc.; **a decir —** to tell the truth; **de — que** really (e.g., **¿De verdad que murió en el incendio?** Did he really die in the fire?)

verdadero real, true

verdoso greenish

verdugo executioner

verdura vegetation, foliage, greenery; *pl.* green vegetables

vergüenza shame, embarrassment

vericueto difficult terrain

verja iron railing (fence)

verosímilmente understandably, logically

verter (ie) to pour, spill

vértice *m.* apex, tip

vertiginoso dizzy

vértigo dizziness, dizzy spell

vestíbulo hall

vestido *n.* dress, clothing; *p. part.* dressed

vestimenta dress, clothing

vestir (i, i) to dress (*trans.*); **—se** to dress, get dressed

vete *imp. of* **irse** Go away!, Get out!, Leave!

veteado streaked

vez time; **alguna —** ever, sometime; **a la —** at the same time, simultaneously; **a su —** in turn; **cada — más** more and more; **de — en cuando** from time to time, now and then; **de una (buena) —** once and for all, finally; **en — de** instead of; **otra —** again; **tal —** perhaps

vía track, line (*railroad*)

viajar to travel

viaje *m.* trip, journey; **— de prueba** trial run

viajero traveler; *adj.* traveling

víbora viper, snake

victimario person responsible for someone else's misfortune or suffering

vida: con — alive

vidriera large window

vientecillo *dim of* **viento** wind

vientre *m.* belly, abdomen

viga beam (*wooden*)

vigésimo twentieth

vigilante *m.* watchman, guard

vigilar to watch over, stay on guard, keep an eye on

vigilia wakefulness

vilano down of a thistle

vilo: en — up in the air

vinagre *m.* vinegar

vincular to link, connect, bind, tie

vínculo link, bond, tie

violáceo violet

violado violet

virtuosismo virtuosity

viruela smallpox

víscera *also pl.* inner organs; entrails, bowels

visera bill, peak (*cap*)

visita caller, visitor (*lit.* visit)

visitante *m.* visitor

vislumbrar to glimpse, catch a glimpse of

víspera eve, night before

vista sight; **a la —** in sight, before you; **perder (ie) de —** to lose sight of

vistazo look, glance, perusal

visto *p. part. of* **ver; por lo —** apparently

vistoso showy, attractive

vitral *m.* stained glass window

vitrina china cabinet

viuda widow

viudo widower

víveres *m. pl.* food, provisions

viveza cleverness

vivo alive; lively, active; **—amente** in a lively way, keenly, intensely

vocablo word, term

vocación calling, vocation

vocecita weak voice

vociferar to shout, scream

volandas: en — in the air, as if flying

volante *m.* balance wheel; steering wheel

volar (ue) to fly; **—se** to fly away

volcar (ue) to overturn

voltear to overturn, demolish, knock down

voluntad will

volver (ue) to return, go (come) back; to turn; **— a** + *inf.* to do something again (e.g., **Volvió a ocupar su asiento.** He sat down again.); **— en sí** to come to (regain consciousness); **—se** to turn around; to become; to return

voto vow

voz *f.* voice; shout, call; the "word": **voces** rumors, news; **dar voces de socorro** to call (for help)

vuelo flight; expanse; grip (*of a tool or instrument*); **levantar —** to take off (*as a bird or plane*)

vuelta return; turn, movement around (*something*); **a la — (de)** around the corner (from); **dar —** to turn around; **dar —s** to walk around; **dar una —** to take a walk, turn; **dar la — (a)** to go around; **darse una —** to turn around; **estar de —** to be back, return; **ida y —** round trip

vuelto *p. part. of* **volver;** turned

vulgar common, ordinary

Y

ya already, then; now, right away; ¡— **está!** There! *expl.,* OK!; ¡— **lo creo!** Of course!, Yes, indeed!; — **no** no longer, not anymore; — **que** since
yacente reclining
yacer to lie
yema fingertip
yermo *n.* wasteland; *adj.* deserted, barren
yerno son-in-law
yerto stiff

Z

zafiro sapphire
zaguán *m.* entrance hall
zampar to gobble, wolf down
zángano drone
zapateo stamping, foot-tapping
zarpazo blow with the paw
zoco Arab market
zorro fox
zozobra sinking, floundering
zumbar to buzz
zurcir to mend
zurdo left-handed; clumsy

Acknowledgments

We wish to thank the authors, publishers, and copyright holders for their permission to reprint the stories in this book.

Jorge Luis Borges, *Los dos reyes y los dos laberintos,* copyright © 1995 by María Kodama, first printed in *Obras Completas.* Reprinted with the permission of The Wiley Agency, Inc.

Enrique Anderson Imbert, *El leve Pedro,* by permission of the author.

Isaac Aisemberg, *Jaque mate en dos jugadas,* by permission of Susana A. Arbuschi de Aisemberg.

Manuel Peyrou, *El señor Alcides,* by permission of Olga de Balbiano.

Horacio Quiroga, *El hombre muerto.*

Eduardo Goligorsky, *Orden jerárquico,* by permission of the author.

María Elena Llana, *Nosotras* from *Cuentos cubanos de lo fantástico y lo extraordinario* (Colección Escuela Social, 1968).

Alfonso Ferrari Amores, *El papel de plata,* by permission of the author.

Marco Denevi, *Las abejas de bronce,* by permission of the author.

Marcos Victoria, *Un suicida,* by permission of Carmen Aguirre de Victoria.

María de Montserrat, *El pajarito de los domingos,* by permission of Marta Canessa.

Rodolfo Jorge Walsh, *Cuento para tahures,* by permission of Patricia Walsh.

Conrado Nalé Roxlo, *Fósforos de madera,* by permission of the author.

Rubén Loza Aguerreberre, *El hombre que robó a Borges,* by permission of the author.